FORGOTTEN FAMILIES

Jody Heymann

FORGOTTEN FAMILIES

Ending the Growing

Crisis Confronting

Children and

Working Parents

in the

Global Economy

UNIVERSITY PRESS

2006

OXFORD
UNIVERSITY PRESS

Oxford University Press, Inc., publishes works that further
Oxford University's objective of excellence
in research, scholarship, and education.

Oxford   New York
Auckland   Cape Town   Dar es Salaam   Hong Kong   Karachi
Kuala Lumpur   Madrid   Melbourne   Mexico City   Nairobi
New Delhi   Shanghai   Taipei   Toronto

With offices in
Argentina   Austria   Brazil   Chile   Czech Republic   France   Greece
Guatemala   Hungary   Italy   Japan   Poland   Portugal   Singapore
South Korea   Switzerland   Thailand   Turkey   Ukraine   Vietnam

Copyright © 2006 by Oxford University Press, Inc.

Published by Oxford University Press, Inc.
198 Madison Avenue, New York, New York 10016

www.oup.com

Oxford is a registered trademark of Oxford University Press

Library of Congress Cataloging-in-Publication Data
Heymann, Jody, 1959–
Forgotten families : ending the growing crisis confronting children and working parents
in the global economy / Jody Heymann.
     p. cm.
Includes bibliographical references and index.
ISBN-13 978-0-19-515659-1
ISBN 0-19-515659-5
1. Work and family. 2. Dual-career families. 3. Children of working parents.
4. Globalization—Social aspects. I. Title.
HD4904.25.H478 2005
306.3'6—dc22   2005008503

9 8 7 6 5 4 3 2 1

Printed in the United States of America
on acid-free paper

Injustice anywhere is a threat

to justice everywhere. . . .

whatever affects one directly,

affects all indirectly.

—Martin Luther King, Jr.

To Steve, Cindy, Paul, Becca,

and the role families

play in all our lives

Preface

This book will address two fundamental questions. First, how are work and social conditions in countries around the world affecting the ability of parents to nurture the health and development of their children? Second, in the context of a global economy, what will determine whether there is a progressive race to the bottom among nations, with parents and their children facing worse conditions in each country, or a climb to the top?

Beginning to answer these questions could not be done without a new focus and breadth of research. If you placed a pin on a world map for every study that has been conducted on working families, North America and Europe would be so littered with markers that there would be little room left to place any more. The clustering of markers would hide the fact that a far greater number of studies in North America and Europe have been conducted on middle-class and professional families than on those living in poverty.[1] It would, however, accurately reflect the fact that, up until recently, next to no research has been conducted to uncover the experiences of working parents and their children in most of Latin America, Africa, and Asia. In part, these studies were never done because the questions had not been asked yet on a global scale. In part, these studies had not been undertaken previously because of the enormity of the task.

More Than a Decade of Research:
The Project on Global Working Families

I founded the Project on Global Working Families in order to address these unanswered questions and to shed light on the experiences of working families across the boundaries of class and country. Since the 1990s, my research group at Harvard has talked to and learned from thousands of working families around the world. Our studies have ranged from in-depth interviews of more than 1,000 families in Latin America, Africa, Asia, North America, and Europe, to analyzing survey data on 55,000 families around the world, to examining the extent of public policies supporting working parents and their children in 180 countries. More than thirty research and staff assistants and thirty students have contributed. The intense research efforts I have been fortunate to lead are based on a series of beliefs:

- First, it is important to know the conditions that working parents and their children are facing worldwide.
- Second, it is essential to understand what conditions families face across all social groups, from the working poor to the affluent.
- Third, it is important to use a methodologically rigorous approach to gathering the evidence, so that one can rely on the ascertained facts.
- Fourth, knowing the facts in detail is the best foundation for learning how to improve the opportunities available for children and families.

As this book is based on our research, what follows is a brief overview of the studies conducted. For those interested in greater detail, it is provided in the appendixes.

Mapping the Demographic Transition

In the first global studies we undertook, we asked how families and the nature of the labor force have changed. We looked at how many children parents are having, how often adults are caring for the elderly, how often they receive help from other family members, and where they are living, among other questions. At the same time, we examined who is joining the workforce, how extensively they are working in the formal sector, what kind of work they are doing, and what conditions they are facing. To do this, we drew on data that we were able to obtain from the World Bank;[2] the World Health Organization;[3] the International Labor Organization;[4] the United Nations Educational, Scientific and Cultural Organization;[5] and other global organizations covering more than 180 countries. When data were available only for recent years, we examined information from those years in detail. However, whenever possible, we looked at historical trends by examining data for those 180 nations over a forty-year period. Understanding what has changed for families and for work over the past forty years around the world is essential to understanding why we face the current dilemmas.

The broad strokes painted by the statistics we were able to obtain and analyze were clear: There has been a dramatic transformation in the workforce worldwide, with hundreds of millions of people leaving the home or farm to join the formal labor force; the majority of both men and women are in the labor force in nearly every region in the world; more than 930 million children under fifteen are being raised in households in which all of the adults work;[6] and elderly and disabled adults are increasingly in need of new solutions for how their basic care needs will be met.

National and Regional Surveys
of Households from around the World

The global data, however, did not allow us to examine any details behind the statistics. What effect have these changes had on infants, six-year-old girls starting school, or eighty-three-year-old grandfathers no longer able to care for themselves? In carrying out the first analytic studies of working families that are truly global in scope, my goal was to understand the experiences of working men and women worldwide when they had to balance earning enough money to survive with caring for those they love—their daughters and sons, their parents, disabled family members, and others. The daunting aspect of this research was determining how, given our resource constraints, to begin to cover this important topic on a global scale.

We analyzed closed-ended data from national household surveys of more than 55,000 people in five regions and seven nations that are diverse geographically, economically, and politically: the United States, Mexico, Brazil,

Russia, South Africa, Botswana, and Vietnam. (See appendix A for details on these studies.) We were able at look at how commonly children are being raised in single-parent, two-parent, and extended-family households; how often they are being reared in families in which all adults work; the frequency of health problems that working parents need to address; the availability of early childhood care; and the extent to which school-age children were being pulled out of school to act *in loco parentis.*

We supplemented the analyses we could conduct using available national data by conducting large surveys of our own—both at national levels and within diverse urban areas. Sometimes these large surveys were designed to give us a new kind of information that no one had ever collected before. For example, working with colleagues in the United States, we asked a representative national sample of more than 1,000 Americans every day for a week the extent of cutbacks they needed to make in their work and other daily activities to care for family members. At other times, the surveys were designed to gain more knowledge of especially pressing issues. For example, in Botswana, we interviewed more than 1,000 working caregivers about the critical issues they were facing as they struggled to care for their children, care for family members affected by AIDS, and economically survive (see appendix B).

Interviews with Families Worldwide

In order to be able to interview hundreds or thousands of people and to be able to summarize what is learned, those conducting large surveys typically ask closed-ended questions. However, closed-ended questions are, by definition, limited in their response options. For example, a survey question might ask, "Do you spend time caring for your mother or father while working?" whereas an interviewer conducting an open-ended interview could say, "Please tell me about all the different people you are caring for, what you do for each of them, and what their relationship is to you." More importantly, closed-ended questions are limited to the ideas that the researcher, journalist, or other interviewer had in designing the study. Open-ended questions and in-depth interviews—when done well—allow the individuals being interviewed to raise whatever they believe to be the most important issues. The respondents may cite problems, concerns, successes, and opportunities for and barriers to improvement that the interviewer had never considered. Particularly rich data can result from the participants' ability to raise these new issues and to discuss the important topics of the interview in different ways. To add to our analyses of large multinational surveys the insights unique to in-depth, open-ended approaches, my research team and I conducted lengthy interviews of more than 1,000 parents, childcare providers, teachers, and healthcare providers about the experience of working parents and their children in North America, Latin America, Africa, Asia, and Europe. This book will share the stories these families shared with us, as well as the statistics that resulted from our research.

Wherever possible, we interviewed representative samples of those using public services or samples representative of all households in a geographic area.[7] Additionally, in the studies I've led, we have always invested time and resources in ensuring a high response rate.[8] Our studies' response rates average over 80 percent. (Details on individual studies can be found in appendix C.)

Analyses of Public Policies Affecting Families Worldwide

Finally, having developed both a qualitative and a quantitative understanding of the difficulties that millions of families around the world are confronting, we wanted to understand what was already being done about these difficulties before making any recommendations. Therefore, my group looked at public policies from around the world that have been designed to meet working families' needs. We examined what 180 countries have been doing to improve the working conditions that all of us face, as well as what countries have been doing to help struggling families ensure that the basic needs of their children, elderly parents, and other family members can be met.

In particular, we examined both the extent to which basic rights were guaranteed in the workplace and the availability of social supports in the community. We conducted primary analyses of all legislation that was available either in the original or translated into English, French, or Spanish. This included legislation from 128 countries. We analyzed data on social security systems from 160 countries and conducted an extensive review of educational and service data available from a wide range of UN agencies and other global intergovernmental organizations. (See appendix D for details.)

Acknowledgments

It is because of the mothers, fathers, brothers, sisters, sons, daughters, grand-parents, aunts, and uncles with whom we spoke that this book was possible to write and important to write. Many gave generously of one of their scarcest resources—time—because they are deeply worried about what is happening to all of our lives. We are all indebted to these families for their openness, candor, and generosity in sharing their lives.

This project would not have been possible without generous support from the Canadian Institute for Advanced Research, the Ford Foundation, and the Rockefeller Foundation.

The research behind this book is the product of extraordinary teamwork. Large research programs, like many accomplishments, say more about the team than about any one individual named. One person lands on the moon, but thousands of engineers and scientists are the engine that made it possible. A single cyclist wins the Tour de France but not without a team that gives him the chance in the first place. The teamwork required for research is little different.

In every country in which we ran studies, we have had the assistance of exceptionally committed local colleagues. Our work in Mexico was made possible by doctors, nurses, and other health-care providers working in Mexican social security hospitals and public health clinics and hospitals. In Botswana, colleagues at the Botswana Harvard Partnership led by Ibou Thior and health-care providers at hospitals and clinics in Gaborone, Lobatse, Mochudi, and Molepolole provided invaluable assistance. In Vietnam, colleagues in public health, medicine, and education guided us. In Honduras, Mariano Planells and Humberto Romero paved the way for our work. In Russia, the help of Valentina Bodrova was indispensable.

Although I founded and led the research team at the Project on Global Working Families and wrote this book, understanding the conditions that working-poor families face around the globe as they try to raise children, exit poverty, and survive has truly been a team effort. In each country where we conducted in-depth interviews, we had multilingual team members. In addition to the interviews I conducted in each country, Cara Bergstrom and Francisco Flores interviewed parents, childcare providers, teachers, and doctors in Mexico. Sarah Russell and Divya Rajaraman interviewed adults caring for children and HIV-infected family members in Botswana; Adepeju Gbadebo interviewed professionals there. Phuong Vo interviewed mothers and fathers and education and health-care professionals in Vietnam. Lindsey Leininger conducted interviews in Honduras, as Michal Engelman did in Russia.

In total, the in-depth studies involved more than 1,000 families. This element of the project was made possible by the exceptional coordination of Stephanie Simmons and Jennifer Eckerman. All interviews were transcribed, translated, and analyzed by multiple readers. The country-specific research staff and Alyssa Rayman-Read contributed greatly to the analyses. Research assistants who added to the transcription, translation, analytic, and literature review efforts included Amina Arbi, Lan Bui, Ngan Dam, Anna Gallardo, Primrose Koloi, Sarah Liebschutz, Renat Lumpau, Obakeng Matsietse, Gopolang Mogotlhwane, Tumelo Molelekwa, Anne Nguyen, Inosentia Puso, Uyen-Khan Quang-Dang, Merav Shohet, Dung Thai, Mimi Trinh, Gani Uzbekov, and Erika Veley.

In addition to the in-depth interviews, we fielded large closed-ended surveys in Mexico and Botswana. Divya Rajaraman led a project which surveyed more than 1,000 families on their experiences of work, caregiving, and HIV in Botswana. She was ably assisted in data collection by Kgomotso Magagane, Shaidah Maposa, Kgato Ntereke, Khumo Mookane, Tsholofel Ntebela, and Luciah Madisakwane, in database creation by Erik Widenfelt, and in data entry by Kenneth Onyait, Kiston Moyo, and Luso Mnthali. Francisco Flores ran our field study in Mexico of 1,500 households, half of which were working families split across the Mexico-U.S. border and half of which were working families living together in Mexico. Edmundo Berumen, who has directed statistics for the Mexican National Statistical Agency, carried out the survey we designed with the excellent team he has brought together in his survey group.

In addition to the primary data we collected in large surveys in Mexico and Botswana, we analyzed survey data on more than 55,000 households across eight countries. Alison Earle did a remarkable job leading this effort with the able assistance of Karen Bogen, Amresh Hanchate, and Jeff Hayes. Longitudinal demographic trends were examined in 170 countries, led first by Nitzan Shoshan, then updated by Amresh Hanchate.

Our team also examined the public policies affecting the lives of working families in 180 countries. This massive project involved looking at all of the legislative frameworks that were available in French, Spanish, and English, as well as looking at collected data on services available within a wide range of countries. Aron Fischer helped to initiate our efforts in this area. Stephanie Breslow, Stephanie Simmons, and April Kuehnhoff led these efforts through to the first major global report. Lola Kassim joined to carry out ongoing analyses of their relationship to employment and productivity. Francisco Flores analyzed legislative frameworks in Latin America. They received important assistance from Tom Clarke and Karen Tseng.

At Oxford University Press, Dedi Felman patiently guided this book to fruition, shaping it in important ways with her probing questions. As this book goes to press, we are incredibly fortunate to have Kate Penrose coordinating team members' efforts and providing exemplary research and staff assistance with immense intelligence and good cheer.

While I have led the team since its inception, many people have served as indispensable glue in keeping us together. No contribution has been greater than that of Alison Earle. The senior member of my team, Alison's deep commitment and thoughtful insights have left her fingerprints on nearly every piece of our work. She has brought to the team her endless attention to detail, a profound understanding of the big picture, an enormous capacity as teacher and colleague, and an unwavering commitment to working-poor families.

Colleagues in a wide range of settings have provided immensely helpful feedback on our project, ranging from provocative questions to insightful commentary to advice on how to bring the research to the next level. In very important ways, this research would have been less rich without their support, generosity of time, and insights. Harvey Fineberg, Richard Zeckhauser, Mary Wilson, Shanta Deverajan, Paul Cleary, and Barbara Gutman Rosencrantz taught me skills that would prove indispensable—even before the project had been conceived. Harvey Fineberg and Barry Bloom provided ongoing support as the research of my team increasingly focused on how social conditions affect the health of children and families. Michael Marmot and his research group at the University College of London provided an intellectual home during a sabbatical as this global program became increasingly active. Max Essex, in his role leading a large HIV/AIDS initiative in collaboration with the Botswanan government, brought important support to the notion that addressing critical health problems can best be done with tools that span from the social sciences to the basic lab sciences.

The Canadian Institute for Advanced Research's Population Health Network provided a uniquely rich environment for doing this work. I am grateful to all of the members for their input as this research developed, to Clyde Hertzman for his extraordinary support as director of the program, to Bob Evans for his ability to go right to the heart of a matter with humor, to Margaret Lock for her understanding of the value of in-depth studies, to John Frank and Cam Mustard for their insights into work's impact on health, to Michael Wolfson for his questions about data, to George Kaplan for his ability to question fundamentals, to Lise Dubois for her understanding of nutrition, to Morris Barer and Noralou Ross for their eye to implications for health services, to Chris Power for her approach to the life course, and to Jonathan Lomas, Christina Zarowsky, John Lavis, Greg Stoddart, and the whole network for their pursuit of the translation of research into policies and programs that improve lives.

Helpful comments on different pieces of this work were generously provided by colleagues from the University of Botswana, the Princess Marina Hospital, the Ho Chi Minh City School of Public Health, and the Colegio de Mexico. Colleagues from around the world contributed to a meeting we held on inequalities at work. The depth of their understanding of individual issues enriched ours. They included, among others, Leonor Cedillo, Catalina Denman, Kimberly Elliot, Luiz Facchini, Parvin Gharayshi, Antonio Giuffrida, Amanda Glassman, Peter Glick, Zafiris Tzannatos, and Susanna Yimyam. I'm indebted to the wide-ranging insights provided by colleagues with whom I discussed different stages of this project, including, among others, Joy

Phumaphi at the World Health Organization; Catherine Hein, Lin Lian Lim, and Franklyn Lisk at the International Labor Organization; Carolyn Hannan at the United Nations; Soo Hyang Choi at UNESCO; Shanta Devarayen at the World Bank; and their colleagues.

There is a tremendous group of researchers committed to different aspects of the lives of families at work in North America and Europe who have been remarkable colleagues. Our work has been further enriched by colleagues in the field who work in policy and nonprofit settings. Particular thanks for the energy and urgency they have brought in one country that has a long road to travel: the United States.

Many other friends and colleagues gave encouragement and posed challenges often without knowing how important their words were. This was particularly true of Larry Aber, Patricia Baird, Mary Jo Bane, Linda Bauer, Seth Bauer, Chris Beem, Bob Blum, Allan Brandt, Marie Chevrier, David Christiani, Ophelia Dahl, Leon Eisenberg, David Ellwood, Paul Farmer, Nancy Folbre, Byron Good, Mary Jo Good, Janet Gornick, Heidi Hartmann, Don Hernandez, Alice Hill, Jerry Jacobs, Paul Jargowsky, Jim Kim, Cathy Knott, Suzan Lewis, Hannah Mahoney, Martha Minow, Fraser Mustard, Helen Neuborne, Kathy Newman, Harriet Presser, Julie Richmond, Juliet Schor, Leslie Simon, Theda Skocpol, Len Syme, Al Tarlov, and Mary Waters.

The Project on Global Working Families has been a large undertaking and a labor of love. Like most such undertakings, it has changed my daily life and touched my family. Tim has seen most of the valleys as well as the mountaintops with me and provided immeasurable support. Ben was my first teacher about the challenges and the inestimable value of being committed to both children and work. Jeremy kept me honest about when it was important to be away—generous about his mom traveling when it really mattered, but always questioning where it would make a difference. My parents provided the kind of practical and moral support that is essential to anyone taking on an impossible task. They have always supported working on the world's biggest problems rather than on the easiest ones.

As for many of us, family and friends have brought many of life's greatest blessings to me. My brother, Steve, has always brought a fountain of humor and love to daily life and exceptional courage and strength to adversity. Some of my earliest memories are of him teaching me these. We were fortunate, unlike many of the brothers and sisters whose stories are told in this book, as neither of us had to drop out of school to care for the other. But, like many of the children whose stories are told in this book, our lives were indelibly intertwined. As we grew into adulthood, we had the tremendous joy of sharing the lives of those we love. His wife, Cindy, has become a sister; the lives of their children, Paul and Becca, have become a central and joyous part of mine. This book is dedicated to Steve, Cindy, Paul, Becca, and the role that families play in all our lives.

Throughout the world, nearly all human beings work—whether for pay or not. All have had families—parents or partners, spouses or siblings, sons or daughters, nieces or nephews. When work and family are so fundamental to human life, it is long past time that society should make room for both.

Contents

FORGOTTEN FAMILIES

1

Dramatic
Transformations

Gabriela

Gabriela Saavedra's home in Tegucigalpa, Honduras, had been crudely built with scrap wood and cardboard and was now old and falling apart.[1] While in elementary school, Gabriela, along with her three siblings, had inherited the house when her mother died of uterine cancer that had gone undiagnosed and untreated for too long. Now nineteen years old, Gabriela was renting out the eight-foot-wide downstairs of the shack, although "renting out" was more a figure of speech: the woman downstairs was dying of uterine cancer herself and hadn't been able to pay rent for months, but kicking her out or demanding rent was the last thing Gabriela could do after having witnessed her own mother's painful demise.

To get to Gabriela's room in the shack, you had to climb an outside wooden ladder, which had the top two rungs broken—a ladder she had to climb holding her nineteen-month-old toddler, Ana Daniel. Gabriela's own room was slightly wider than the one below, but it certainly was no wider than ten feet, and its length was no more than a dozen feet. The walls were made of bent wooden boards with gaping holes as a result of age and their poor initial quality.

The spaces between the boards were large. Recently, after Ana Daniel had come down with repeated respiratory infections, Gabriela had covered the boards with cardboard so the walls would let in less air. Her daughter had been at heightened risk for respiratory infections since Gabriela had had to stop breast-feeding less than two months after Ana Daniel's birth in order to return to work. With long hours of factory labor and no leave allowed, Gabriela couldn't take Ana Daniel to the clinic during the day when she got sick. "Sometimes I would come back late from work, very tired, and she would be very sick, barely being able to breathe," Gabriela explained.

Sitting in a chair in a weathered Nike sweatshirt, Gabriela described what the sweatshop in which she was working was like. She worked making clothes for export from 7:00 a.m. until at least 6:00 p.m., seven days a week. But many nights, with no advance warning, the Korean owners would require everyone to stay until at least 9:00 or 11:00 p.m. There had been several shifts when they had been required to stay until 5:00 the next morning, leaving no time for sleep after getting home. Gabriela and the other workers had been told that if they refused to work the mandatory overtime shifts, they would lose their jobs.

The dangers of her job increased with the sleep deprivation. "I was sewing at 3:00 a.m., and I couldn't do it any more because I was so tired. I almost cut off a finger." She told us of others who had worked at the factory longer and suffered serious injuries because of extreme fatigue. Overtime pay was minimal, even lower than her normal wages. Gabriela noted, "I've heard that overtime at night should be paid at 200 percent of normal wages, but they pay only 75 percent [of normal wages]."

There was no leave time at the factory, and there were barely breaks for lunch. "When we get our lunch break, we only get fifteen minutes, but they take five minutes away from that. We are a thousand people working in the factory, and we all get our lunch break at the same time. We all have to exit through the same gate. We have to stand in line. Sometimes we don't even eat before we hear the buzzer."

For working seven days a week from eleven to twenty-two hours a day and making 100 shirts an hour, Gabriela still earned only 400 lempiras, or 26 U.S. dollars a week. Food was expensive at the factory—$1.00 to $1.50 a meal—but the fifteen-minute break left no time for alternatives. Even if she ate the factory food only once during an eleven- to twenty-two-hour day, Gabriela spent $7–10 of her weekly salary on her own meals. The next $10 went for formula and diapers for her daughter. That left $6–9 a week for any other necessities. Gabriela couldn't afford to lose any of the limited wages she earned, so she worked when she was sick. She also worked when Ana Daniel was sick.

While her mother-in-law had cared for Gabriela's daughter at first, that was no longer an option. On September 10, the day before his birthday and the eve of a children's holiday, the Day of the Child, Gabriela's husband, Daniel, for whom Ana Daniel was named, was coming home with a gift for their daughter. With a full two weeks' wages in his pocket, Daniel was attacked and murdered. After his death, Gabriela's mother-in-law would only agree to care for Ana Daniel if Gabriela would give the child up. For a while, Gabriela's stepmother was able to care for Ana Daniel, but then she, too, had to return to work. Not long before our interview, Gabriela's ten-year-old stepsister had started caring for the toddler, but she was to return to school within weeks of our departure. Gabriela had no idea what she would do then.

It was clear that her daughter was the light of her life. Gabriela's face lit up as she displayed the clothes she had made for Ana Daniel out of scraps she had stolen from the factory. She explained that at the factory they threw out old scraps of cloth—burned them—but wouldn't let the employees take them home. When asked what she would change in her life if she could change one thing, she answered without hesitation. She spoke immediately, not of the condition of her house or of her wages, but of caring for Ana Daniel: "I would like to work fewer hours. I would like to have someone who could take care of my daughter over here. And I would like to leave work earlier to be able to spend more time with her." As she explained this, Gabriela went to get a picture of Ana Daniel to show us how green her eyes were.

Despite her mother's adoration, Ana Daniel didn't have a chance at a healthy childhood if her mother remained in the sweatshop where she worked. The pay was too low for them both to eat adequately. There was no money to repair the burned-out holes in the side of their shack, or to fix the missing rungs on the ladder that one day could trip Ana Daniel and cause her to fall more than a dozen feet to the ground. There was not enough money to pay for water cleaned of the diarrhea-inducing pathogens that are one of the leading causes of malnutrition and death for children younger than five. Moreover, the punishing work schedule necessary for subsistence left Gabriela no time to be a parent, and Ana Daniel was at risk of being locked alone at home with no one to care for her when her aunt returned to school.

On the cardboard walls of their room, Gabriela had written her name and Ana Daniel's with a felt-tip marker next to the shelf on which she kept the doll Daniel had tried to bring home. Gabriela had put "&" between her name and Ana Daniel's and had marked *forever*, as though they were teenagers in love. But the wall next to the scrawled names was blackened from a recent fire. Gabriela had had to work until 11:00 p.m. and had not gotten home on the bus and to bed until past 1:00 a.m. She had gotten up at five o'clock the next morning to bathe. Exhausted, she had left a candle burning by the wall as she went down to bathe. There was no electricity in her hovel, so candles were her only choice. When she came out of her bath, the wall was on fire.

Gabriela and Ana Daniel are far from alone. There are at least 900 million children being raised worldwide in households in which all adults work; the actual number may be closer to a billion children.[2] Millions of their parents labor under conditions that damage their children's lives, as well as their own. The anti-sweatshop movement has brought much-needed attention to the draconian conditions under which many adults must labor around the world. But globally, we've turned a blind eye to how the grim working conditions many adults face are ravaging their families.

Indelible Transformations

During the past fifty years, three striking forces have led to major transformations of family life that offer the potential to either lift families out of poverty or place children at heightened risk. A labor force transformation has increasingly drawn fathers and mothers worldwide into the formal labor force—simultaneously providing more opportunities and creating new obstacles to caregiving. Urbanization has pulled nuclear families toward new job opportunities and away from extended-family support. And all of this has occurred in an era of increased economic globalization, which has brought with it access to lower-cost goods and services but also less ability to bargain for decent wages and benefits. These transformations are affecting every family from Detroit to Delhi. Moreover, the lives of families across the planet are becoming more interdependent and the likelihood that parents and children in Great Britain and Gabon, the United States and the Ukraine, will either sink or swim together is rising.

Labor Transformation

During the twentieth century, there were dramatic global shifts in the labor force. Men and women moved from jobs in which they often controlled the hours and location of their work—either because they were laboring on their own farms or because their work involved crafts and services they produced and sold themselves—to jobs in factories, in agribusiness, and in the more formalized service sector, where employers controlled the hours and location of their work and where it became far more difficult to simultaneously look after children. In many countries, this movement was first made by single women without family responsibilities and men who were not primary care-givers. But as discriminatory bans against work by married women and mothers were dropped, and as the economic need of families to have all adults in the workforce rose, the number of women with families in the managed labor force rose worldwide.

While global data are not available from the late nineteenth and early twentieth centuries, when the majority of men's movement into the formal labor force took place, longitudinal data on the second half of the twentieth century are available. These data provide insights into the magnitude of the changes in mothers' labor force participation.[3] While previous attention has focused on North America and Western Europe, the data demonstrate that the transformation in women's paid labor has been truly global. The percentage of the paid labor force that is made up of women increased between 1960 and 2000 from 26 to 38 percent in the Caribbean, from 16 to 33 percent in Central America, from 17 to 25 percent in the Middle East, from 23 to 31 percent in North Africa, from 31 to 46 percent in North America, from 27 to 43 percent in Oceania, from 32 to 41 percent in Western Europe, and from 21 to 35 percent in South America.[4] The global movement of women into the labor force without equally large reductions in men's labor has led to a substantial increase in the number of children in households where all adults are in the workforce. A conservative estimate is that 340 million of the world's children under six live in households in which all adults work for pay.

In Mexico, while a substantial number of children are being raised in extended-family households, all adults are working for pay in 30 percent of households with children younger than five. In Botswana, in 29 percent of the households with children under five, all adults in the household work for pay. While it is again fairly common for children in this age range to live with extended family, in a quarter of these types of households, all adult members of both the nuclear and extended family are employed. In other nations, an even higher percentage of homes with young children have all adults in the labor force. In 41 percent of households with young children in Brazil, all adults aged 18 and older are working for pay. In 50 percent of households in Russia in which there are young children, all adults in that age range are working for pay. The numbers are still higher in Vietnam. In 68 percent of Vietnamese households with young children, all adults are working for pay.[5]

Living in a household where all adults work for pay is even more common for school-age children. Thirty-one percent of school-age children in Botswana, 34 percent in Mexico, 49 percent in Brazil, 63 percent in Russia, and 78 percent in Vietnam live in households in which all adults work. Globally, we estimate that at least 590 million children between six and fourteen years old live in households where all parents and adult extended-family members work.

Urbanization

At the same time, over the course of the twentieth century, a rapidly rising proportion of the world's population began to live in urban areas. Only 18 percent of the world's population lived in urban areas at the beginning of the twentieth century. But by the century's close, nearly half of the world's population did.[6] The greatest changes in the developing world happened in the second half of the twentieth century, with the percentage of the population living in cities more than doubling from 18 to 40 percent. The United Nations estimates that by the year 2030 more than 56 percent of the developing world's population will live in cities.[7] Globally, more than 60 percent of the world's population is expected to live in cities by the year 2030.

Poor individuals and families living in rural areas without land or means to support themselves often moved to cities in hopes of finding decent work. Some found improved work opportunities; for others, cities were merely a cruel illusion of opportunity and offered no exit from poverty. While some migrated to cities truly of their own free will, others moved to cities when droughts, expropriation of land, and "development" projects like dams left them landless, or when falling agricultural prices in the context of first-world trade barriers to agricultural goods left these families with no way to support themselves in rural areas.

Why does urbanization matter to families? Often, when adults move to cities, they become separated from their extended families and, thus, from a critical source of help.[8] At the same time, parents living in cities are more likely to work in the formal labor force—and even those who work in the informal labor force are more likely to work at jobs where it is difficult or impossible for them to take their children to work.

Globalization

Families are not in jeopardy because of these transformations in labor and location alone. Indeed, conditions might have improved and families might not have been placed at risk were it not for the concurrent economic pressure resulting from globalization.

Of the myriad of changes that characterized the marked rise in globalization during the twentieth century, it is the increasing flow of jobs across borders that has had the greatest impact on working families. Companies can now readily move their jobs to the country with the lowest labor costs. In the past, barriers in communication made running operations efficiently around the world difficult. Savings from using less-expensive labor in poorer countries did not offset high transportation costs, which made producing goods in one market and selling them in another difficult. Dramatic improvements in the speed and costs of communication and transportation have lowered both of these obstacles. At the same time, free-trade zones and agreements have dropped the barriers that countries used to erect in the form of taxes and tariffs. Companies now readily move jobs from the United States to Mexico in search of cheaper labor, and within a few years the jobs move from Mexico to Honduras to China and elsewhere in search of even more poorly paid labor.

The scale of this relocation of jobs is unprecedented and has led to a series of consequences for families. In industrialized countries first and then in industrializing countries with decent working conditions, millions of jobs were lost. As a result, there has been increasing pressure placed on workers to accept lower wages and fewer benefits in order to keep their jobs. While this trend began in high-income countries, it has already spread to middle-income countries, and consequently labor standards have declined in many regions.

At the same time that workers have lost their leverage in the fight for decent working conditions, nations have lost the power to mandate that all companies within their borders provide adequate working conditions because of their own need to compete for corporations to bring jobs. These changes, which are occurring in America and Australia, France and Fiji, are increasingly intertwined, but so too are the opportunities for solutions.

While presenting real threats of a perpetual "race to the bottom" in labor conditions, globalization also presents the possibility of reversing this and setting a floor of decent working conditions globally. Organizations like the World Trade Organization are influencing national economic behavior more substantially than any previous form of governance with global participation. The problem lies not with its potential, but with its execution. To date, global trade agreements have been used to protect the economic interests of those with substantial capital, not the human and economic interests of laborers.

Perfect Storm

When these three major historical shifts in labor, urbanization, and economic globalization occurred simultaneously, they dropped working families into the vortex of what is in many ways a perfect storm. There was no inherent problem with the migration of families from rural to urban areas or the movement of men out of fields, rural jobs, crafts, and individual service work into the industrial and post-industrial labor force. Yes, the changes were disruptive, but they also offered new and real opportunities for economic growth and better living conditions. Nor was there any inherent problem in the similar movement that followed in women's work. Women's entry into the paid labor force away from home offered similar economic advantages to families and increasingly equal opportunities for women and men. Had families alternated whether it was the woman or the man who worked away from the home and farm, then the equal opportunities could have been present while an adult was home to care for any children and other dependents. Had changes in reproductive-age women's and men's productive labor occurred without the simultaneous changes in the availability of extended family, then grandmothers and grandfathers, great-aunts and great-uncles, would still have been available to help rear children—at least for the first generation of the transformation. (After that, as adults stayed in the workforce until older ages, the question still would have arisen, because older family members, even living nearby, would have themselves been working at jobs that made it difficult to help care for children at the same time.) Moreover, had working conditions and social supports been developed that took families into account, changes in the labor force could have gone smoothly.

The perfect storm arose because the changes in residence and work occurred concurrently with increasingly one-sided pressures from globalization. With the power of workers to press for changes in private company policy diminished because of companies' threats of taking jobs to other countries, globalization eroded the ability of working families to bargain for basic decent working conditions at the exact same time that these conditions became increasingly critical to their ability to adequately care for their children. With its weakening of the ability of individual countries to guarantee decent conditions for their workers, the current form taken by globalization also decreased the ability of the public sector to provide solutions—exactly when children and families needed them the most. It was the confluence of changes in labor force participation, urbanization, and the current form of globalization that placed families worldwide in the eye of the storm and raised critical new questions and concerns on a global scale, among them: Who will care for infants and toddlers? Who will care for six- and seven-year-olds when school is not in session in different countries? How will adults keep their jobs while caring for children who become sick with fever, diarrhea, or pneumonia? How can parents ensure that their young children receive essential preventive care, such as immunizations, or receive breast milk, the best protection against the frequent malnutrition and illnesses accompanying infancy in poor nations around the world? Have the transformations helped to lift parents and children alike out of poverty around the world? If not, why not?

But families can survive this storm strengthened, and poverty and gender inequality can be decreased as a result of the labor and economic transformations, if we address the needs of working caregivers. With *Forgotten Families* I hope to make clear the urgency of the need to collectively address the problems that working families face in industrialized and developing countries alike, and to demonstrate how feasible and affordable it is to solve these problems and how costly it is to us all to do nothing.

Book Overview

Chapter 2 of this book will examine the experiences of families raising children from birth through preschool in Latin America, Asia, Europe, and North America. Chapter 3 will focus on school-age children, the care they lack, and the caregiving gaps they are forced to fill when no one else is available. Chapter 4 will examine the consequences of the changes discussed above for children's health. Chapter 5 will examine the implications of these transformations on family income, the ability of children and parents to exit poverty, and the degree of equality between girls and boys, men and women. Chapter 6 steps back and asks the question of whether the dilemmas that families face, as great as they are, continue to be relevant in the context of other crises from epidemics to natural disasters to the long-term aftermath of wars. Having looked in detail at the impact on the health and development of children of all ages, the economic welfare of families, and equality, chapter 7 provides some answers to what can be done about meeting the critical needs of children and families in the midst of globalization.

While much has been written about the lives of working parents and their children in the United States and Western Europe, far too little has been written or done about the conditions faced by the more than 930 million children under fifteen and their working parents living in countries in Latin America, Africa, Central and Eastern Europe, the Middle East, and much of Asia. This book is dedicated to telling their stories—stories that together paint a picture of how the global economy has left out working parents and their children.

Only the thickest armor of indifference would enable anyone to emerge unchanged, intellectually and emotionally, after witnessing the conditions under which children in the world economy are being raised. Only myths and lack of will stand in the way of implementing effective solutions to this worldwide dilemma.

2

Who Cares for Preschool Children?

When you ask the leaders in most countries who is caring for infants, toddlers, and preschoolers, they have similar answers: "Grandparents play a large role in our culture." When pressed, they make clear that they mean grandmothers. What about when grandmothers aren't available, you ask? "There's lots of informal care," they inevitably reply, "other family members, neighbors, women in the community." "Many mothers can bring their children to work." The answers are vague because they describe a world that has been kept out of sight, unexamined.

Ramon

I met with families in Tegucigalpa, Honduras, early in 2001. The slums of the city rose rapidly on the escarpments on either side of Rio Choluteca, which divided the Honduran capital from its twin city, Comayagüela. In 1998, Hurricane Mitch had led to devastating floods and massive mudslides. Years later, the reverberations of the natural disaster were still felt in the precarious work and family lives of the poor.

Ramon Canez's family lived in a room in a lengthy metal barracks that housed families who had lost their homes to the floods and mudslides of Hurricane Mitch and who still had not been able to replace them more than two years later. When I met Ramon, he was leaning against a metal pole beside a set of communal sinks. He stood watching members of the neighboring families wash clothes. At ten years old, he was small and slight for his age. He wore black jeans that were several sizes too big at the waist and too long at the ankle. A girl in the neighborhood barracks had told me that Ramon was caring for his younger siblings. When I asked Ramon about this, he led me thirty yards from where he stood, back to the single room that the eight members of his family shared.

Ramon recounted on the walk to his family's one room that he was caring for five siblings. When he opened the door, three of his younger sisters swarmed around him. Scared to have been alone in the darkness, they were clearly delighted to see him come home. Martita was five years old, Cari was four, and Justina was three. At first we couldn't see the other two in the darkness; even when Ramon pointed out Laurita, it was difficult to recognize her. There appeared to be a doll placed on a chair in the dark room, but not the toddler he described. The object was completely immobile, unlike any healthy two-year-old. Even her eyes did not respond to our entry. Only with Ramon's insistence did it become clear to me that this was in fact Laurita. Farther inside the dark room on a bed lay Beni, Ramon's infant brother.

There had been nothing wrong with Laurita at birth. But during her first two years of life, according to Ramon, at best she had been eating one meal a day when their parents were gone. In reality, it was unclear whether she had even had the chance to eat that one meal and, if so, of what it may have consisted. All of the children depended on their fourteen-year-old brother, Miguel, to come back for them to have a meal since Ramon had no money to purchase food nor means to get to the market. Because Laurita's thin, bent legs were welded with rickets from malnutrition, she never used them. Ramon explained simply that she couldn't walk yet. But there was also no one there to get her out of her chair or to encourage her to walk. She didn't move her eyes. She barely moved anything.

At five months old, Beni was on his way to becoming equally malnourished. There was a bottle at home, but Ramon didn't know how to prepare it. He said Miguel would feed Beni when he got home. Ramon also said that Miguel would feed Beni when he cried, but Miguel seldom was present when Beni was crying. Beni had a deep, penetrating cough—one far deeper than most infants would ever exhibit. There was medicine in the neatly kept room for his cough. The medicine's label clearly indicated that he was meant to take it three times a day, but there was no one who could give it to Beni during the twelve hours that his parents were at work. Concerned that the side effects would be dangerous if Beni received too much, his parents had specifically instructed Ramon never to give the medicine. Because no adult care providers were available during the day, Beni was receiving far too little medication and was growing dangerously ill.

Ramon was tender with his siblings and as attentive as one could expect a ten-year-old to be, but, like any other ten-year-old, he was unable to provide adequate care for five children aged five years and younger. Ramon was about to start third grade. He had already repeated the second grade because of time lost from school when his parents had asked him to care for Martita, then age three, who had had convulsions and high fevers. As a result of the limited care he could give, his younger sisters' teeth were rotted with bottle mouth, a condition occurring when a young child is left with a sweetened bottle in her mouth for hours on end without supervision.

Although Ramon's parents left the children alone at home, it was clear they were caring for their children as well as they could with the scarce resources available. Ramon's mother cooked and sold food in the street from six in the morning to six in the evening, all but one day a week. His father worked equally long hours as an electrician. In their one-room home, there were no signs of even a small amount of money having been spent on the parents themselves. Neither a radio nor an old black-and-white television was visible, as in many of the other rooms in the barracks, and only a minimum of adults' clothes could be seen. The small shelter was neat and clean, and carefully arranged on one wall were stuffed animals the parents had bought for their children. They had clearly taken the time not only to get medicine for Ramon's youngest sibling but to ensure that he understood it was unsafe for him to administer the medicine. Needing to work to try to provide for their family's basic needs of food, clothing, and shelter, these parents had no choice but to leave their preschool children in the care of their school-age brother, a young child himself. As a result, their children's health, basic development, and education were all being sacrificed.

When asked about a child like Ramon in their own countries, most of the leaders I met in different nations would say, "It's sad. It may happen. But it's rare. Normally the families can provide care or a neighbor can or parents can bring the child safely with them to work." But they don't know how often it happens. This chapter will report findings from my research team's in-depth studies of more than 1,000 parents, childcare providers, and employers worldwide, as well as findings from our analysis of survey data from 55,000 households in seven countries and five regions.

Who Is Caring for Preschool Children around the World?

Extended Family: An Answer for a Minority, Absent or Insufficient for a Majority

Before presenting findings from our interviews of families in Botswana, I explained to an audience at the largest teaching hospital in Gaborone why we were looking at the conditions that working families face. A hand went up. "Those issues don't affect us here. Everyone has extended-family members they can rely on so they never have any problem getting care for their children." Though the belief was satisfying, the problem was that the experience of the families we had interviewed in Botswana belied it. We interviewed many families in which parents had no choice but to leave young children home alone, pull older children out of school to provide free care, or take children to the workplace even when doing so threatened the children's health and development or the parents' jobs. But before I could respond to the fantasy the first speaker relayed by sharing the experiences of some of the 250 families we had already interviewed, a Motswana[1] surgeon raised his hand and interjected: "A lot of parents have no one they can rely on. I see the children who, because of that, end up being left home alone when they come into the emergency room or into my operating room with broken bones and burns."

When we began our work in Russia, one of our colleagues, who was otherwise knowledgeable about many of the problems challenging Russian families, explained, "You won't find any parents to interview in Moscow who don't have extended-family members they can rely on. Everyone in Russia has a babushka. Problems may arise in other countries, but not here. Russia is different. Everyone has a grandma who helps." But once again, that was not the reality.

What, then, is the global reality? There is no doubt that both having two parents in a nuclear family and having extended family can make an enormous difference to children's care. Among families we interviewed, 33 percent of single parents had left their young children home alone compared with 22 percent of parents living with a spouse or partner.[2] When single parents have no other adult caregivers in the household, young children are even more likely to be left home alone (56 percent versus 23 percent). When extended-family members outside the household are also unavailable, the increased risk of being left home alone is dramatic: 67 percent versus 23 percent.

But the myths that extended families alone solve the problem are mistaken in at least three ways. First, many working parents and their young children have sporadic, limited, or no contact with extended-family members they might ever turn to for help. Worldwide, with urbanization and the increasing mobility required to get and keep jobs, the number of working adults who live near enough to their own parents to be able to turn to them for regular assistance is rapidly declining. Second, even among those who continue to live near their children's grandparents, many cannot rely on them for help. Grandparents themselves may need to work and may be as constrained as parents in their ability to provide routine care or even to take time off to care for a grandchild who is sick, Third, all too often those adult family members who might be able to help—because they are close by and are not working themselves or already caring for a full house—face physical and mental health constraints. In fact, when extended-family members are close, they are as likely to be in need of care as to be able to assist with it.

In situations where extended-family members are in need of care, preschool children often get less care than if no extended family were nearby. When mothers or fathers are caring for other sick family members, children are twice as likely to be left home alone. Forty percent of working parents caring for a sick spouse and 41 percent of parents caring for extended family had to leave a child home alone (see figure 2-1). When extended-family members don't require assistance, they may still be too physically limited, frail, or sick to provide adequate care for their grandchildren, nephews, nieces, and other dependents because the same constraints on age and health that limit extended-family members' ability to work affect the quality of the care they can provide. Motshamiki Tshwaragano's experience provided an example. She worked in Botswana cleaning churches, and she relied on her niece to care for her disabled grandchild, Bagitle, who was paralyzed on his left side. Her niece was available because she couldn't work for pay—partly because she had a significant mental disability. Motshamiki explained:

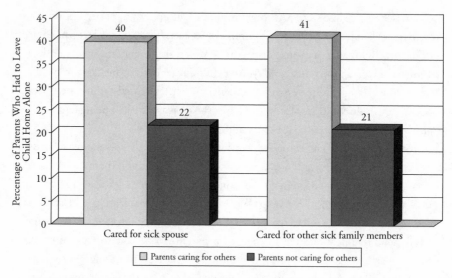

Figure 2-1

**Parents with Other Caregiving Responsibilities Are More Likely
to Have to Leave Their Preschool Children Home Alone.**

Note: Data from Project on Global Working Families' in-depth interviews with working caregivers. Analyses in the above figure are based on households with a zero- to five-year-old child.

She helps, but she's very forgetful. She takes a long time to learn things, too, so you have to remind her all the time how to do things. She gets tired easily and she forgets easily, so every day you have to tell her what to do and how to do it. She can cook, but sometimes she'll cook something for ten minutes and then take it off the heat for no reason and start dishing it. I have to help her all the time. I can't leave her alone for a long time because she'll mess everything up while I'm gone. . . . When I'm at work, I can't come back and guide her, so there may be times in which she gets very little done. . . . The problem is that Bagitle is paralyzed and can't do things for himself. He comes home at lunch and that's when he needs help. I get worried because my niece gets his medication confused at times, too. He's supposed to take two pills, three times a day. Sometimes she gets confused and gives him three pills, twice a day.

While the extent may vary, similar problems of family members being unable to provide adequate care because of poor health arose in every society we examined. Grandparents, in-laws, aunts, uncles, and other relatives who, at one point in time, are able to provide help often cannot continue to do so as they age. While these natural life transitions occur under all economic conditions, the timing of transitions is another way in which those who are in greatest need face the greatest obstacles. The poor develop chronic and disabling conditions at younger ages.[3]

Worldwide, it is the poorest parents in the poorest countries who because of a lack of any other options end up needing extended-family members the most to provide childcare. Yet while poor families have the greatest need, they are also the least likely to be able to rely on extended family for help as their extended-family members are the most likely to have to work or to be in need of care themselves. While less than a third of low-income parents can rely on extended family for help without needing to provide assistance, nearly half of low-income parents are providing assistance to extended family (see figure 2-2).

Taking Preschool Children to Work

After "grandparents care for all the preschoolers in need," the most common myth is that parents can care for their children well, if need be, while working. While some policy makers acknowledge the improbability of such safe care in factories and the unlikelihood that parents will be given permission to bring children to work elsewhere in the formal sector, they assume it is not only possible but a decent solution in the informal sector. The image conjured up is of a parent—nearly universally a mother—working with an infant swaddled tenderly on her back or a toddler playing happily at her side as she sells goods in a market or cleans a home.

In our studies, we met many women who had lost formal sector, decent-paying jobs in order to care for their children. At times, they subsequently found informal sector jobs which allowed them to bring their children. But even those women, who had the better experiences of the lot, did not have any romanticized fantasy of their children's lives spent at their mother's side while they worked. Most shared a bleak view of children at work with their mothers who had started in the informal sector because of lack of education and job choices and had never been able to leave because of caregiving responsibilities.

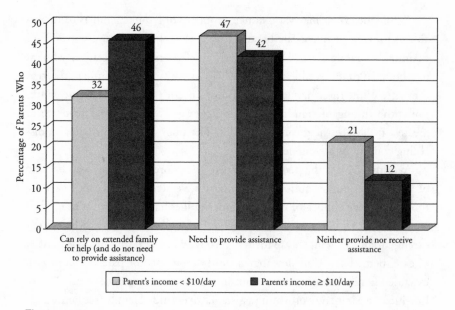

Figure 2-2
Low-Income Parents Are Less Likely to Receive Help from and
More Likely to Need to Provide Caregiving Assistance to Extended Family.
Note: Data from Project on Global Working Families' in-depth interviews with working care-givers. Analyses in the above figure are based on households with a zero- to five-year-old child and represent family help and needs over the life course. Income data from each survey have been converted to a common currency using the World Bank's purchasing power parity (PPP) conversion factors.

Even when children taken to work are not at high risk of sustaining sudden life-threatening injuries, their opportunities for normal growth are often degraded daily. Amalia Montoya, born and reared in Cancun, Mexico, was raising her son as a single mother. She had been cleaning houses since age fifteen and never had the chance to finish school. Living far from her family, she had no one to turn to for help. Without sufficient publicly supported slots available, childcare was far beyond her economic reach. Amalia took her infant son to work with her because she had no other choice. "It was really difficult because it's not the same as being in your own house. When he began to cry because he was hungry, I couldn't tend to him at the same time as working." For example, when her employer's family wanted to eat at the same time that her son was hungry, she had to leave her crying infant—who, like all other infants, needed more frequent meals than did the adults—and serve her employer. She went on to describe how she grew depressed over the situation and her son's consequent malnutrition.

Beyond Amalia's inability to feed her son regularly, she couldn't care for him adequately when he was sick. She explained how, during the first year of his life, he became ill often (which was not surprising for an inadequately nourished child). "I had to take him [to work] as he was—sick—because I didn't have anyone else to leave him with." However, she couldn't care for him adequately while working. Like any other sick infant, hers needed extra attention—far more than she could provide. When Amalia gained access to a childcare center, perhaps the most telling summary of her son's experience was her delight in the most basic elements: "I dropped him off at seven-thirty in the morning and picked him up at five o'clock in the afternoon. He ate there and everything." She was grateful even for care that consisted of the most fundamental features: enabling her to work, providing her son with adult supervision, and ensuring that he could eat.

Among Mexican parents we interviewed, nearly one-half reported that they had to take their preschool-aged children to work either regularly or occasionally. Some parents had to bring their young children with them every day because they lacked any other care options. For other parents, taking children to work served as a stopgap when childcare fell through or when a child was sick and not allowed to attend childcare.

The same stories echoed among the parents we interviewed in Botswana and Vietnam. What differed across national borders and economic circumstances was not the nature of the problem but the level of parents' desperation. Preschool children in the poorest families were taken to work under the worst circumstances because their parents, who faced more hazardous conditions at work, had fewer alternatives to fall back on when no childcare was available. One in four parents earning less than $10 per day have to take their children to work regularly, as do one in four parents who have just a primary or middle school education themselves. Parents who work in the informal sector are the least likely to have access to formal childcare. As a result, half of the parents we interviewed who worked in the informal sector needed to bring their children regularly (see figure 2-3).

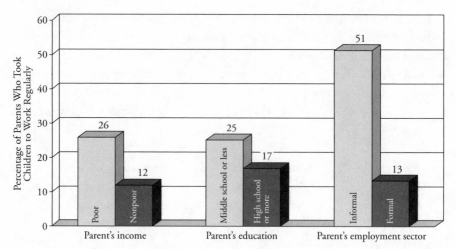

Figure 2-3
Parents with Fewer Resources and Those in the Informal Sector
Are More Likely to Lack Formal Childcare and Bring Child to Work.
Note: Data from Project on Global Working Families' in-depth interviews with working care-givers. Analyses in the above figure are based on households with a zero- to five-year-old child. *Poor* was defined as having an income below $10 per day. Income data from each survey has been converted to a common currency using the World Bank's purchasing power parity (PPP) conversion factors.

Informal Care: When Quality Formal Care Is Unaffordable

The final fiction about preschool childcare is that inexpensive informal care is a viable solution. It's clear that low-income families and many middle-income ones cannot currently afford or find space in childcare centers for all of their children. But it's also clear that there is a large and apparently less expensive informal sector market for care. Public policy makers often ask, without beginning to examine the double standard implied as they support early childhood care and education centers in higher-income countries, "Isn't informal care the solution for young children in poor countries?" These experts argue that it is less expensive and assume it is as good as formal care. Our experience is that, in the majority of cases, parents reported only that it was cheaper.

In Botswana, Mmapula Sikalame had five children, aged six months to thirteen years. Like others who could barely afford informal childcare, she had little choice about whom to hire. She told us:

> Initially, I didn't want to hire a small child. I tried a very old woman who was even older than myself. Then my husband was in an accident, and he was admitted at [a major hospital in the capital, Gaborone]. He had a head injury, and I had to spend the majority of my time in Gaborone, and this old woman was left to care for my kids. Apparently, she was drinking and left my kids alone to go and drink. I came back from Gaborone to find she was no longer with my children.

After that experience, Mmapula hired a thirteen-year-old girl, who it seemed at first could at least be taught what was important in caring for the children. But the girl, like many others her age, failed to care well for young children. Mmapula explained, "Sometimes I spend a lot of time at work, and I find that my children don't have any food, there is no water, and all sorts of problems have come up."

Because there was no public support for childcare and because she earned so little, Mmanko Chikopo similarly wrestled first with low-quality care and then with the lack of any childcare. Mmanko, a cleaner, earned $46 a month, so she struggled to provide enough food for her four children. Hiring somebody to care for her children in her home was her only childcare option, since she could not afford a childcare center at $52 per month: the center care would cost more than she earned. So she hired a young girl to help her at home and care for her children during the day. But she knew that her children were receiving inadequate care:

> I'm not satisfied with the care that this girl provides. Sometimes I come home and she's not there. There was a time when I forgot the keys at home. When I got there, she wasn't home. She had gone with her friends. That was around ten o'clock in the morning. It looked like she hadn't cooked anything. Until that time, this child [of mine] hadn't had anything to eat.

Her daughter who had been left home alone was three years old. "I do have very serious problems with [the baby-sitter] because she leaves the child alone and she doesn't even lock up the house. She just goes. I just have to keep moving on because I can't afford any better help. I've always had problems with household helpers because of the amount of money that I can afford to give them."

In the countries we studied, many parents reported that they had to leave their young children in the "care" of other children. In Vietnam, 19 percent of the working parents we interviewed had to leave children home alone or in the care of an unpaid child, and 4 percent relied on a paid child for childcare. In Mexico, 27 percent of the parents we interviewed had to leave children alone or in the care of an unpaid child, and 9 percent left their sons and daughters with another child who was paid as a provider. While Botswana had a nearly identical GDP per capita to Mexico and one that was more than seven times as high as Vietnam's, Botswana families had the highest rate of leaving children home alone. With next to no publicly supported childcare, 48 percent of working parents in Botswana had to leave a child home alone or in the care of an unpaid child (see figure 2-4).

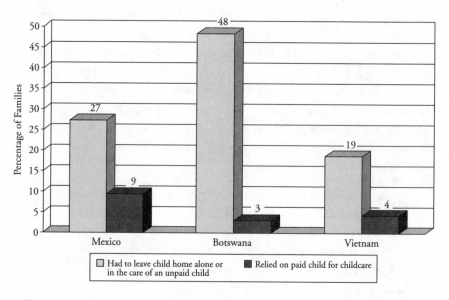

Figure 2-4
Frequency That Children Are Left Alone or in the "Care" of Other Children.
Note: Data from Project on Global Working Families' in-depth interviews with working caregivers. Analyses in the above figure are based on households with a zero- to five-year-old child.

There was a clear social class gradient in informal care. Parents who were poor and parents who had the least educational opportunities themselves were the most likely to have to leave their preschool children in the care of another child. Parents with a middle school or less education were twice as likely (22 versus 9 percent) to have to leave their children in the care of other, unpaid children as parents with a high school education or more, who as a result earned more money.

"You get what you pay for" may be true, but whatever wisdom the old adage contains offers little to those who have no resources with which to pay for decent childcare. When poor families were able to afford informal childcare, the care was often inexpensive because it was provided by a child who was too young or an adult who had too many problems to find another job. Since they could not find a better-paying job, they were willing to accept the minimal pay that parents making very low wages could offer, even when the pay was too low to survive on. Middle-class parents did better in the informal care market, since they could afford to pay more and, therefore, could hire someone who might otherwise have gotten a different job.

The calculus is cruel: 2.7 billion people live on less than $2 a day, and 1.1 billion live on less than $1 a day.[4] Even those who manage to feed their children on less than $2 a day simply cannot afford to pay, on their own, even for informal care of their preschoolers that will ensure the children's safety and good health.

Home Alone

In every country where we interviewed families, preschool children were being left home alone or in the care of other children because parents had no choice. When parents were poor and couldn't afford to pay for childcare, when parents had limited education themselves and therefore fewer job opportunities, and when parents faced costly penalties at work for caring for their children, they were more likely to leave children home alone on either a regular or an intermittent basis. Forty-six percent of those who lost pay because of caregiving responsibilities ended up having to leave children home alone (see figure 2-5). Parents with a middle school or less education were more than twice as likely (39 versus 18 percent) to have to leave their children home alone or in the care of other, unpaid children as were parents with a high school education or more.

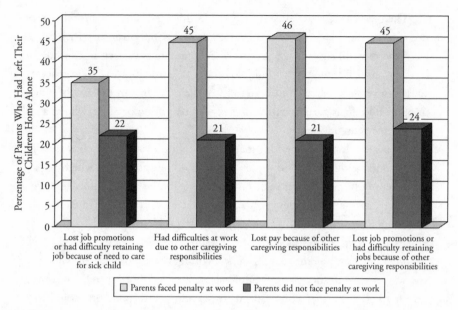

Figure 2-5
When Parents Face Penalties at Work for Caregiving,
Preschool Children Are More Likely to Be Left Home Alone.
Note: Data from Project on Global Working Families' in-depth interviews with working caregivers. Analyses in the above figure are based on households with a zero- to five-year-old child.

Paucity of Quality Care: Consequences for Children and Parents

Once it becomes clear that parents have few options regarding where to take their young children, that children are not being cared for by a healthy grandmother or grandfather, that informal care is as likely as not to be provided by another child, that children brought to work are not enjoying quality time with their parents but may be tied up for their own safety to protect a parent's job, some unspoken questions still hang in the air: How do the children fare? Are the circumstances, while less than ideal, nonetheless leaving the children with their basic needs met? What happens to the parents?

No Chance for Healthy Development

When children are left alone or left in inadequate informal care, they have little chance for healthy development. In two out of three families where parents had to leave children home alone or in the care of an unpaid child, the children suffered in accidents or other emergencies while their parents were at work. In more than a third of cases where children were left home alone or in the care of a child, the children had suffered from developmental or behavioral problems (see figure 2-6).

Forty-two-year-old Maribel Mendoza Reyes was raising her three children

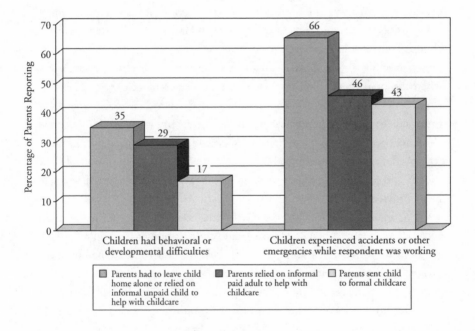

Figure 2-6
When Parents Have Poor Childcare Choices,
Preschool Children's Development and Health Suffer.
Note: Data from Project on Global Working Families' in-depth interviews with working caregivers. Analyses in the above figure are based on households with a zero- to five-year-old child.

in southern Mexico. In her town, there was only one childcare center, and far more people wanted slots than were available. Unable to get a space for her children, she hired the only type of baby-sitter she could afford to come to her house: inexperienced and untrained. The baby-sitter would hit Maribel's children too often in failed attempts to discipline them. Eventually, she left them home alone. Maribel recounted: "The last time she left my children locked up. I had to leave for work in [a city more than an hour away by bus], and when I got back, my children were locked up. They had been [alone] for four hours and she had left. She left them under lock and key. When I got home, my children were crying because they were hungry." Both the lack of food and lack of positive interaction with an adult for many hours a day affected their cognitive development.[5]

Often unable to live on the low wages they earn, informal childcare providers frequently end up leaving children alone or taking them along when going to a second job. At other times, poor-quality providers leave the children out of a lack of commitment or no sense of responsibility. Clearly, preschool children do not have an adequate chance for healthy development when the poor-quality informal care they receive results in lengthy periods alone or locked up. Parents who have extensive support networks are sometimes able to draw on family, friends, or neighbors to look in on the informal childcare providers and make sure that adequate care is being given. But those who live far from their extended family or are poor enough that most of their friends and neighbors are also working have few means to supervise the care being provided.

When parents have to bring their children to work because they have no access to adequate formal or informal care, children under five still often lack a fair chance for healthy development. In Mexico, Edith Merino had been orphaned as a young child and, to survive, had gone to work as a domestic servant at the age of eight. She had never had a chance to complete her education. Her husband was a laborer and earned too little for their family of nine to survive on his income alone. When her first two children were young, Edith continued to work as a domestic servant and explained: "At the time, I had to take my two little children with me. [My daughter] was about a year and a half. I had to tie her up by the foot of the table with a shawl in order that she not fall while I was cooking. . . . That's how it was. . . . My children had to suffer." Toddlers need active play time in order to develop motor skills. Lacking any affordable childcare, Edith had little choice but to tie her daughter up. But while tying her up kept her daughter safe in the short run, it was virulent in the long run as she fell increasingly behind other children developmentally.[6]

Injuries, Illness, and Malnutrition

The consequences of poor-quality informal care for young children's health and development—for their nutrition, as well as for the frequency of infections, injuries, and accidents—can be nearly as devastating as the consequences of no care. In Lobatse, Botswana, for instance, Ame Seleke came home from work in a meat-packing plant to find her infant, who had been left by her baby-sitter, alone and injured on the floor. Sometimes, parents never know the true sources of the injuries, even though it is clear that serious injuries are more frequent in poor-quality care. Refilwe Keetetswe, in Gaborone, came home from work to find her son scalded from boiling water. The burn was bad enough that years later he still had a scar. The baby-sitter reported that the scalding had occurred when the child took a cup of hot tea from his older brother. But it was impossible to know whether that had really happened, whether the baby-sitter had been there to supervise at all, or whether, if there, she had been watching the children closely enough.

When extended-family members are overburdened or have diminished capacities, the care they provide can jeopardize the health of children, just as poor-quality care by paid providers does. Vu Truong Khanh worked as a laborer making furniture in Vietnam. Her husband suffered from depression and had been unable to work for many months. During that period, Khanh had to take sole responsibility both for earning the income to sustain their family and for caring for their two children. Since she could not afford childcare, she had left her son and daughter in the care of her mother-in-law. But her mother-in-law was often either too overburdened or ill prepared to provide adequate care. During one of the worst episodes, Khanh's daughter had nearly died from untreated meningitis when Khanh's mother-in-law put off taking the child to a doctor for her high fever. Khanh summarized her concerns, which went beyond this single crisis and included the daily risks. "We left the child at home with her grandmother. She was old, so she could not care for the child as a mother could. But there was nothing we could do when our family faced economic difficulties. After the child would go, I cried a lot. I was very worried."

While injury and illness can surely happen anywhere, the data clearly indicate that children in poor care have higher accident and injury rates (see chapter 4).

Impact of Unreliable Care on Parents' Jobs

Unreliable care takes its toll on parents' jobs and ability to earn enough for their families to survive, as well as on children's health and development. Mmanko Chikopo, a forty-two-year-old single mother who lived in Lobatse, worked as a cleaner. There was constant turnover in her children's caregivers. Mmanko explained, "I would hire a caregiver who would stay on for a few months and then she would leave. I have never had a steady or reliable caregiver." She had not even been able to rely regularly on having *any* childcare. She told us:

> There was a time when I paid my helper at the end of the month.
> Following day, she didn't report for work. I was supposed to go to
> work, and I had to call my supervisor. I told her I couldn't come. My
> supervisor told me she couldn't accept that report from the phone, so
> I had to come in. I tried to explain that there was no one to look after
> my kids, but she said I had to bring them with me. I had to go there
> by taxi and report that I couldn't come to work. Then she said okay. I
> had to take three days' leave so that I could look for a baby-sitter. I
> couldn't get a baby-sitter. I knew my supervisor wouldn't take a re-
> port over the phone, so I took my kids again and talked to her about
> it. She told me to take my kids home. So I tried to explain to her that
> I couldn't because there was no one to watch the kids. . . . I looked
> and found somebody who wasn't good either. She was a drunk. She
> would just disappear. I had to make do, even though I knew it wasn't
> the best care I could get.

Mmanko longed to be able to send her children to formal childcare centers or to preschool.

While informal care was often unreliable because the low pay meant it was regularly performed by children or adults unable to get other jobs, care provided by family members could be equally unreliable because of the declining health of poor, older family members with serious consequences for children and parents alike. Modiegi Tatedi lived in Lobatse and worked as a conductor on a bus from 6:00 a.m. until 9:00 p.m., seven days a week. She had only four days off from work a month. When Modiegi returned to work after the birth of her children, her mother cared for them. But when Modiegi's children were thirteen, ten, and five years old, her mother died. She struggled to find someone who could help her with childcare and eventually turned to an elderly aunt. But that solution ended after a year because the aunt had a stroke. After her aunt's stroke, Modiegi had to leave her job because she lacked any adequate care for her children. The job loss plunged her family further into poverty. Modiegi's story is not uncommon. Poor families we interviewed were at heightened risk of job and pay loss due to caregiving. Fifty percent of poor parents we interviewed had lost pay and 15 percent had lost a job promotion or had difficulty retaining a job when caring for a sick child.

The Problem Is Not That Solutions Do Not Exist

The natural question that arises is: Are there effective ways to provide affordable high-quality care to poor families in affluent countries? to poor and middle-class families in low-income countries? The remarkable success stories—remarkable for what they have done and for the fact that we have failed to replicate them—provide a clear yes to the question of feasibility. Still, questions remain regarding the global community's failure to replicate these experiences. The question of widespread change will be addressed in the book's final chapter.

For now, it is important first to document the answer to the question: Do sustainable and effective responses currently exist in poor countries? The San Isidro Center of Honduras provides just one example.

Supporting Children Whose Parents Work in the Formal and Informal Sectors

In operation for more than thirty years, the San Isidro Center provides care to children whose parents work in the informal sector, as well as to those whose parents work in the formal sector. Located near the central marketplace in Tegulcigalpa, Honduras, it has a long history of serving children whose parents work selling goods in the *mercado*. The childcare center had more toys and supplies before a fire in the nearby market burned down the center one night in 1996. When we visited in 2001, five years after the fire, the center occupied a far smaller building. Due to inadequate funds, the overcrowded center could not move to a larger space and lacked sufficient toys. Even under these difficult, far from ideal circumstances, the center provided essential services to scores of children. It was one of only three public childcare centers in the whole capital, however, and the need far outstripped the number of spaces.

The infant room, approximately twelve by eighteen feet, held fifteen cribs, in which children often slept two to a crib because there were twenty-five infants enrolled. With cribs lining every wall of the room and an additional row of cribs up the middle, there was only a small circle where one could walk in order to reach each baby. This small circle and a roughly four-foot-wide area at the entrance were the only places in which the infants and toddlers could crawl and walk. There were no toys in the room, and the director explained that the center had no budget to replace the games lost in the fire.

The children in the center, who ranged from eight months to six years old, were grouped by age. The classroom designated for infants had eight- to eighteen-month-olds. The toddler room, which had been designed to be limited to twenty, held twenty-five children. The kindergarten room held thirty-four. Supplies, such as paper and crayons for the youngest children, were scarce. Although the children were being left in crowded conditions, their parents had no alternative, and the director didn't have the heart to turn these children away. Lined up around the walls and squeezed next to each other, the preschool children were sitting on the floor and building things from some old popsicle sticks and a few wooden blocks. In the toddler room, children were running around the circular walkway that was used to access their cribs.

While the building was small and the supplies limited, the staff members were well trained. Each classroom had two childcare providers. The center had a nurse, a nutritionist, and cooks, as well as access to a doctor. The staff took care to visit every home so that they would know about the enrolled children's living conditions. The small center rooms were scrubbed every day while the children were taken into a yet smaller room, where they watched cartoons on TV as their own room was cleaned. The childcare providers played games and sang songs with them when toys were unavailable. Even when the center was overcrowded, undersupplied, and inadequately financially supported, the care and attention that all of the childcare providers gave the children still made for the best alternative many of the families had.

Every parent we spoke to made that fact readily apparent. Damaris Leal was a twenty-five-year-old mother of four children: an eight-year-old boy, a four-year-old girl, a one-and-a-half-year-old boy, and a two-month-old boy. She worked providing outreach services to agricultural workers. Although Damaris's mother cared for her two-month-old grandchild, she couldn't care for the other grandchildren because she worked in the informal sector, making and selling tortillas. Damaris worked six days a week. She explained that she knew people who did not use the childcare center because of the time involved in trying to get a child admitted and registered. Damaris also knew of mothers who felt that too many children were being cared for at the center, but Damaris had seen what could happen to children left home alone. She had watched friends leave cold food for their children, who had grown sick while eating inadequately alone. She had observed others teach their children how to use a stove, only to find the children getting burned when home alone. The childcare center first and foremost offered safety. Moreover, it offered Damaris's four-year-old daughter and one-and-a-half-year-old son the chance to play with others of the same age.

Chavela Salinas had been trying for three years to get her four-year-old grandson enrolled in the childcare center, but there hadn't been space. The center director had told us that there were easily more than two hundred children looking for space in her center whom she hadn't been able to serve. Chavela had kept checking back for three years until space had become available. She had been persistent because the benefits, going beyond safety, had been clear to her. She spoke to us of how the children learned more while in the center. She noted proudly that they learned to sing, to count, and to distinguish colors and that they got to paint. "They know a lot by the time they go to school," she said.

Alejandro Estrada was thin and neatly dressed in poor-quality clothes when we spoke with him. He had come to pick up his five-year-old daughter, Rosa, from the center. Far more women than men picked up their children, but Alejandro's wife, Gladys, was out of town. Alejandro and Gladys couldn't make enough money when they both worked in the city market, so Gladys would leave town for the countryside for four days at a time. She went from one small town to the next selling goods. Alejandro spent his time alternating between selling goods in the market and going out to build a new home for his family in Divina Paraiso (Divine Paradise). Before Hurricane Mitch, his family had lived in Nueva Esperanza (New Hope), but the hurricane had devastated their home and left them homeless. They had spent a year living in shelters—six months in a school turned into a shelter and six months in a purposely built one—before one of Alejandro's extended-family members had rebuilt a house that they could share with Alejandro, Gladys, and their children. Throughout this period of upheaval, Alejandro and Gladys had continued to work, out of necessity. One of the most important pieces of stability they had throughout this time was their ability to take Rosa to the daycare center.

Alejandro explained that it simply wasn't safe for his daughter to stay with him in the market while he worked. As soon as she had been old enough to walk, that setting had been dangerous because of cars speeding past all of the stands. He had been worried about what would happen to Rosa while he was busy selling goods. She had witnessed daily devastations close up that he did not want her to see at her age. He described in detail one instance in which she had seen a man die after he was hit by a car. Moreover, her body had been wracked with repeated respiratory infections during her stays in the market. Since starting at the San Isidro Center, she had grown healthy again, and the respiratory infections had ceased. When we interviewed him, Alejandro was going through the process of getting his one-year-old son enrolled. Children couldn't be enrolled before they were eight months old, so for a year Alejandro's infant son had been cared for by Alejandro's twelve-year-old stepson. But this arrangement had meant no school attendance for the stepson, and Alejandro was anxious for him to be able to return to his education.

The center in San Isidro needed more space and better equipment. The center director would have been the first to say that with more resources she could have provided care to more children, expanded the play space, and offered them better facilities. But there was no doubt that even with such limited resources, the care and educational services she was providing to the children of families in the informal sector made an enormous difference in their health and safety, early childhood development, and education. The center's services affected the welfare not only of children who would otherwise have been left alone but also of children who, according to their parents, had previously been in grossly inadequate informal care settings, as well as children who had been cared for by siblings who had been pulled out of school, and the older siblings themselves.

Local Contexts, Universal Needs

Can childcare centers in Honduras teach us anything about what to do in Botswana? Is there really any similarity between family experiences in Mexico and Russia? Can one country really learn anything from another? The assumption behind such questions is usually that the experience of working parents and their children is so divergent across national borders that there is little commonality in the problems and the possible solutions.

Clearly, there are relevant ways in which the experiences of children, parents, and grandparents differ significantly across national borders. The differences are largely due to the substantial variation between countries in the extent of poverty and the strength of the safety net. Notwithstanding these differences, in every country where we have spoken with parents, physicians, and teachers, we have found that a large number of children are being left home alone in the absence of adequate safety nets. Where poverty is greatest and the safety nets nonexistent, one- and two-year-olds are being left home alone. Where the safety nets are slightly better but still inadequate, older children—that is, six- and seven-year-olds—are being left home alone. Similarly, in every country in which we have worked, we have found children getting injured because they have no adults to care for them or because their parents have no choice but to take them to dangerous work situations. The nature of the injuries varies. In the poorest regions, where families depend on firewood for cooking, burns among children are far more common. But children's accidents occur in underserved areas of wealthy countries as well, though they may reflect the different material conditions—a child's arm being cut when a glass door gets broken, for example.

The commonalities overwhelmingly trump the differences in other ways as well. Around the globe, working parents of young children spend a lot of their time worrying, first, about how to find and afford any decent care for their children and, second, what to do when the care falls through. The barriers to low-income families finding affordable, decent childcare are often insurmountable.

Around the world, low- and moderate-income parents were often desperately searching to meet similar needs. Parents were concerned about their children being adequately nourished in their absence. They were concerned about their children's safety and about the opportunity their children had to grow and learn. Working parents urgently needed reliable, affordable childcare. They all knew that the training, education, and diligence of the child-care providers mattered, that monitoring the childcare providers and teachers and having a reasonable number of children per teacher would significantly affect how well their children were cared for and taught.

In the overwhelming majority of cases, parents preferred formal early childhood education opportunities for their children when those were pub-licly provided, subsidized through work, or made affordable in other ways. Bame Kesupilwe of Botswana chose a childcare center because she knew what the nature of the care would be. "I didn't know what the home helper was doing with my child the whole time I was away, so I then decided that I'd rather take my child to a crèche." Her neighbors had seen a previous baby-sitter carry Bame's daughter on her back and go sell beer as a second job.

Parents appreciated both the social and the educational development their children experienced in childcare. In Vietnam, a wide range of parents—from Pham Dieu Hien, a treasurer at a government-owned company, to Le Thi Thu Phuong, a factory worker—said that the children who went to day care prospered. For many of the poorest parents, who had limited educational op-portunity themselves, childcare and preschool meant a chance for their chil-dren to succeed. Chuong Thi Chinh sold flowers in the market, and she wanted better opportunities for her children. As she explained:

> It was necessary to let the child study from the beginning. The
> teacher would start teaching the alphabet so that when my child
> entered first grade, the child would not be at a disadvantage. . . .
> I'm not highly educated, because at that time, my parents were poor,
> so they did not let me study much. Therefore, I have to let my chil-
> dren study so that they will be as educated as other people.

The short- and long-term developmental and educational benefits of the early childhood care and education these parents were seeking has been well sup-ported by the research literature.[7]

If working parents worldwide agree on the value of early childhood care and education programs, why don't more of them send their children to such programs? The cost outstrips their wages. This same reason explains why poor families don't send their children to primary and secondary schools if public ones aren't freely available. Phatsimo Ramokate of Botswana explained sim-ply, "Most of the Batswana do not take their children to a crèche because of financial problems." Nkakaemang Mbaiwa, who longed for his daughter to have opportunities that he could not afford, explained, "I'd wanted to have her be prepared for school, to go to a preschool before she goes to normal school. It looks like she will not get that preparation. I'd wanted to take her there when she was three, but now even next year I won't manage to take her to the preschool." He barely had enough money for rent and transportation to his job after paying for food. For those parents who could afford the fees for preschool, they often could only barely afford them. The loss of wages when a parent cared for a child with a common childhood illness could result in the family not being able to make ends meet. Moreover, there is a catch-22. To exit poverty and afford childcare, many families need the second parent to work, but he or she cannot get a regular job until the child is in childcare.

Addressing the Dramatic Needs

We, as a global community, have agreed that all children have a right to a free public primary education. However, by doing nothing for most children in the critical developmental years from birth to five, we have effectively left hundreds of millions of children globally with little chance to succeed in school. Before they are six, they have no adequate chance to develop in a healthy way, let alone learn the requisite basic skills for beginning school.

Strides Taken by Some Nations

We need to ensure that all children have access to early childhood care and education. The public sector in some countries and the private nonprofit sector in others have begun to address this problem. However, the gap between the care that is available and the number of families that need it is enormous.

As a nation that has made important strides, Mexico illustrates both the difference that services can make and the size of the existing gaps, even in the countries with better-than-average services. In Mexico, those adults who are working in the formal sector for employers large enough to be covered by a social security system have access to childcare through the government-administered *Seguro Social.* For those who have coverage, it makes a tremendous difference. Liany Rivera Barrios was raising two preschool children with the help of her mother. The father of her older son was killed in a car accident within months of his son's birth. The father of her infant left her. Her family was surviving on the income she made as a cashier in a restaurant. If social security had not been providing childcare, Liany could not have enrolled her children in a center. She earned 350 pesos, or 38 U.S. dollars, every two weeks, yet private daycare centers in her area charged 400 pesos every two weeks.

While the Mexican social security system provides critical services, far more families need early childcare and education services than have access to them. In Mexico, workers in the informal sector and those working for small firms in the formal sector are not covered by the social security laws. Moreover, there are not enough childcare slots for those who are covered. As Dr. Fernanda Estrada noted:

> The number [of daycare centers] definitely has to increase. We know this because the public daycare centers—and in particular, those of the IMSS [Mexican Social Security Institute]—are completely full. Sometimes the waiting lists are a hundred people long. We know this because we've gone to the centers ourselves. My own experience . . . is that they're completely saturated. We need more. Mothers tell us many times, "I need to work, but I don't know where to leave my children. I don't have any relative who can take care of him, and the daycare centers are full."

Martina Guzmán, a childcare provider in Nuevo Laredo, Mexico, made clear just how few slots there were. Nuevo Laredo, with a population of 316,000, had 208 spots available in the only two social security daycare centers that existed. She explained: "[My child's] daycare center has a capacity of 112 children. . . . There are very few places for the large number of working women in this city. . . . There are over 130 applications on the waiting list in this center." More people stood on the waiting list than in the center.

While the centers provided critical services to the children enrolled, problems remained. One doctor pointed out the real concern about young children who were falling in the age gaps:

> Many daycare centers admit children until they're four years old. Afterwards, the parents are still working. But the five-year-old or six-year-old ends up without a place to go. . . . The IMSS daycare

centers, which are supposedly the better ones, admit children only until age four. After that, children enter kindergarten with fixed schedules from 9:00 to 12:00. The problem arises for parents of who's going to pick up the child and who's going to take care of him or her in the afternoon.

While different countries may choose a wide range of models, fundamentally all nations need to ensure that childcare is available when parents work away from their children. A number of nations have made important strides. In Vietnam, for example, a 1999 law organized responsibility for preschool programs within the Ministry of Education and Training. The range of active public sector efforts in Vietnam has increased the number of families being served and decreased the disparities in access to early childhood care and education. The greatest headway has been made in access to early childhood care and education for three- to five-year-olds in urban areas. In Brazil, it is the responsibility of municipalities to provide childcare for children under three years, with the support of the state and federal governments. These policies have led to higher enrollment of preschool children in early education. In Vietnam, 44 percent of children three to five years old in dual-earner families and 51 percent of children in single working-parent families are enrolled in early childhood education programs. In Brazil, similarly 44 percent of children three to five years old in dual-earner families and 40 percent of preschoolers in single working-parent families are enrolled in early childhood education programs. In contrast, in Botswana, where the government has made substantial investments in health and education but not in early childhood, less than a quarter of preschoolers are enrolled (see figure 2-7).

Still, more remains to be done in nations that have taken first steps, as well as in those that have not. Currently, children's needs all too often are unmet because they fall in the abyss between the time when employers require parents to resume work after childbirth and the age at which childcare services are available. Tran Thi Cat Khue of Vietnam worked in a supermarket. Cat Khue had a nine-year-old son and was expecting her second child. She did not yet know how she would handle her newborn's care. While there were excellent public school options, little was available for infants. She explained, "When the baby is four months old here, there are not yet any childcare centers that accept four-month-old children. But my husband and I have to go to work. I only have four months off for maternity leave."

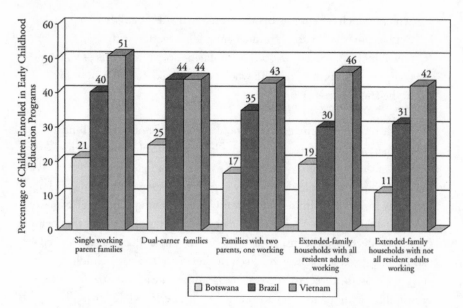

Figure 2-7
Percentage of Children Three to Five Years of Age in Early Childhood Education Programs.
Note: Data from national household surveys.

Setting Clear Indicators

In the health arena, the greatest strides have been made when clear goals were set with measurable and important outcomes, such as the eradication of smallpox or the elimination of polio. Similarly, clear-cut goals against which global progress can be measured should be set for early childhood care and education. As a first step, the global community needs to realize three critical goals:

1. No preschool children should be left home alone.
2. All preschool children should be cared for in settings that promote their health and protect their safety.
3. All preschool children should receive care that supports their development and early learning.

The first, most basic, essential step is to ensure that no young children are being left home alone. Children who are left home alone at young ages are at enormously high risk of having preventable and serious injuries and illnesses. They have little chance to have normal social or cognitive development. Yet, currently, a substantial percentage of low-income families have to leave their young children home alone some of the time. In the countries where we have conducted interviews, 10 to 40 percent of parents of preschool children have left their young children home alone at least some of the time. Parents with good childcare options are substantially less likely to have to leave their children home alone (see figure 2-8). Nineteen percent of those who used

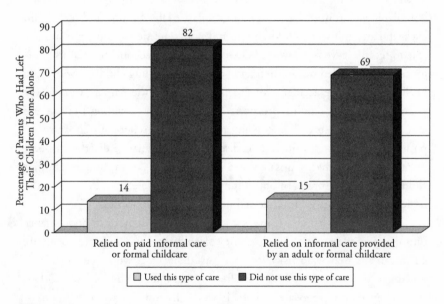

Figure 2-8
When Parents Have Access to Affordable Childcare Provided by Adults or Other Paid Caregivers, Children Are Less Likely to Be Left Home Alone.
Note: Data from Project on Global Working Families' in-depth interviews with working caregivers. Analyses in the above figure are based on households with a zero- to five-year-old child.

formal childcare had left their child home alone compared to 82 percent of families who used an unpaid child to care for a preschooler. While parents with formal childcare left children home alone at markedly lower rates, it is important to note that these parents were not immune; although child-care centers are generally more reliable, they do occasionally close, for example, due to weather or holidays. In Vietnam, where public early childhood care was more widely available, the number of children left home alone was lowest.

HEALTHY AND SAFE CARE

In our studies, parents reported increased rates of injury, including severe burns, trauma from falls, injury from knives, and assaults, when children are left alone or in the care of other young children. As detailed in chapter 3, there are children in countries around the world who are pulled out of school on short- and long-term bases to care for their younger siblings when no care is available on a routine basis, when routine care falls through and there is no back-up care, and when children five and under are sick and parents are not able to receive leave from work. When parents of preschool children used informal care provided by children and youths, their young children were more likely to experience accidents or emergencies while the parents worked (57 versus 35 percent). The life prospects of the children providing the care are also greatly diminished due to being removed from school. Parents also reported increased rates of infectious diseases, in particular of diarrheal disease due to children drinking unsafe water when left alone or in the care of other children. These high rates of both injury and illness were also observed by the health-care providers we interviewed in a number of countries.

Children being left alone, in the care of other children, or in poor-quality informal care were not the only causes of children being exposed to unsafe environments that were risky for their health. Parents who were unable to find or afford adequate childcare often brought their children to work—even when they were aware that their work environments were perilous—because they lacked any other alternative. Children were brought to unsafe, informal work settings where they were exposed to risks ranging from toxic chemicals to motor vehicle accidents. They were also brought to factory settings which were not safe for children and where children were not legally allowed.

When children had adults caring for them, the parents we interviewed pointed to two critical factors in determining the developmental opportunities their young children faced: first and foremost was the quality and commitment of the childcare provider; the second was the supervision the childcare provider received. On average, the low-income parents we interviewed were able to find better childcare providers who received more supervision in formal centers.

While in theory, care provided by adults in informal care settings could be of equal quality to formal settings, this was not the common experience of most parents we interviewed, and in particular, this was not the experience of low-income families. Though many countries have some degree of subsidy for low-income families using formal childcare settings, far fewer subsidies and little public provision or supervision exist in informal settings. As a result of this and of parents' low wages, those low-income parents using informal care typically could afford to pay little. This resulted in their having extremely limited choices in childcare providers. The low wages they could afford to provide meant that, in general, they were hiring either adults who could not find other work or adults who provided the informal care while working at another job. The low skill level of those hired and the fact that those hired were, at times, simultaneously doing other work led to poor-quality care when it was provided. Moreover, problems that began with the poor quality of childcare providers in the informal sector were exacerbated by the lack of supervision in the informal sector. Parents we interviewed repeatedly recounted stories of going home to find that informal childcare providers had left their children home alone for all or part of the day.

When families used formal childcare, their children were less likely to develop behavioral or academic difficulties than when they used informal childcare. Parents with preschool children who used unpaid children to provide informal care were significantly more likely to have children with behavioral or academic difficulties (39 percent versus 22 percent).

In short, we need to ensure that all preschool children in working families have access to affordable, healthy, safe, and developmentally appropriate care.

For this care to reach children in working-poor families, if wages do not rise substantially, the services will either need to be publicly provided or privately provided with public subsidies. This is feasible if countries and global institutions make the same commitment to early childhood care and education as they have to the provision of primary school education. There are numerous excellent examples of how early childhood care and education can be provided in formal settings in the public and private sector. Wider availability of early childhood care in Vietnam already leads to fewer children left home alone. IMSS, the Mexican social security system, provides an example of how formal childcare services can be integrated well into workplace benefits. If informal care models are followed, ensuring high-quality care providers with adequate supervision will be an essential part of the solution. Finally, to hold leaders accountable, just as we follow other educational, health, and economic indicators on a routine basis, we need to monitor the affordability, availability, and quality of early childhood care and education globally. We should know not only how many children in a country have not been vaccinated but how many are being left home alone as preschoolers, left in the care of other young children, or left in unsafe settings. Finding the national gaps in early childhood care and actively filling them is essential to ensuring that all children receive a decent chance at life.

3

School-Age Children:
Getting a Chance

If the problem with the rhetoric surrounding preschool children is that it assumes extended-family members fill much of the need and that high-quality informal care fills the rest, then the problem surrounding school-age children is that there is no rhetoric. Only silence.

When pressed about who is caring for school-age children, popular unspoken presumptions emerge: that most school-age children can fare adequately when left alone, that school-age children can usually care for each other well, that needing to rely on themselves and each other can teach responsibility. Because of these underlying but unconfirmed suppositions that school-age children can manage on their own before and after school, far less is done to meet the needs of school-age children than those of preschool ones.

In some ways, the disparity between the visibility of the needs of preschool children and those of school-age children in the United States is a microcosm of the world. In the United States, where the need for quality care for children under five far outstrips the supply, attention is beginning to be paid to this problem by politicians as they talk about the need for better childcare. Some companies already provide care for the preschool children of their employees. Several states are considering providing early education for all children. In marked contrast, the dialogue about the needs of school-age children in the United States is at a mere whisper. Most employers do next to nothing to help working parents address the needs of children six and over. Federal funding amounts to less than the equivalent of two afternoons' care for school-age children.[1]

Similarly, where attention is being paid by global organizations to children in working families, such as by UNESCO and the World Bank, it is almost exclusively paid to early childhood care and education. Virtually nothing is being said or done about school-age children in working families. This discrepancy begs the question: Are the needs of school-age children worldwide already being met reasonably well so less notice should be given? or is there a hidden crisis? To begin to answer these questions, we interviewed families globally who were caring for elementary-school children, pre-adolescents, and teenagers.

How Are School-Age Children Faring?

Physical Safety and Health

We asked parents in North America, Latin America, Africa, Asia, and Europe about the impact of their working conditions on a wide range of aspects of their school-age children's lives. Clearly, there were enormous benefits to children from parental work—particularly when parents were able to succeed at work. Rising incomes brought families out of poverty, increased the food available to children, improved their home living conditions, and often were the primary reason that the children could attend school for more years than their own parents had. We heard little bad and a great deal of good about the impact of parents' ability to work per se. Rather, parents' predicaments arose when the length and timing of their work hours—combined with the absence of quality affordable care for their school-age children—meant that their children were left home alone.

As with preschool children, when parents face poor working conditions with few social supports, they are markedly more likely to have to leave school-age children home alone. The question is: Do school-age children fare far better than preschoolers? What are the consequences of the lack of adult care on the children's health, education, and development?

Naledi Mmereki worked one of the lower-wage jobs in Botswana's mining industry. She described how sad she was about her ten-year-old son, Tumelo's, care during her work times:

> In the morning I do take care of him. I prepare him for school, bathe him, give him breakfast. But the problem is that before I am home from work, my child is back from school. That's the time when I think he really needs someone to be caring for him. He is at home with my sisters' kids. They too are small so they need someone to take care of them.

One time when Tumelo was home alone, he grew hungry and tried to cook a meal for himself on a woodstove. He lost control of the fire and burned his leg. Naledi explained, "My neighbors heard him crying, and they took the child to the clinic for treatment." There had been no way for Naledi to know what had happened until she returned from work, no phone on which to telephone her. Her son had been lucky in having neighbors who were at home when the fire broke out, who were able to hear his cries, and who were willing to take him for medical care. He would have been luckier to have avoided the entire event in the first place by not having to be alone.

Leaving children alone at home is often the only option that low-income parents have when out-of-school childcare is neither available nor affordable. Fifty-six-year-old Nunuko Ndebele was the mother of seven children and the primary earner in her family. In April 1999, Nunuko's thirty-year-old daughter died of AIDS. Her daughter left behind an eleven-year-old who was healthy, Mosadi, and a six-year-old who was infected with HIV, Kgomatso. Nunuko cared for both of these grandchildren, in addition to her own younger children who remained at home. She had worked full time as a maid in a church since 1993 to earn enough income for her family. After she had put her earnings toward what the family needed to survive physically, her first priority was to pay her children's and grandchildren's school fees, as she noted:

> Although at times I lack, . . . working has done a great deal for my children because I am able to pay their school fees. Despite the poverty that I'm in, they will not suffer like I've suffered. It won't be that poverty cycle. . . . If I was not working, I wouldn't be able to pay school fees, and all of them could have dropped out very early from school—not because they're not intelligent, but because I couldn't pay what I needed to pay.

Nunuko's work hours allowed her to get her children ready for school before she went to work, but they came home from school long before she returned. During after-school hours, the youngest children were in the care of the older ones who were still at home. In 1994, Nunuko's young daughter switched on the gas without lighting the stove correctly as she tried to cook food in the afternoon. While the children escaped, the resultant fire burned their house to the ground. At that time, Nunuko was earning 38 U.S. dollars a month. Just to survive, the family became dependent on their neighbors. It took six years for Nunuko to save enough money from her wages, after paying living expenses and school fees, to reconstruct a house of four rooms for her family. But at the time of our interview, she had not yet been able to save enough to pay for the roof.

In every country we studied, young school-age children had their health and safety placed at risk when they were left alone regularly.[2] While injuries from broken glass were more common in the United States and Russia and those from fire in Honduras and Botswana, in all countries school-age children's serious accidents and injury rate rose when they were regularly alone during out-of-school hours. In the families we interviewed where parents had to leave school-age children home alone, 55 percent experienced accidents or other emergencies while their parents were working. Furthermore, working conditions presented large barriers to parents meeting preventive and curative health care needs of their elementary-, middle-, and high-school children (see chapter 4).

Education, Development, and Emotional Well-Being

The educational, developmental, and emotional strains are as great as the physical. At age thirty-five, Serafina Prado was supporting her family as a housekeeper in Mexico, earning less than $1.25 a day. Frequently, she had little choice but to leave her two daughters home alone without adult supervision, locked inside to prevent them from wandering the streets. The toll was starting to show in both her children's health and their schoolwork. There was also the emotional toll. It was gut wrenching for her to describe how her eleven-year-old daughter felt while caring for the seven-year-old, a responsibility she had already borne for years:

> How does she feel? She misses me because I'm not there. Because sometimes they both cry. They hug each other. "Calm down, don't

cry," one says to the other one, but sometimes she stumbles. Sometimes she falls. They start to crawl, my daughter and her sister. "Don't cry, don't cry, Mamita. Calm down, pretty Mamita," she says. And that's how they calm down. Sometimes when I come home, they have their things laid out on the rug. I leave them locked there so they don't get out.

Mexican physician Fernanda Estrada described a few of the many health problems resulting from children being left alone:

The older siblings clearly are not qualified to take care of children. Sometimes there are malnutrition problems. We've also faced enuresis—psychosomatic problems like enuresis—in children who are not supervised by their parents, but rather by elder siblings. We've also found sleeping disorders in these children. They wake up in the middle of the night, or they have insomnia, or they require the mother to be with them at night in order to sleep.

Teachers, as well as parents, were well aware of the impact that adult availability for school-age children could have on their children's education and development. Twenty-one-year-old Elizabeth Ramirez lived and worked as a kindergarten teacher in Villa Franca, Honduras. She was an astute observer of the four- to six-year-olds who were in her care from 7:30 a.m. until noon. Elizabeth explained that about half of the children were left largely on their own by their families. She taught forty children, twenty of whom came to school and went home in the care of a brother or sister, parent, or other family member. But the other half came to school and left school alone. Elizabeth held monthly weekday conferences with parents, but only about half could come. If the conferences were scheduled for Saturdays, a few more parents were able to participate, but many still had to work on Saturdays.

Elizabeth recounted her experiences with some of the children who were left on their own. One six-year-old boy who arrived at and left school alone had a mother who worked in a *maquila* (a foreign-owned company producing goods for export) and a father who was a carpenter. He spent his afternoons without adults around in the care only of his two sisters, aged nine and ten. The boy rarely participated in any school activities. He didn't know what to do, and Elizabeth often needed to take him aside to explain. Even with her help, the boy often withdrew from the activities. Another five-year-old boy whom Elizabeth taught was also cared for by a ten-year-old sister. The sister was looking after him and their seven-year-old sibling. Elizabeth was struck that he, too, stayed apart from the other children. While sometimes he would seem happy at school, he often seemed sad. He would arrive late and not have any food for lunch or snacks. His homework was done only sporadically. These were not isolated cases. Elizabeth explained that most of the children who were left on their own participated less in class, came later to school, did less homework, more often came without any food, and experienced ill effects on their studies because of their lack of adult support at home. Even among kindergarteners, the effect of lacking adult supervision was great. In our studies, in families where parents had to leave school-age children home alone, 50 percent of the children had behavioral or academic difficulties at school.

Teachers of older elementary- and middle-school children had similar reports. In Buenas Nuevas, Honduras, Lola Oslan described what a difference having a school lunch program had made to her students. Because so many of the children who were home alone didn't eat well or didn't eat at all when at school, their attention was on their hunger instead of on their lessons. In Villa Cristina, Honduras, Selena Diego de Calderon described how children she taught who spent time with their parents felt more secure in the classroom than children who were left home alone. The children who were left alone often came to class without having eaten. Sometimes, children who had not eaten all day fainted at school. They were more rebellious during the academic sessions and more likely to get into fights during recess—which was when the children who had been left on their own came to school.

In our studies, families whose children were facing academic or other developmental problems were nearly twice as likely to have had to rely on another child to provide unpaid care (37 percent versus 21 percent).

Why Are School-Age Children Being Placed at Risk?

School-Age Children Left Home Alone

Most parents we interviewed worried about the risks to their elementary-school children's health and development if they were home alone, and many worried about the educational outcomes and risk behaviors of their older children if they had to be routinely alone for extended periods of time.

If most parents shared the assumption that school-age children fare well enough alone, then there would be as many school-age children who are affluent and middle income as there are poor children left alone. Parental circumstances wouldn't determine which children have adults available to them during out-of-school hours. But that was not the case for the families we interviewed. The Robleses' experience was tragically typical.

Both Crista Robles, thirty-five, and her husband, Ernesto, worked; they earned too little for either to stay home and care for their children and too little for their children to attend after-school programs. Neither their workplaces nor their communities provided access to that care. As a result, their elementary-school daughters were home alone after school. On days when their two-year-old brother was sick, the girls had to miss school in order to stay home and care for him. Crista explained:

> My son, who is two, I had just left with his older sister, the one who is six years old. I told her I was coming home soon. Because it's very important that she did that for me. And that's how it was. I left him with her, and they were alone. . . . They feel sad, because sometimes they tell me, "Mamita, don't work any more, because we don't want to be alone." And I tell them, "But if I don't work, we won't be able to afford food." Then they understand me.

Beyond poverty, what determined whether children were home alone were parental working conditions and social supports (see figure 3-1) as well as the availability of affordable programs for school-age children. Parents who lacked support at home and at work were more likely to have to leave a school-age child home alone. Eighty percent of single and married parents who had no paid leave, no other caregivers in the household, and no regular family support had left a school-age child home alone compared to 45 percent of other parents. Eighty-eight percent of parents who were single, had no paid leave, and did not have other caregivers in the house had left a school-age child home alone compared to 47 percent of other parents.

School-Age Children Filling the Care Gap

In addition to being left alone during after-school hours, school-age children are placed at risk when they are pulled out of school. School-age children from the United States to Russia, Honduras to Vietnam, are taken out of

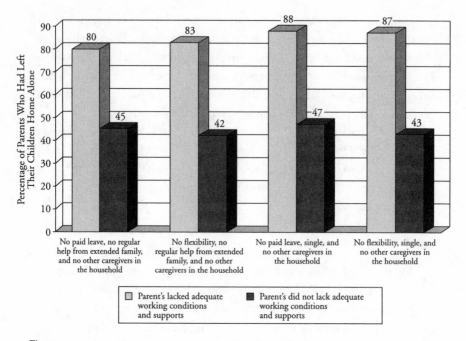

Figure 3-1
When Parents Lack Decent Working Conditions and Social Supports, They Are More Likely to Have to Leave School-Age Children Home Alone.
Note: Data from Project on Global Working Families' in-depth interviews with working care-givers. Analyses in the above figure are based on households with a six- to fourteen-year-old child. The category "No other caregivers in the household" includes one- and two-parent households for which there is no extended family and no other caregivers besides the parents living in the household.

school to provide care for other children and adults. We analyzed data from large national household surveys in five countries in five different regions. These national surveys allowed us to look at the relationship between school attendance and having a preschool-age brother or sister. We found that the presence of newborns to five-year-olds in need of care in the home was as-sociated with a lower probability of school attendance by six- to fourteen-year-olds in single working parent and dual-earner parents' households in all five countries: Botswana, Brazil, Mexico, South Africa, and Vietnam (see figure 3-2). In Botswana, 14 percent of single parent families with preschool

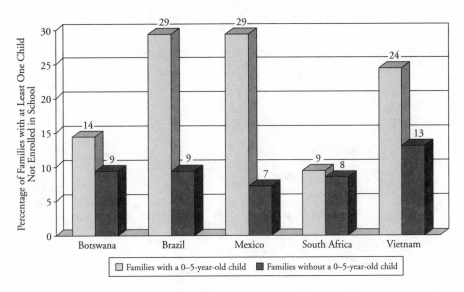

Figure 3-2

Single Working Parent Families: When Parents Have Young Children Needing Care, School-Age Children's Enrollment Falls.

Note: Data from national household surveys. Analyses in the above figure are based on households with a six- to fourteen-year-old child.

children had at least one school-age child not enrolled in school—one and a half times the rate of families without preschool children. In Brazil and Mexico, 29 percent of single parent families with preschool children had at least one school-age child not enrolled—more than three times the rate of families without preschool children. While in general dual-earner families were more likely to be able to keep their children in school, the presence of preschoolers in the family diminished the chances of school-age children being enrolled in every country (see figure 3-3). Even in extended-family households where all adults worked, having a preschool-age sibling put an older child's education at risk in four out of five countries (see figure 3-4). The one country we studied that did not demonstrate a similar impact on school-age children in extended families was Vietnam. It is noteworthy that Vietnam was the only country in which the majority of families with school-age children interviewed in the national survey (80 percent) lived in rural areas.

While the need to care for preschool children affected school-age children

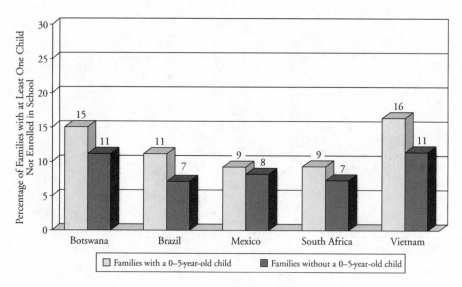

Figure 3-3
Dual-Earner Families: When Parents Have Young Children Needing Care,
School-Age Children's Enrollment Falls.
Note: Data from national household surveys. Analyses in the above figure are based on households with a six- to fourteen-year-old child.

across social class, having a newborn to five-year-old at home particularly decreased the likelihood that six- to fourteen-year-olds in poor households would be attending school. We were able to examine the experiences of low-income families in detail in two of the national surveys; these two surveys both collected information on income and interviewed a large enough group[3] of single working parent, dual-earner, and extended-family households in which all adults worked. Analyses of these surveys documented that the burden of pulling six- to fourteen-year-olds out of school to care for newborns to five-year-olds fell particularly hard on families living in poverty, and among these, children in single-parent families were most severely affected. For example, in Brazil, 42 percent of low-income single working parents with preschool children had to keep some school-age children out of school, as did 37 percent of low-income single working parents in Mexico (see figure 3-5).

While data from these large national household surveys were strongly suggestive of how the need to care for newborns to five-year-olds negatively af-

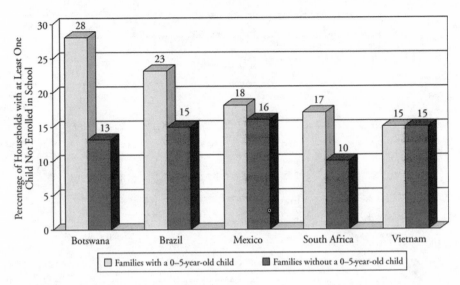

Figure 3-4
Extended-Family Households: When Parents Have Young Children Needing Care, School-Age Children's Enrollment Falls.
Note: Data from national household surveys. Analyses in the above figure are based on households with a six- to fourteen-year-old child. The publicly available childcare in Vietnam and the childcare available through social security in Mexico succeeds in narrowing the gap in these two countries.

fected the education of six- to fourteen-year-olds, the surveys were not designed to directly address this question. We supplemented these studies with analyses of the in-depth interviews we have conducted of working families. We found that a significant number of working parents with newborns to five-year-olds relied on children to provide childcare some or all of the time. Even when parents are able to find care for their preschool children when they are healthy, poor working conditions often prevent them from providing essential care when their youngest children are sick. Prohibited from taking leave from work, unable to afford pay loss, and threatened with job loss, mothers and fathers cannot stay home themselves. Too often this leads to nearly inconceivable "choices" between leaving sick infants and toddlers home alone or pulling young children out of school to care for them. Twenty percent of Mexican families with preschool children with whom we discussed

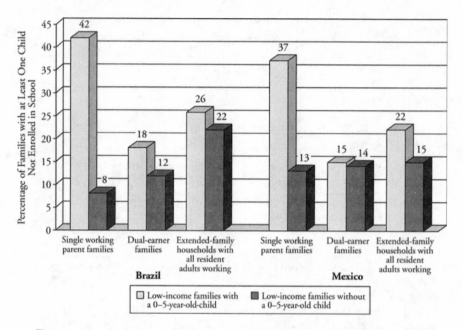

Figure 3-5
When Low-Income Single Parents Have Young Children Needing Care, School-Age Children's Enrollment Is at Highest Risk.
Note: Data from national household surveys. Analyses in the above figure are based on households with a six- to fourteen-year-old child.

childcare relied on children to care for their children, as did 25 percent of respondents in Botswana and 18 percent of respondents in Vietnam. Across the three countries, an average of 21 percent of families with newborns to five-year-olds had relied on children to provide childcare. Moreover, when parents had to rely on school-age children as unpaid childcare providers, the children were substantially more likely to have problems in school (59 versus 38 percent).

In short, these analyses of quantitative national household survey data and of local in-depth interviews from our studies in diverse countries have documented the following. First, while parental work, in general, may increase the likelihood that all children in a household will attend school, when parents of newborns to five-year-olds have to work and no affordable early childhood care and education is available for these children, parents may be forced to take six- to fourteen-year-olds out of school to care for younger children in the family. Second, while being pulled out of school to care for younger children affects both boys and girls, it disproportionately affects girls' chances of attending school. At the same time, by increasing family income, work makes it more feasible for parents to pay school fees, buy uniforms and books, and otherwise afford the costs that often even attending state schools involves. Moreover, an increase in parental earnings makes it less likely that children themselves will have to work for pay so that families can afford such basic necessities as food, shelter, and clothing. Work itself is not the culprit; working conditions and lack of early childhood care and education are.

Barriers to the Involvement of Parents

School-age children need their parents to have the chance to be involved in their lives. Extensive research documents the fact that a key factor affecting how children fare in school is parental involvement.[4] When parents are involved in their children's education, children achieve more in both primary and secondary school.[5] Parental involvement is associated with children's higher achievement in language and mathematics, improved behavior, greater academic persistence, and lower dropout rates.[6] The critical role which may be played by parents' support for and ability to become involved in their children's education has been documented in developing and transitional economies as well as in industrialized ones. Studies have been carried out in countries ranging from Australia to Latin America and the Caribbean, from Turkey to Peru, from Guinea to the United Kingdom, from Indonesia to Brazil.[7]

While the number of working parents facing obstacles to helping with their children's education varied across countries, a majority in all countries faced barriers. The percentages of parents facing barriers to helping with homework, participating in school events, or other involvement in their children's education due to work responsibilities and restrictions were 66 percent in our study in Mexico, 51 percent in Vietnam, and 82 percent in Botswana (see figure 3-6).

Juana Duran Ochoa, who lived in San Cristobal, Mexico, had long workdays with little or no access to leave, which made it next to impossible for Juana to meet with her children's schoolteachers. Juana cleaned rooms in a hotel while her husband waited tables. She earned 32 pesos (less than $3.50) a

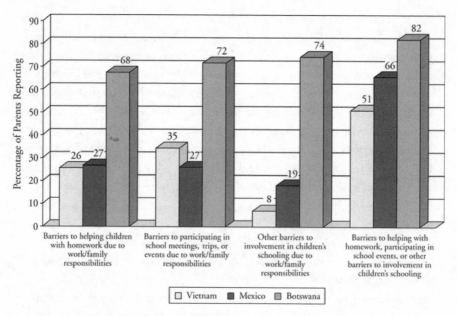

Figure 3-6
Frequency of Barriers to Helping with Children's Education.
Note: Data from Project on Global Working Families' in-depth interviews with working care-givers. Analyses in the above figure are based on households with a six- to fourteen-year-old child.

day. She had been working at the hotel for eight years, but the hotel had re-cently come under new ownership and had instituted new policies. The pay remained the same, but the number of employees was cut, so that fewer women had to clean the same number of hotel rooms. Consequently, Juana became responsible for cleaning 50 percent more rooms. After long days at work, she went home to a second shift of domestic responsibilities made lengthier by the time-consuming nature of fulfilling basic needs while living in poverty. As Juana was working longer hours, her younger two children began to do less well in school than her older two had. She explained, "Fif-teen days ago, the teacher of my son in secondary school called me to come in and talk [about the situation], but I couldn't." She just couldn't get the time off work. "I don't know what the teacher wanted to say to me, because my son told me that if I didn't get there in three days, the teacher wouldn't receive me. I couldn't go within three days . . . [so] I don't know what the teacher wanted." She could not get time off to consult her child's teacher about his academic problems; she could not help him study or learn how to better address his difficulties.

In Botswana, there was little work for Akayeng Gabotalwe in her small desert village of Gootau (named after "the den of the lion"), so she moved to the city to find work. At first, she could find only temporary work, but she sent money home. Because of the tenuous work situation, she left her ten-year-old son, Kitso, with family members in the village, but there was no one to help him with his schoolwork. She explained:

> During that time, he wasn't doing very well in school. I'd asked my younger sister to make sure that he stopped playing so much and made time for school. But he was failing. . . . I think the reason he wasn't doing well in school was because there was no one really there to monitor his schoolwork. Sure, when he woke up, someone would make sure that he went to school, and he was dressed okay. But when he got back, no one asked him about what he was taught in school, what was hard, what was easy, what couldn't you understand. There was no one to monitor and help him with his homework. . . . He would return late at night, and he would be tired and hungry. He was just there, trying to do it himself as a kid.

By the time of our interview, Kitso had come to live with his mother in the city. But because Akayeng was working as a hospital cook, her shifts rotated among morning, evening, and overnight. Some of the time she could be there with her son, but some of the time no one was there:

> I try my hardest to provide for my child, but the problems come in when I work night shifts. I knock off at 8:00 p.m. and get home very late. I find him sleeping, and sometimes he's gone to sleep without bathing or without having much to eat [or having done his homework].

In our studies in Mexico, Botswana, and Vietnam, we examined the children who were experiencing academic and developmental problems. It was clear that several of the most important factors that placed children at risk were the disadvantages that families faced in working conditions. When parents' long work hours or poor schedules limited the time they could spend supervising and helping their children, their children were at greater risk. In those families where parents faced barriers to helping children with homework, 66 percent had children who were experiencing behavioral or academic difficulties at school (compared to only 31 percent of children in families where the parents were able to help with homework). Similarly, in those families where parents faced barriers to participating in school meetings and other school events, 58 percent of their children experienced behavioral or academic difficulties in school (compared to 33 percent of children in families where parents were able to become involved in the school) (see figure 3-7). Poor working conditions—in particular, the lack of paid leave and flexibility—played a critical role in parents' abilities to help school-age children. Those parents who were unable to alter their work schedules or get leave from work for caregiving were substantially less likely to be able to provide the assistance their school-age children needed. This resulted in far higher levels of behavioral problems and academic difficulties (see figure 3-8).

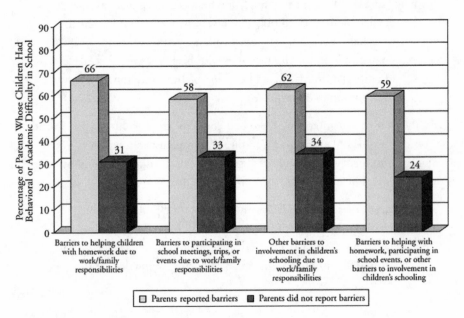

Figure 3-7
When Parents Report Barriers at Work, Their School-Age
Children's Education and Development Suffer.
Note: Data from Project on Global Working Families' in-depth interviews with working caregivers. Analyses in the above figure are based on households with a six- to fourteen-year-old-child.

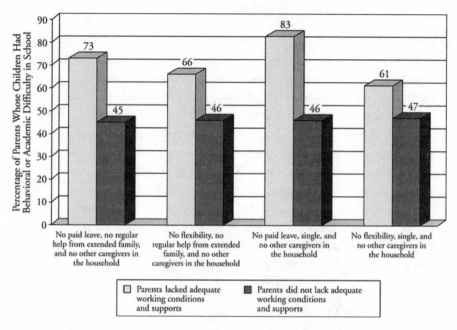

Figure 3-8
When Parents Lack Decent Working Conditions and Social Supports,
Their School-Age Children's Education and Development Suffer.
Note: Data from Project on Global Working Families' in-depth interviews with working care-givers. Analyses in the above figure are based on households with a six- to fourteen-year-old child. The category "No other caregivers in the household" includes one- and two-parent house-holds for which there is no extended family and no other caregivers besides the parents living in the household.

Lacking Options, Not Commitment or Judgment

If parents are living the all-too-often demeaning and devastating conse-quences of having been pulled out of school too early themselves, why do they do the same to their own children? If the parents did not work, their children often could not afford to attend school. Even "free" public schools have costs for books, supplies, and clothing. The parents we interviewed knew they had to work. Moreover, the problems that their school-age chil-dren faced came as a result of the working conditions the parents faced and the lack of adequate social supports, not the mere fact that they worked.

Thirty-eight-year-old Dang Thi Tho had worked since age sixteen as a vendor selling pickled fish and, at the time of the interview, worked as a seamstress. Her husband, Cao Van Luong, worked painting cars and buses from 8:00 a.m. to 6:00 p.m. Tho and Luong had four children, ages sixteen, fifteen, ten, and four years. Tho had been pressed to quit school in fifth grade to help on her parents' farm. She and her husband wanted better opportunities for their own children. She explained: "Right now, my husband is working to support their schooling. In our youth, we did not do as well as others in school and now we have to labor. We have to try to help our children so they will do work that is lighter, easier than their parents'."

From one month to the next, Tho and Luong often did not have enough money for the children's school fees. When they could afford the school fees, they could not afford the teacher they hired to tutor their children in preparation for exams. Regarding the tutor, Tho explained:

I had such a low level of education. Now I don't know enough to teach them. If I see that they are having difficulties, I hire the teacher to come and teach them. . . . So when I see that my children are not doing well, especially when they have exams to go to the next grade, I have to try any way possible so that my children would have a tutor to help them advance to the next grade.

When she was asked to attend a parent-teacher meeting, Tho went, but otherwise she was absent from the school. She couldn't afford to be there and still earn the amount of money needed to cover even the public school fees. "It's my family's economic situation. It doesn't allow me to participate in my children's schools. We have to worry about earning a living to raise our children."

She and her husband were desperately hoping to get all of their children at least through the level-two exams at the end of middle school. But no matter how much value Tho placed on education, Tho still needed her oldest daughter, sixteen-year-old Nhu, to help care for her youngest children. She described the problems involved:

My oldest daughter suffers the most. In the morning, at 5:30 a.m., she wakes up and reviews her older siblings' schoolwork. She then studies until 6:30 a.m. Then they all go to school, except for the youngest, who goes at 7:00 a.m. At 11:30 a.m., they come home. The oldest takes care of the meals for the younger siblings. All done. Then 1:00 p.m., they return to school. From 12:30 p.m. to 1:00 p.m. they look over their schoolwork before they return to school. About 6:00 p.m., they return from school. They have their dinner. The oldest cleans up the house and washes the clothes. . . . The oldest gives her younger siblings baths, washes the clothes, irons the clothes.

Although Tho needed to rely on Nhu to help provide essential care for the younger children while Tho worked, she knew it was negatively affecting her daughter's chances at school. Tho explained, "She can't finish her studies at home, so she has to go to school and squeeze in her studying." If the childcare Nhu already had to provide didn't keep her from passing her exams, she would at least make it through middle school. Still, after that, Tho and Luong planned on pulling Nhu out of school to help their family full time.

Among the people we interviewed, parents who pulled their children out of school to care for younger siblings did so because they had little other choice. Three quarters had had to leave children home alone, and over half had children who had experienced accidents or other emergencies while the parents were working. Nearly nine out of every ten who pulled an older child out of school to provide childcare had experienced difficulties at work because of the need to care for a sick child, had lost pay, or had been forced to leave a sick child home alone.

Recently, a number of global organizations have been considering the expansion of efforts to provide parenting education to adults. How could anyone not be in favor of parental education who knows what it feels like to bring a small, vulnerable newborn home for the first time or what it means to suddenly have teenagers? Yet any notion that parents' lack of knowledge about how to raise children is a major factor affecting the health of children living in poverty is some mix of naïveté and prejudice.

Is there information that would help working-poor families raise their children? Undoubtedly. There is information that would help any parent. But for the majority of families, the problem is lack of options, not lack of knowledge or judgment. How this issue plays out in families' lives when it comes to providing childhood's essentials can be particularly excruciating.

In Russia, the United States, Botswana, Vietnam, Mexico, and Honduras, the parents we interviewed all knew that their children would have advantages by attending school for as long as they could. While families living under varying conditions assessed the value of further education to their children somewhat differently, all knew it would help to lift their children out of poverty. Moreover, while differences did exist in their assessments of the value of schooling, parents were, by and large, accurate in their assessments. In certain economies, the additional opportunities provided by getting a high school degree or an advanced education significantly increase expected wages. In other economies, there are not yet enough jobs for those with advanced skills for realization of as high a return on the investment in education.

The parents who had lacked any opportunity to go to school themselves often were acutely aware of the indelible footprint their lack of education had left on what kind of jobs they could get and what income they received. These parents, as much as any, sought to do everything they could to ensure that their children had a better shot at education. It was not a lack of information, a lack of knowledge, or a lack of will or parenting ability that stood in the way. The problem was impassable roads. When a parent stayed home to care for preschool children, too often the family could not afford to have their older children attend school. When all of the adults in the household were at work, too often school-age children had to miss school in order to care for the youngest children in the house because no supports for raising those younger than five were available. Finally, when young children were able to attend school, the indecent working conditions many parents faced and the lack of social supports their children received meant that these children spent too much time alone without basic needs—like food and safety—being met and with no help in persisting with their education.

What Can Be Done to Give School-Age Children a Chance?

Three changes need to be made for school-age children to have a fighting chance. First, the caregiving gaps for preschoolers need to be filled by formal early education programs staffed by adults so school-age children are not pulled out of school to bridge the gulf. Second, school-age children themselves need care by adults during out-of-school hours when their parents are at work. Third, school-age children need their parents to have a real shot at being involved in their lives.

Preschool Programs Are Essential to School-Age Children

It is a spurious question to ask: Which matters more, investing in preschool or school-age children? First, these are the same children. If we provide care to preschool children only to allow their future opportunities to be destroyed once they turn five, we have done little for them. At the same time, it is unlikely that we will ever be able to provide adequate support for school-age children if we have not adequately cared for their development before they reach school. A child's preschool education and development is highly predictive of her success when she reaches school. Moreover, as documented earlier in this chapter, a significant number of school-age children are being pulled out of school to care for their preschool-age brothers and sisters. Only by meeting the pressing need for preschool programs can we ensure that older siblings can attend school.

School-Age Children Need Adults in Their Lives throughout the Day

The efficacy of programs beyond the school day for school-age children is well documented in industrialized countries. In affluent nations, a wide range of before- and after-school programs has been shown to improve academic achievement across social class.[8] Studies have shown that children who participate in after-school programs not only spend more time on their homework but are also more likely to complete their homework and prepare it better. The ability to read well, like the ability to demonstrate mathematical skills, is at the core of educational achievement in all countries, and after-school programs have been shown to have important effects on reading. The National Academy of Sciences' study on preventing reading difficulties confirmed that children who receive extra time and reading instruction beyond the school day have significant improvements in their achievement.[9] Both children already succeeding in school and children who are struggling benefit from after-school programs. For example, after-school tutoring in reading by volunteers has been shown to lead to improved skill in elementary-school children who had previously been poor achievers in reading.[10] Among at-risk youth, aspirations for completing high school also improve when they participate in after-school programs, and these youths are less likely both to drop out of school and to be held back.[11]

While these studies are based in North America and Europe, given what parents reported to us about the problems their school-age children face without any adults available, it makes sense that the availability of adults to work with children after school would be equally effective in Latin America, Africa, and Asia. If a question still remains as to whether after-school programs have these same positive effects in low-income countries, it is clearly time to find out.

The importance and viability of after-school programs in widely varying settings should not be underestimated. Not only is there a gaping need for programs for school-age children, but programs such as the Dula Sentle in Otse, Botswana, have demonstrated their feasibility and importance under dire conditions. Otse is a village of 3,500 inhabitants in southern Botswana. While developed to serve the stark needs of the increasing number of orphans created by AIDS, Dula Sentle could serve as a model for any after-school program. Dula Sentle was designed to serve primary- and secondary-school children. Many of the children had been home alone with other children before attending Dula Sentle. The program offered them several invaluable things every afternoon: the presence of adults, help with homework, and a chance to spend time learning and growing up—instead of having to work as if they were adults trying to care for younger siblings. The program is divided into two groups: the beetles are five- to ten-year-olds, the grasshoppers are children ten and older. Two teachers are responsible for each age group, and with approximately thirty-five children attending on any given day, all of the children are able to receive the help they need with their schooling. The facilities include a playroom filled with toys, which give the children a chance to develop as well as to enjoy themselves. Children receive help with their homework every day. Moreover, the connections between the after-school program and the school are tight. Whenever children have difficulties at school, the after-school teachers visit the school to learn what can be done about it. Children bring their report cards to the after-school program so the teachers know where they need greatest assistance. The children's parents, when they are living, and other guardians when the parents have died, come regularly to Dula Sentle—every three months, more often than they would have teacher meetings at any school.

When older and younger children from the same family begin attending Dula Sentle at the same time, it is often the first time that the older siblings have a chance to focus on their school work, get the help and support they need from adults, and not have to act *in loco parentis* because their parents are too sick, working too far away, or otherwise unable to help. A volunteer at Dula Sentle described what it had been like for one of the secondary-school students before she had come to the center. The student had been caring for her mother for two years as she grew progressively sicker before she died. Then, the student took on raising her younger siblings while living with her aunt. By providing care for her younger siblings during the day and providing her with a place to go and be mentored after school, Dula Sentle changed her life. She began to attend school full time again and was thriving.

Simple Steps Matter to Parents' Involvement in Schools

While far too many of the mothers and fathers we interviewed were denied by their employers any chance to help their children make it though school, there were employers in every region whose quiet practices demonstrated the feasibility of enabling working parents to support children in school. At forty years old, Guadalupe Alfaro Dominguez was the mother of two daughters aged ten and thirteen. She worked as a janitor at a government clinic in Mexico. In her conversation with us, she underscored the advantages of her current job in the formal sector, where she was able to take leave from work to meet her children's essential needs—unlike in the past, when she had worked in the informal sector as a domestic servant:

> Sometimes I ask for permission for a little bit of time from my job,
> "I'm going to go ask how my daughters are doing in school." If there
> is a meeting, I ask for leave from my boss, "I'm going to the meeting
> at my daughter's school." Because it's also important that I look after
> my daughters. . . . Now where I am we have to ask for leave but
> they give us permission. It's the right of the worker. You have to have
> your leave. [In contrast,] working as a servant is very difficult.

Among employers who did not provide paid leave, only a fraction allowed flexibility. Eva Acevedo had children ages eight, ten, twelve, and fifteen. School was important for all of them. While the private bakery she worked at did not give her paid leave to attend to school needs, at least it allowed her the flexibility to change her schedule to attend meetings with teachers:

> Yes, we have meetings. Every two months there are meetings and you
> have to go to them to see how the kids are doing: if they're getting to
> class, if they're not in the streets, if they're learning, if they want to

learn because they're doing homework. They have the meetings to see how the child is doing. . . . Well, on a day that there's a meeting I have to go to work earlier to get out early so I have time to go to my children's meeting. So if I usually go in at eight, I'd have to go in at six.

In caring for children's extended needs—health and educational—the benefits of paid leave clearly far outstrip the benefits of unpaid leave to low-wage workers. Parents living on the edge economically simply cannot afford extended unpaid leave. While it is often impossible for parents working long hours for meager pay (in addition to long unpaid hours to survive in poverty) to make up multiday absences with "comp time," working additional hours to compensate for the shorter work absences needed to attend a school meeting is more feasible, if still difficult.

The ultimate changes required globally are clear. How children fare in school fundamentally depends on parental involvement. Parents need a small amount of paid leave each year to attend to their children's school needs— twenty-four hours per year would be adequate to address critical needs in the majority of cases. Businesses can afford to provide the necessary leave. This amount of paid leave is the equivalent of only slightly more than a 1 percent increase in wages, and wages are themselves a fraction of most businesses' costs. Until paid leave is universal, all supervisors should allow workers to shift schedules when it is important for them to attend educational meetings for their children. These schedule shifts can be planned ahead in most cases, making the required schedule adaptation feasible for the widest range of occupations. While taking these needed steps would be straightforward, the costs to schoolchildren of not taking the initiative—and in particular the long-term cost to schoolchildren in low-income families—is inestimable.

Addressing Needs of School-Age Children: The Keystone to Breaking Intergenerational Cycles of Poverty for Working-Poor Families

While school-age children are important for their own sakes, supporting their success is particularly critical because it is the linchpin to breaking intergenerational cycles of poverty. Perhaps the most compelling stories that parents recounted were those that described how they themselves had needed to leave school at young ages to become caregivers for their younger siblings, to earn money their families needed to survive, or simply because no one could help them over the bumps in the road. Then, as a result of not finishing school, the parents had so few job options that they, in turn, had to sacrifice the care and opportunities they could provide to their own school-age children.

If low- and middle-income children in developing countries and poor children in affluent nations are to have anything resembling the shot at life that the majority of middle-class children in industrialized countries have, they need to have a real opportunity to succeed in school. Children six and older need to have the chance to attend school and not be removed to become unpaid childcare providers; they need adults in their lives throughout the day; and their parents need decent working conditions so that it is possible for them to provide essential support to school-age children. Providing the early childhood care and education essential both for the cognitive development of children five and under and for the ability of older children to attend school and having workplaces and schools provide the small amount of flexibility that parents need to be able to be involved in their children's education is feasible in every country around the world if we make a commitment.

4

Parents' Working Conditions and Children's Health

The global transformations in the type of work adults do, where they labor, and who controls their hours and leave have raised fundamental questions about how working adults can meet the health needs of children and adults alike. Who is currently taking responsibility for maintaining children's health when their parents are working? Who cares for children when they get sick and are not allowed to attend childcare or school? Who cares for infants and toddlers who cannot be left home alone sick? Who cares for school-age children who are too sick to care for themselves but not sick enough to be in a hospital? Is our ability to prevent illness and injury improving with higher incomes or declining with less time available to provide the care needed? Likewise, is our ability to address the health needs of those who are already sick with acute or chronic conditions rising in the global economy or rapidly declining? This chapter begins to address these questions.

Hien

When we interviewed her in Vietnam, thirty-three-year-old Pham Dieu Hien seemed already to have lived several lifetimes. Born during what Americans call the Vietnam War and what Vietnamese call the American War, Hien's early childhood was overshadowed by that war. Before her father went into the army as a paratrooper, they lived in the countryside and her mother stayed home to care for Hien and her three siblings. When her father died in the war, everything began to change. Hien's mother had to go to work in the market to earn money if her children were to survive. As a result, Hien, the eldest at eight years, had to take on all the responsibilities of caring for her siblings. She cooked for them, bathed them, and tried to address all of their needs while also attending school. She explained: "My mother, at that time, was alone, and yet she had to care for her children while trying to earn a living so that her children could go to school. When her children were sick all the time, my mother had to stop selling to care for her children. In general, she met hardships." For Hien, the word *hardships* summarized that period in her life.

Hien's life continued to follow the history of her country. Years later, as the Vietnamese economy reopened to outside investment by foreign companies and to private ownership under Doi Moi—a program which transformed the centrally planned Vietnamese economy into an increasingly open market economy—Hien went to work as a seamstress in a Taiwanese-owned athletic shoe factory. She worked six days a week from 8:00 a.m. to 8:30 p.m., with only one break. After getting married, she became pregnant with her son, Liep. Hien worked through the majority of her pregnancy. The hours and days were long and difficult. When she didn't feel well, she would try to rest at the factory and then return to work. She knew she would receive limited maternity leave and wanted to save as much of it as she could for after her child's birth.

When Liep was born, he seemed healthy, but that proved true for only a brief time. His grandmother described caring for Liep while Hien was recovering from her cesarean section. "After two weeks, each night I had to hold him. . . . I held him and observed that his arms shook. I had raised eight children and hadn't seen that. I didn't understand what was happening to my grandson. I told my husband." After two months had passed, the grandmother witnessed an episode where Liep's whole body convulsed. She explained:

> I took him over to a nurse nearby. The nurse said it was all right to take him home. He became well. But the next day, around the same time, I didn't go to market. The child shook again. I took him to the

nurse again, then took him to Children's Hospital. I then called his mother home. He was admitted to the hospital. His mother stayed with him [in the hospital for weeks].

Liep was diagnosed with epilepsy. Like most of the health problems that affect children living in poverty, epilepsy can affect children of any income or social class. But, as with most of those other conditions, there are reasons that poor children are more likely to have seizures and, if they do, for the condition to more markedly affect their lives. Some cases of epilepsy in young children are *idiopathic*, meaning that doctors can't determine the cause. But other cases in infants and toddlers are due to trauma at birth; exposure to toxins and poisons; or meningitis, encephalitis, or other illnesses. When families are too poor for women to receive adequate prenatal care or when poverty prevents them from having a midwife attend a birth or having a physician's care from a sufficiently early stage, the chances that their infant will experience these and other problems—such as a serious illness or injury going undetected or being detected too late, asphyxia during birth due to an umbilical cord wrapped around the baby's neck, or the mother's significant blood loss—rise. Immunizations are now available to prevent many of the most severe infections that affect infants and young children. But it remains the case that children living in poor nations, as well as children living in poverty in affluent nations, are more likely to lack immunizations or be immunized too late. They are more likely to get preventable communicable diseases, such as polio and measles. Moreover, if they are infected with one of the pathogens against which vaccinations do not exist, children living in poverty are less likely to receive prompt medical attention—the kind of attention that can mean the difference between a full recovery from and serious sequelae to an illness.

Liep's parents didn't know what had caused his seizures, so there was no way for us to know. It is certainly possible that he had had a traumatic birth. The boy's grandmother and father both wondered if the cesarean section performed could have, by itself, caused seizures. No well-performed cesarean section would cause seizures, but if the baby had been in trouble during a lengthy labor—if the baby had been stuck in a birth canal that was too small and had gone into distress, or if the cord had been wrapped around his neck (two potential reasons for a cesarean section)—delays in Hien's receipt of care could have meant time when Liep didn't get adequate oxygen to his brain, resulting in seizures.

Alternatively, his first seizure at a few months of age could have resulted from meningitis, which, if detected and treated too late, could have led to brain damage. Liep could also have been exposed to toxins prenatally. Agent Orange, a defoliant used during the war, led to countless fetal defects in Vietnam and among the children of American veterans returning to the United States. Moreover, Agent Orange has a long half-life. A quarter century after the war's end, the toxin was still detected at levels too high to be safe for humans in the soil of a number of Vietnamese agricultural areas where it had been sprayed. It was also still detectable in laboratory tests conducted on people who had been exposed a quarter century earlier.

If poverty and poor health were two strikes against Liep's chances, the third strike against him was the penurious working conditions his parents faced. As a job, his father played a wind instrument at funerals—of which there were many. But he was paid on a piece basis—when he worked, he received payment; on other days, he did not. His mother's working conditions were far more egregious, as Hein explained:

> Each time when I took time off—I was working for a Taiwanese athletic shoes employer—the schedule was very demanding. If I took off one day, then three days' salary would be taken off. . . . When I had my son, I couldn't continue to work there because I couldn't take time off. If I took time off, the days off would be subtracted from my salary and I would end up not having any income.

Under these conditions, Hien's "job" grew ever closer to unpaid, forced labor. For the period that Hien continued to work in the factory, her mother-in-law would go to the hospital during the day to care for Liep. Hien would return from work and then go to the hospital at night to care for him and thus would barely sleep.

As a seamstress in the shoe factory, Hien had no time with her family even when they were well. She often was required to add a seventh twelve-hour day to her work week. "In a month, there were two Sundays I had to work and two I was allowed off," she said. "If I were to take another Sunday off, three days of salary would be taken away in addition to that Sunday's salary. Additionally, at the end of the year, the bonus money would be reduced." She described the factory's approach to the ten days of leave per year that each employee supposedly could take:

Although they said ten days, they didn't let us take those days off. They would pay us a little more when we worked on those permitted leave days. They said that a production factory needs people. If people took time off there would be no one. When I worked there for a few years, I didn't take any days off. Although they said that I could take the permitted leave, I couldn't really. They would fire me if I had taken those days off.

Unable to see her son or her husband, losing more money every day she took off than she had earned on multiple days at work, Hien eventually decided to leave the factory's low wages for even lower wages in the informal sector. The hours in the informal sector were as long, but at least she wasn't triply penalized when she needed to take time to care for Liep. She explained: "About seven o'clock in the morning I already left the house. I helped sell until eight o'clock at night when the stores closed. I helped to sell goods like blankets. It demanded a lot of time. I had to sell at night."

When Hien finally found a job in an import-export company that didn't fine her when her son got sick, she felt like she had won the lottery—even though the wages were poor compared to those of most other jobs. "The salary in my office, my salary is the lowest. But that is okay. I work to earn money to care for my son." Liep continued to need a great deal of special care. Settled into her new job, Hien was finally able to take leave, but she remained worried. "I am afraid to take time off, especially working at this new place. I'm afraid it would affect my work. What if they let me go? What would I have to care for my son?"

Finances were tight. Regarding each of her son's trips to the doctor, she explained: "I pay cash, because we don't have health insurance. The doctors give us the prescription that we would go out to fill. In general, when working as hired workers like ourselves, it is extremely difficult to raise a sick child like this one." She went on to describe the times when she and her husband had had to borrow money to pay for Liep's care: "Our family has to spend wisely to save so that our son can go to childcare. What is left, the family spends on daily needs. If our son is not sick, then we don't have many hardships. But when our son is sick, then we do suffer hardships."

Hien's husband helped with their son's care while she worked. He also helped care for his own father, who had hepatitis B, and his mother, who had severe arthritis. Referring to the demands of the caregiving and work, he said, "There is no time when I am free." Hien's own physical and mental health were hit hard by the stress, as she noted:

> I am also often sick. I often worry. I worry about my son being sick,
> my family's economic situation. . . . I have to worry about my son's
> childcare fee, the rent, my son's health-care fees, and the like. I think
> a lot; therefore, sometimes, my memory is reduced. I often forget.
> Although I go to work, I am always thinking of my son.

Liep needed someone who could care for him when he was sick: a teacher who had been trained to handle children with health needs, a parent who was able to take leave from work, or a healthy adult family member who could afford not to work. His grandmother was home because she was no longer well enough to work but, increasingly disabled, she was in need of help herself.

Hien's story was only one of hundreds we heard recounted which told of the indelible ways that working conditions and social supports determined whether families could meet children's preventive, curative, and care needs while working.

Promoting Children's Health: How Do Working Conditions Affect Prevention?

The major killers of children worldwide are all preventable. Periodically, reports review the tragic statistics about the millions of children who die needlessly of avoidable diseases worldwide, as well as about the far greater number who live with preventable illnesses, injuries, and disabilities. Organizations have been developed and initiatives launched to increase rates of vaccination, breast-feeding, and preventive prenatal care, among other approaches. Many of these initiatives are critically important to the health of our world's children.

But amid the talk and action aimed at improving children's health, a hole in the safety net has been growing. Prevention requires the time and active involvement of children's parents and caregivers as well as of health-care workers to ensure, for example, that children receive immunizations on time, have access to clean water to prevent diarrhea, and receive life-saving treatment if they develop diarrhea or respiratory infections. Yet, little or no attention has been paid to who actually has the opportunity to care for children's health and safety.

- Do mothers have any chance to breast-feed in the jobs they must work at in order to feed their families?
- Do working parents living in poverty have any realistic way to take their children for immunizations at the times and places those are being given?
- Are adults available to care for young children so they do not face serious risks of injury and illness? or are children left home alone with no one to ensure their safety?

Breast-Feeding

Breast-feeding provides an important example of why it is important to know about parental working conditions. The leading four causes of death of children include problems related to delivery in the first month of life (20 percent), respiratory infections (18 percent), diarrhea (17 percent), and vaccine-preventable diseases (15 percent).[1] Breast-feeding plays a critical role in preventing two of these four: diarrheal diseases and respiratory infections. Two million children die in developing countries from diarrheal disease each year,[2] and the risk is dramatically increased when infants are not breast-fed. Breast-fed infants have significantly lower rates of gastrointestinal infections,[3] respiratory tract infections,[4] otitis media,[5] meningitis,[6] and other infections.[7] Overall, breast-fed children are one and a half to five times less likely to die prematurely.[8]

While the benefits of breast-feeding are many and well established, and while there is no inherent conflict between employment and breast-feeding, many working women aren't able to breast-feed for long because of the conditions they face at their jobs. When women lack an adequate maternity leave, when they need to return to work early without any opportunity to take breaks during the day to breast-feed, and when infant care is distant—making breast-feeding during the day impossible—mothers often have to end breast-feeding dangerously early even when they are unable to afford or obtain adequate nutritional substitutes for breast milk.

The family of Maria Gonzalez, who lived in Buenas Nuevas, Honduras, had an all-too-common experience. Neither Maria nor her husband had had the opportunity to learn to read or write, but they had managed to put their daughters through school. Their oldest daughter, Leti Marta, aged twenty-three, was working as a bilingual secretary. Leti had a seven-month-old baby,

Marcela, who Maria was helping to raise while Leti worked to support her baby. The baby's father had abandoned Leti during her pregnancy. Leti's job provided her with only forty-two days off after her daughter's birth. Maria explained that when Leti's official maternity leave ended, so did the breast-feeding. Leti tried to express milk, but she was not able to sustain that practice while working. Maria fed her granddaughter milk "from a can," but by the age of seven months, the girl was as pale as a ghost from anemia. Having been weaned too young, she suffered from acute malnutrition and was falling off the growth chart, weighing, as a seven-month-old, what she should have weighed as a four-month-old.

While the lives of millions of children are currently placed at risk when their mothers cannot breast-feed while working, the problem is not that good solutions do not exist. When children fall sick and die because they do not have the protection that breast milk would have offered them, their illnesses are *not* the result of the impossibility of their mothers' breast-feeding while working. Workplaces around the world have demonstrated that when child-care is available near work sites and when mothers are given breast-feeding breaks, they are able to work while breast-feeding their infants throughout the first year of life.

When employers are committed to providing the kind of working conditions that make it feasible for parents to contribute at work while caring for their children, breast-feeding becomes possible in a wide range of settings. Mandipa Kazapula described her experience breast-feeding while working in Botswana. At twenty-nine years old, Mandipa was the mother of three children between one and ten years old. She worked as a local police officer, but Mandipa's employer understood the importance of making it feasible for her to care for her infant while working. Because of this, Mandipa explained, "I had a feeding hour at 11 o'clock [in the morning] so I could come home. In the evening I could come home and feed."

Halfway around the world from Mandipa's job as a police officer, Truong Thi Nhu Quynh worked as a public-school teacher in Vietnam. She recounted to us how she had been able to work while breast-feeding her son for eighteen months:

While my son was little . . . while I was working, I often came home to nurse him every two classroom periods. Having done so, I felt near my son, although I went to work. The headmaster used to care for teachers in the school. By doing that, the teachers could work well. The assigned workload would never be four or five hours continuously, which would have made it impossible for me to go home to nurse my child. . . . I would teach two periods straight and then could go home. I would have to come back for more teaching, but that type of arrangement helped me nurse my child.

Immunizations, Safe Drinking Water, and Infectious Diseases

Vaccinations provide another important example of a critically important, theoretically readily feasible method of preventing childhood illness and death. Yet, immunization programs in many parts of the world are currently structured so that parents, or other adult care providers, must take time off from work to bring their children to clinics or physicians' offices for shots or be home during the day, when immunization campaigns occur.

Dr. Marcelo Javaloyas was the director of a health clinic serving many of the neighborhoods we visited in Tegucigalpa. He spoke compellingly about the salience of patients' working conditions and social supports to their children's health and welfare. He explained that his clinic was in the middle of a vaccination campaign, and he spoke of how difficult it was to effectively immunize children in many of the households with working-poor parents who lacked childcare. Since the parents worked all day and received no leave, they could never take their children to the clinic for immunizations. The doctors and nurses went to countless homes where children were home alone. The children couldn't find their *carnets*, or immunization cards, so they couldn't be vaccinated. No adult was available who knew which immunizations the children had received and which they had missed. Studies in Haiti, Indonesia, and the United States have all found that parents report conflicts with work schedules as a significant barrier to getting their children immunized.[9] Our studies suggest that if parents had basic benefits, such as paid leave from work and schedule flexibility that would enable them to take their children to clinics and doctors' offices, children would be more likely to receive a full complement of immunizations on time. Because of poor parental working conditions, children in lower-income families are currently more likely to lack immunizations than children in higher-income families—even when the vaccines are "freely available." This does not need to be the case. If parents received basic benefits at work, they would be able to bring their children for immunizations and other essential preventive care. If immunization campaigns occurred on weekdays in childcare centers and preschools (where they exist) or in clinics on weekends or evenings, the children of working parents could also be reached.

Diarrheal disease provides further examples of potentially life-saving approaches that currently rely on the availability of parents and other caregivers. Life-threatening diarrhea affects millions of children worldwide annually. Oral rehydration therapy provides a critical opportunity to effectively treat diarrheal disease and prevent deaths in poor countries. The simply made rehydration solution—consisting of water, sugar, and salt—can keep children from dying. But the solution must be administered by an adult who can give the child one sip at a time, every minute, for hours. No one has asked or determined whether these adults are available.

Dr. Javaloyas also told this story as representative of how having no adults available increases the chances that children will suffer repeated episodes of diarrheal disease and consequent malnutrition:

> A boy of one year of age comes to the health center. The doctor who sees him finds out that the medical record at age one is extensive, and that attracts his attention. He starts going through it, and he realizes that the kid has had diarrhea problems. He then checks that the diarrhea problems started at six months of age. The doctor then asks the mom if she breast-fed the kid. She says that she did, but only for the first six months. That means that for that time the kid was better protected. . . . Then the doctor asks: "After six months, who was taking care of the child?" "My ten-year-old daughter." "How many children live at home?" "Six."

All of the children are cared for by the ten-year-old girl, who is the eldest.

Dr. Rosa Dominguez was one of many other physicians who reported on readily preventable illnesses resulting from no adequate care being available to children. She explained: "Last year I had a patient who got sick very often. I told the mother that there had to be something wrong with the child. She told me that since both she and her husband worked, the child had to stay home with his younger sibling, who was seven years old. She told me that once she found that the younger one had defecated a lot because he had eaten rotten food."

Much is known about what it takes to prevent diarrhea. First and foremost, the delivery of safe drinking water is necessary. The most straightforward solution is having either indoor plumbing or outdoor standpipes that deliver water free of microbes. But for the many parts of the world where water is drawn from rivers or streams and the many more places where water from pipes still carries bacteria, water need only be boiled and fruits and vegetables peeled or cooked to avoid the spread of most sources of diarrhea. But to do those things, adults need to be able to spend substantial amounts of time making the necessary preparations. Fuel needs to be gathered; all drinking water must be boiled. Safe water and food preparation takes a great deal longer under these circumstances. As a global community, we have known these facts for a long time but have failed to examine whether any of the required steps are feasible for adults in poor countries. Are there adults even available to take these precautions for their children? or do parental working hours and the paucity of programs for preschool and school-age children mean that children are left alone or in settings where these preventive measures cannot possibly be taken? Worldwide, poor parents' working conditions and long hours are all too often unaccompanied by any supports for families and therefore are associated with a deep void in preventive health measures for their children.

Injuries

Preventing injury as well as illness requires that adults are available to care for children. The rates of accidents occurring while parents were at work were high in all countries due to the inadequate availability of care. In 53 percent of families we interviewed in Botswana, children experienced accidents or emergencies while parents were at work. Accidents and other emergencies took their toll on children while parents were at work in 47 percent of the families we interviewed in Mexico and 38 percent of the families we interviewed in Vietnam (see figure 4-1).

When children are left home alone or in the care of other children, injury rates skyrocket. Eva Martinez, a single mother of five children, lived in Villa Franca, one of the poorer neighborhoods high on the hills surrounding Tegucigalpa. Eva's home consisted of one adobe room that served as living room, kitchen, and play area. There was a wooden ladder in the middle of the room that ran straight up to the roof. In a small eave below the roof, the family kept their bedding and clothes. Eva's home was typical of other poor families' homes in this impoverished neighborhood in that the common area had only

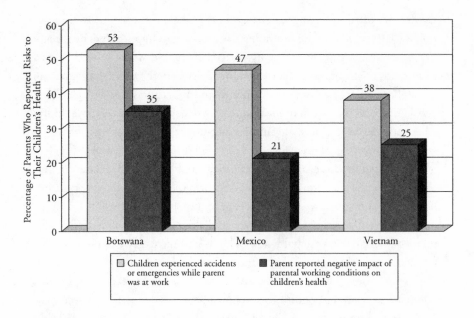

Figure 4-1
Frequency That Parental Working Conditions Affect Children's Health.
Note: Data from Project on Global Working Families' in-depth interviews with working care-givers. Analyses in the above figure are based on households with a zero- to fourteen-year-old child.

one chair, which she generously offered to any visitor. Their single-room shack smelled heavily of the cheap gasoline she had to use to cook.

Eva was raising her five children on her own and had to support them on the small earnings she made washing and ironing the clothes of other families. Each day, she went from house to house in another poor neighborhood asking how she could help families for the small amount of money they could afford to pay her in return. Her earnings barely fed and clothed her children. There was clearly nothing left to pay for childcare, so she had no choice but to leave them alone when she went out in search of work.

She spoke to us about the traumas that occurred when her children were alone. When her son was seven and caring for her then three-year-old daughter, they went off alone to buy some food. Her daughter fell down one of the hillside escarpments surrounding the capital and broke her leg. Another time, a different daughter cut the tip off her finger as she tried to cook. She sliced all the way through the nerves, damaging them irreparably. One day, when her four daughters had been left alone with her oldest son, one of the preschool girls climbed the wooden ladder in the room and fell from the roof to the ground, fracturing her skull. When Eva returned from work, her daughter was unconscious. Still bleeding, the toddler was taken to the hospital, where she had to stay for weeks. The hospital bill, more than 2,000 lempira ($115), sent the family further into debt. The amount was far more than Eva's typical monthly earnings—earnings that were too meager to allow any savings. Eva was painfully aware of the risks of leaving her children unattended, but she knew they would starve if she did not work.

At times, parents left their children home alone because they could not afford any childcare; at other times parents in poverty left their children in the only care they could afford—informal care by poor-quality providers. The result was often the same—children who ended up alone, sick, and injured. Thatayaone Marumoagae lived in Gaborone and sold clothing at the main bus station. Poorly paid, he could afford only low-quality informal care for his young son. One day, the caregiver left the child alone, and Thatayaone's son was hit by a car. "He was trying to go to the other side of the road, just to get out of our house to the neighbor's house. A transport car, taxi, ran over him, and we were informed that he had gotten in a car accident. By the time they informed us, he was already in so much pain he couldn't stand it."

Health-care professionals we interviewed in each country bore witness to the illnesses and injuries resulting from children being left at home alone, in the care of other siblings, or in inadequate care. A surgeon in Gaborone, Botswana, noted that the fraction of children's injuries—from lacerations to burns to broken bones—that occurred when children were alone was high. Dr. Marcia Graciano provided examples of the range of problems she had seen in Mexico:

> Once we had a case of a child who had ingested an object, and another time a child who had fallen from a cradle and had had a brain injury. I've had children in my consultation who stay by themselves at home. In these cases we're talking about children who are between the ages of five and nine. Mothers bring them here when they get sick, but then when we interview the parents, we find out that the child is alone for long periods of time.

Assaults

The problems do not end with accidents and injuries: from North America to Asia to Africa, children left alone are at increased risk of becoming victims of violence. In Molepolole, Onalenna Modise worked as a temporary laborer, receiving a daily wage with no paid leave benefits. A thirty-four-year-old, she was the mother of two daughters, ten and thirteen years old. Onalenna told us what had happened when her children were ten and seven years old. One day after school, her daughter Tebogo came home to an empty house, and a repairman broke into the house and raped her. After the assault, she lay, curled up and crying, in a corner until her mother returned in the evening. Onalenna reported:

> I came back from work and saw that she was in one of our one-
> roomed houses in the yard, crying. She was in the corner and crying.
> I went up to her and asked her what had happened, and she told me
> that a man had had sex with her. A man that I know, a man who
> sometimes helps us repair things in the house, came by when Tebogo
> was home after school. He came into the yard and then forced him-
> self onto Tebogo. Then he left. When I found her, she was still cry-
> ing. I took her to the clinic right away, where the nurses talked to her
> and to me and checked her out to make sure she was okay physically.

However, there was, in fact, no way to know whether Tebogo was "okay physi-cally" because more than a third of the adults in Botswana were already infected with HIV/AIDS, and no tests were available that could immediately determine whether the girl had become infected. After the rape, Onalenna explained, her daughter "was now afraid to be home alone. [I have] to be with her all the time." Onalenna took off time from work, without any pay. "I had to stay at home for the whole week. I had to take Tebogo to the clinic again to ask them to help me with counseling." The loss of pay may have been the least of her worries, but it was nonetheless a real one when they were already so poor that she had not been able to afford the glasses her daughter needed to see.

Fires

Fires were both one of the most common and one of the most devastating kinds of accidents that parents reported when their children were left alone. Since most families lived in wood and mud shacks, fires often left them homeless and deprived of what little they had accumulated as far as clothes and other essentials. In Molepolole, Nunuko Ndebele described what happened when her children were home without supervision:

> They were cooking while I was at work, using the gas stove. I think they switched one button on but didn't light the stove. I can't say what happened, but whatever they did, the whole house was in flames. Everything was burned out. We didn't take a single item out of the house, and when I got back from work, I found what used to be a house was now in ashes.

Fires occurred when children were left home alone; they also happened when parents had to leave children with low-quality, unreliable care. In Gaborone, Larona Muyaluka had left her two children with a housekeeper, who left the children sleeping alone. Larona called home frequently during the day to check on her children:

> Having left around quarter to two, around half past two I called home and was told that "Yes, the children are sleeping." "Where are they sleeping?" "In your bedroom." Around an hour later, I received a phone call from my brother, who had been driving and had seen that my house had caught fire. He said, "The fire brigade is there. They can't even open your bedroom door, and the bedroom is on fire. They can't get to your bedroom." I was shocked. I said, "Where are the children?" . . . I ran home—it was a thirty-minute walk to my house—and as I was running, I could hear the fire brigade there, making that noise. . . . When I got home, I found that many people were there and that the children had been rescued and were outside. I was very shocked. . . . I kept on repeating the same thing so that people thought I had gone cuckoo. They wanted to rush me to the hospital. . . . The house was still on fire at the time; it was still aggressive at that time. Everything was destroyed. . . . The bed caught fire. Then the mosquito net. Then the curtains. My small girl managed to get to the front door, climbed up on a dining room chair, and found that the door was locked. The housekeeper had locked the door and gone out. She knew that I would come back around five and that I would call around half past two and not call again. She went out and locked the door.

Larona went on to describe how, once her daughter got out, a neighbor realized that her son must still be inside. He had locked himself in the bathroom but was rescued before it was too late. Larona was pregnant at the time. She ended up having serious complications and giving birth prematurely as a result of hypertension and preeclampsia induced by the disaster.

The consequences of fires always ravaged lives: lifelong physical injuries, traumas, and deaths. The physical injuries are immediately obvious, the psychological toll often delayed. Dr. Ramón del Mazo of Monterrey explained: "Just imagine the anxiety that a child can feel if a younger sibling has an accident that she can't do anything about. If there's a fire in the house and someone dies, that would be terrible."

Geralda Garcia told us about preschool twins who had been left alone, *encerrados* (closed in), in their house when their mother had to go to work. Their single mother had locked them in for their own safety because she knew that some children who had been left alone and had not been locked inside their homes had been raped or assaulted by strangers; some had wandered off; and others had suffered serious injuries as they walked the streets alone. But in the case Geralda was describing, the preschoolers' home caught on fire, and since the children were alone at the time, no one knew the details—whether they'd been lighting a fire, playing with the fire, or trying to cook. One of the twins died in the fire. The other survived only because Geralda and several neighbors broke the door down, rushed in, risking severe burns themselves, and pulled the child out. The surviving twin was never the same.

Many families were left homeless after fires, literally without anything. In Molepolole, Lebogang Olefetse recounted an incident involving her two-and-a-half-year-old son and seven-year-old daughter:

> I was at work. . . . I have to go to work early in the morning.
> When they come back from school, they are alone and I'm not there.
> It was cold that day and they were trying to warm themselves at the
> fire. Somehow, [my daughter] fell in the fire and got burned. . . . I
> found her when I knocked off [work]. There were no combies [often-
> rickety minivans used as an inexpensive form of public transporta-
> tion] to take her to the hospital. We stayed with her through that
> whole night and took her to the hospital the next morning.

Lebogang went on to describe how the whole house had burned: "We didn't rescue anything from it. . . . It was very difficult, especially since the hut had all of our parents' possessions, clothes, food, everything you can think of."

So why do they take the risk? Most of the parents had left young children alone in order to earn enough to feed and clothe them. They left them alone when there was no childcare available and no other way to earn a living. Their children started fires when they were cold or hungry.

Caring for Sick Family Members

The timing and types of preventive health care that children need are generally predictable. One can tell in advance when children will require immunizations and until what age they need to be breast-fed, and preventing exposure to injury and illness involves the expected: ensuring that children have decent routine care. Addressing the needs of sick children is different. It is made easier than preventive care because of its lower frequency but more difficult because it cannot be anticipated. The fundamental question surrounding preventive care is whether work environments and rules in the global economy allow parents and caregivers to meet the basic needs of children. The fundamental question when it comes to caring for sick children is whether the system has the flexibility to bend when a crisis occurs or whether it breaks down. When children become acutely ill, is anyone available to take care of them? For children with serious health conditions, is anyone with time and flexibility available to provide their needed care?

Parents play as critical a role in caring for children as they recover from illnesses and injuries as they do in preventing health problems. Young children who are sick need their parents or other care providers to take them to the physician, obtain and administer medicine, and provide daily care when the children cannot attend routine childcare or school. Research demonstrating that children recover more rapidly from illnesses and injuries when parents provide care has long been available.[10] Parents' involvement has been shown to speed children's recovery—whether they are having an outpatient procedure or are ill enough to be hospitalized.[11] Benefits to children's health have been shown for a wide range of health problems from epilepsy[12] to asthma to diabetes,[13] among other conditions.

Previously, in the United States, I documented the critical role that working conditions play in determining whether parents are able to care for their children when they are sick.[14] My research team's work in Vietnam, Botswana, Mexico, Honduras, and Russia has demonstrated that working conditions play an equally critical role in determining whether parents can care for their children when they become sick in these widely varied settings.

Having to attend to family illnesses is a common part of human life worldwide. We analyzed data in four countries where information was collected nationally on the frequency of illness for every member of the household. In Vietnam, 50 percent of dual-earner households and 54 percent of extended-family households reported illnesses or injuries among adults and children requiring missing normal activities during the past month (see figures 4-2 and 4-3). In Brazil, this occurred in 31 percent of dual-earner and 44 percent of extended-family households in any given month (see figures 4-4 and 4-5). In Russia, where data were only available on those fifteen and older, 19 percent of dual-earner households and 29 percent of extended-family households reported illnesses or injuries during the past month among youth and adult household members. If data on all members of the household were available, the percentages would be even higher. While living with extended family can provide im-

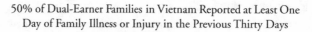

50% of Dual-Earner Families in Vietnam Reported at Least One Day of Family Illness or Injury in the Previous Thirty Days

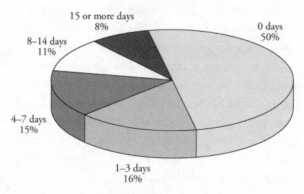

15 or more days
8%

0 days
50%

8–14 days
11%

4–7 days
15%

1–3 days
16%

Figure 4-2
Vietnam: How Many Days Each Month Are Family Members Sick or Injured in Dual-Earner Households?
Note: Data from national household surveys. Analyses in the above figure are based on households with a zero- to fourteen-year-old child.

54% of Extended-Family Households in Vietnam Reported at Least
One Day of Family Illness or Injury in the Previous 30 Days

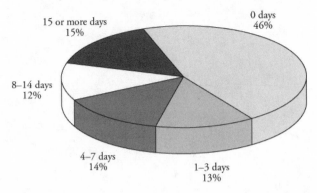

Figure 4-3
Vietnam: How Many Days Each Month Are Family Members
Sick or Injured in Extended-Family Households?
Note: Data from national household surveys. Analyses in the above figure are based on households with a zero- to fourteen-year-old child.

31% of Dual-Earner Families in Brazil Reported at Least One
Day of Family Illness or Injury in the Previous Thirty Days

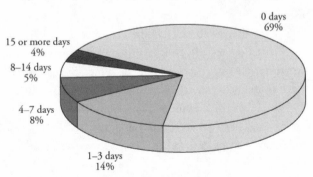

Figure 4-4
Brazil: How Many Days Each Month Are Family Members
Sick or Injured in Dual-Earner Households?
Note: Data from national household surveys. Analyses in the above figure are based on households with a zero- to fourteen-year-old child.

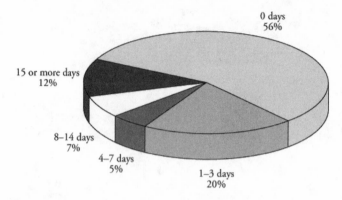

44% of Extended-Family Households in Brazil Reported at Least
One Day of Family Illness or Injury in the Previous Thirty Days

0 days
56%

15 or more days
12%

8–14 days
7%

4–7 days
5%

1–3 days
20%

Figure 4-5
Brazil: How Many Days Each Month Are Family Members
Sick or Injured in Extended-Family Households?
Note: Data from national household surveys. Analyses in the above figure are based on house-
holds with a zero- to fourteen-year-old child.

portant sources of support in caring for children's illnesses, extended families
commonly face a greater illness burden because of the compounding health
problems of grandparents and other older family members.

The at-risk settings children were in when sick paralleled many of the settings they were in when well. Sick children were at times left home alone, at
other times left in the care of young children, sometimes taken to their parents' workplaces, and sometimes left in the hands of inadequate caregivers.
But the grave consequences were more immediate because the children were
already ill. Overall, in the countries that we studied, 17 percent of children
had been left home alone when they were sick: specifically, in Botswana, 28
percent; in Mexico, 16 percent; and in Vietnam, 7 percent.

Causes of Children Left Home Alone Sick

When children are placed at risk, it is not because their parents care less, understand less well what their children need, or have different values or feelings
than do other parents. Time after time, children are placed at risk because

parents have little or no choice: grossly inadequate working conditions do not permit parents to properly tend to their children's needs. In every country we studied, parents faced untenable choices when it came to caring for sick children. Twenty-eight percent of the parents we interviewed in Botswana had lost pay, had difficulty retaining their job, or lost job promotions because of the need to care for sick children, as did 48 percent of working parents in Mexico and 62 percent in Vietnam (see figure 4-6). Parents living in poverty were the most likely to face difficult decisions when their children were sick. Two-thirds of poor families had left children home alone sick or lost needed pay to care for their children (see figure 4-7).

In Botswana, Tshegofatso Walone's experience was illustrative. The mother of five children aged thirteen to twenty-two, she was also the primary

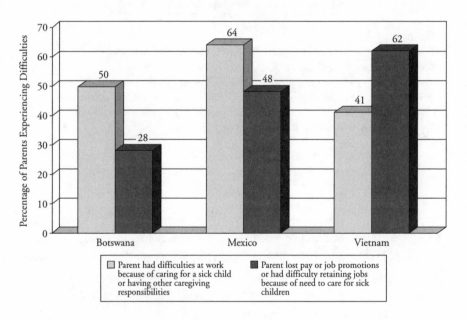

Figure 4-6
Frequency That Working Parents Experience Difficulties
at Work as a Result of Caring for Sick Children.
Note: Data from Project on Global Working Families' in-depth interviews with working caregivers. Analyses in the above figure are based on households with a zero- to fourteen-year-old child.

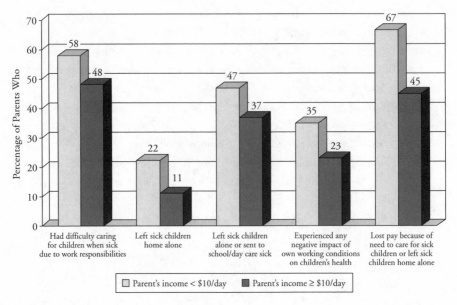

Figure 4-7
Low-Income Parents Are at Greater Risk of Experiencing Difficulties Caring for Their Sick Children.
Note: Data from Project on Global Working Families' in-depth interviews with working care-givers. Analyses in the above figure are based on households with a zero- to fourteen-year-old child. Income data from each survey have been converted to a common currency using the World Bank's purchasing power parity (PPP) conversion factors.

caregiver for her three-year-old grandson. She earned only a few dollars per day as a cleaner of a public building, so her family had to get by on little money. She had found herself having to choose between fundamentals: one month, buying uniforms so her children could attend school and consequently not being able to pay for electricity and, the next month, paying for the electricity but not buying clothes.

Her youngest son, Resego, was blind in his right eye, and she had to save money to pay for his care. Because her family needed her to work to earn essential income, Tshegofatso had little choice about what to do when her children became sick, although she knew that leaving them home alone was a terrible option for them: "When you are away and there is a sick child at home, there is no one to care for that child by giving medication and bathing the child." When asked what she did when a child became sick, she explained: "Sometimes I ask permission to go and take care of this child or even take leave." But often she had no choice besides remaining at work because the leave was not paid. Tshegofatso described what she faced when she ended up going to work under these conditions:

> I think about the condition and about the child at home—how he is feeling at home. I can't cope well with my work. . . . Sometimes I lose my mind, because sometimes you can hear someone say, "Oh Mma Walone, what are you thinking?" Then I would say, "My child is ill." And they comfort me telling me I shouldn't worry because the child will be okay at home and that he will get better.

But she went on to explain why she did, in fact, worry. She described one instance in which she had had to leave a sick child at home alone:

> At half-past seven, when I was going to work, my last born was sick. He was vomiting, had diarrhea and stomach complaints. I left him with my neighbor, but the neighbor didn't care for my child. She just left him there vomiting. Immediately when I came home I thought my child looked worse. I took him to the hospital around half-past six, and he was tired and pale. I had wanted to leave the job, but then I had thought, what would I give this child?

Inadequately paid, unsupervised informal care by poorly prepared providers sometimes differed little from no care. The experience of Arabang Ndlovu in Botswana was representative in many ways. Arabang worked as a kitchen assistant and earned only a few dollars per day. Like many parents supporting their families on barely subsistence wages, she could not afford to pay someone else much to care for her children nor could she come home to supervise. She described desperately how the care her children received was often little different than being left alone:

> Sometimes I come back from work and the kids are very hungry, despite the fact that the caretaker was home and the food was available. There was one incident when one of the twins was sick. [The caretaker] collected them from school. She did notice that [my daughter] was sick, but she left them alone in the house. The other twin went

to the neighbor and told the neighbor that her sister was sick. The neighbor called me at work, but the caretaker had left them alone after taking them from school.

Arabang returned home rapidly to take the sick twin to the hospital to be evaluated.

Many programs are designed around building the capacity of parents, in general, and mothers, in particular, to care for their children when they are sick. By *building capacity*, the designers frequently mean imparting knowledge about how to recognize the signs of different illnesses and what to do when children become ill. But there aren't enough programs or policies aimed at ensuring that parents have the chance to provide the kind of care they already know is important. Tshegofatso Walone, Petra Navarro, Arabane Ndlovu, and the other parents we interviewed were well aware that their children needed them when they were sick. But they couldn't afford to take unpaid leave—and even fewer could afford losing their jobs. The problem involved not a lack of knowledge or parenting skills but a lack of opportunity.

Figure 4-8 shows the number of families that left children home alone sick and the number that sent their sons and daughters to school or day care when they were ill. More than a quarter of families in Botswana, where the impact of illness is devastating because of the HIV epidemic (see chapter 6), had to leave children home alone when they were sick. While the numbers of parents leaving children home alone sick were lower in Mexico and Vietnam, those parents who did *not* leave their children home alone lost pay and jobs at high rates.

No parents wanted to leave their children home alone sick. They searched for every possible alternative. When extended families were available to help, this substantially reduced the likelihood that children would be left home alone sick (see figure 4-9). However, in many cases, parents could not turn to aunts, uncles, or grandparents for help in caring for their sick children. Aunts and uncles often did not live nearby or worked themselves and were unable to take leave, and grandparents who were relatively young were usually working themselves. Many of the older grandparents were not healthy enough to look after sick children. Moreover, rapid urbanization and families moving to look for work had resulted in many living too far from other relatives to be able to turn to them to care for sick children.

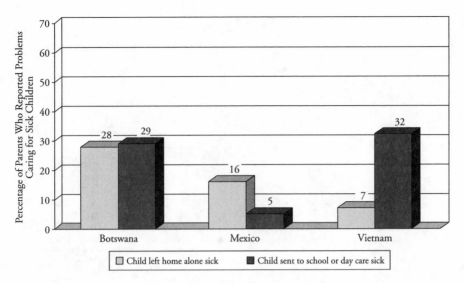

Figure 4-8
Frequency of Inadequate Care for Sick Children.
Note: Data from Project on Global Working Families' in-depth interviews with working care-givers. Analyses in the above figure are based on households with a zero- to fourteen-year-old child.

Children Sent to School or Brought to Work Sick

Lacking flexibility to take leave from work, unable to adjust their hours or take paid leave, the only alternative to leaving children home alone for many caregivers was to send children to school or day care or bring them to work sick.

The same factors which placed children at risk of being left home alone sick also increased the likelihood that children would be sent to school or day care sick. When parents had extended family to whom they could turn, children were less likely to be sent to school or day care sick (see figure 4-10). Whether or not extended-family members were present, the availability of decent working conditions had an enormous impact on the likelihood that children were sent to school or day care sick. Providing parents with any leave from work for caregiving halved the risk of their children being sent to school or day care sick.

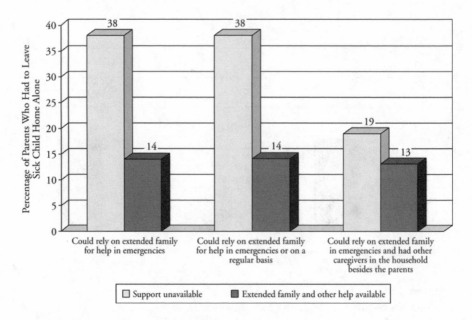

Figure 4-9
When Parents Lack Extended-Family Support, They Are
More Likely to Have to Leave Sick Children Home Alone.
Note: Data from Project on Global Working Families' in-depth interviews with working care-givers. Analyses in the above figure are based on households with a zero- to fourteen-year-old child.

When parents did send their children to school or day care sick, this only led to rapid spread to other children of the infectious diseases that commonly plagued their sons and daughters. When parents brought children to work, they were often unable to provide care. In Vietnam, Le Thi Nhung worked as a teacher. She was more fortunate than many of the people we interviewed because her work sometimes allowed her to find ways of taking leave or rescheduling her obligations. Even so, she didn't always have the option to reschedule, and any leave she took was unpaid. She described one episode when her preschool-age daughter became sick:

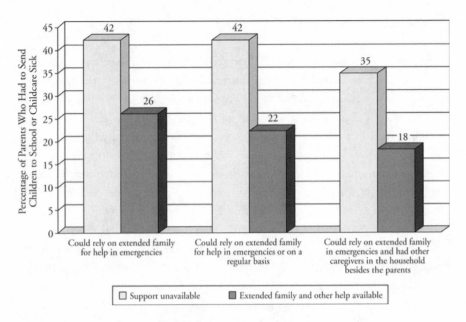

Figure 4-10
When Parents Lack Extended-Family Support, They Are
More Likely to Have to Send Children to School or Childcare Sick.
Note: Data from Project on Global Working Families' in-depth interviews with working care-
givers. Analyses in the above figure are based on households with a zero- to fourteen-year-old
child.

She stayed at home. Her father was at work; he couldn't come home.
It was time for me to go teach; I couldn't stay home. I had to take her
with me to school. I let her sit and play [outside] by herself, although
she was sick. That day she had a fever and a cold. The other people
saw her playing out there. . . . She was very cold. She didn't dare to
say anything nor leave. . . . I was teaching in the classroom. I
couldn't bring her in. . . . Naturally, I was worried because she was
little. . . . I was worried that she would go somewhere and be missing and I can't find her. Whenever a student asked to go out [of my
classroom], I would ask that student to see where my child was, to
see whether she was still there.

Caring for Children with Special Needs

The cruel choices that parents are all too often forced to make between caring well for a sick child and earning an income sufficient to meet their family's most basic needs are magnified many times when a child in the family has a disability or a chronic medical condition. Having to work while caring for children with disabilities and chronic conditions is part of daily life for millions of families. There are 150 million children worldwide who have a disability or chronic condition.[15] Just as it is clear that all children deserve an opportunity for a healthy environment in which to grow and develop, regardless of income, it is equally evident that early opportunities for growth and development are critical to children across all levels of health and ability.

Kereng Seetasewa of Botswana had four children, the youngest of whom, Kesego, had been severely disabled by cerebral palsy. Over time, nerve damage, along with disuse and misuse, had caused the muscles in Kesego's legs to contract, making them barely functional. No early intervention, physical therapy, or childcare was available to Kereng for her five-year-old daughter, nor would any employer who paid a decent wage allow Kereng to bring her daughter to work. For a long period, Kereng could not find a job. In the end, the only work she could find was piecework for women who wanted their laundry done. They paid little but at least allowed her to bring Kesego. Though this was better than leaving her child alone, taking Kesego to work was still difficult for Kereng and her daughter:

> It's not easy, because when I get to work, I have to set Kesego aside
> and do my duties. When she cries, I give her whatever she wants and
> I continue. There are times when she doesn't feel well and I have to
> work with her on my back. When she's really sick, I tell my employer
> that I have to take Kesego to the hospital. With my current employer,
> Kesego has never been hospitalized. But with my first two employers,
> there was a time when she was hospitalized.

While the lack of childcare affected Kereng and her employers, the most devastating effect was on Kesego. Although Kesego needed an operation to get her legs straightened so that they would be more usable, Kereng faced an impossible bind: "They wanted to straighten her legs, but I adamantly refused. . . . If they were to straighten her legs, it could mean that she would only be able to sit [for a long period]. . . . If she's just in a sitting position, she cannot crawl. And if she can't crawl, I can't go to work." Kereng needed Kesego to be able to crawl because she couldn't carry Kesego all day on her back. Getting the operation for Kesego would have meant the loss of the income that the family depended on for survival.

In Vietnam, Bui Thi Phuong Khanh's husband drank heavily. They separated during her pregnancy when she refused to get an abortion. Since her parents were dead, Phuong Khanh, who had a clerical job in a factory, had to raise her son, Toan, on her own. From birth, it was clear that Toan had problems, with his intestines herniating through the abdominal wall. The surgeons recommended that he wait for surgery. Toan's condition made him harder to care for, even as a toddler. Phuong Khanh explained:

> It was hard when he walked. When he ate, he couldn't eat much. He ate smaller portions, but more frequently. Due to his intestines, he could only eat one bowl, where other kids have two or three bowls of meal. He ate several meals; he ate four or five meals in a day. It is not like us—we eat three meals a day.

But developmentally, he was on target. Like other children, Toan needed not only nutrition, but a chance to be with his peers and opportunities to learn and grow. Like other parents who are the sole providers for their family, Phuong Khanh needed to work. But at first, all the odds were stacked against them, as Phuong Khanh explained:

> I was only told by the daycare teacher, "Because of your child's condition, the district yelled at us and wouldn't let me keep your child here. It would be very dangerous. I have to return [him] to the mother of the child because this is a very special situation." That was what happened. However, I didn't hear directly from the Department of Health. I was very sad. I cried in front of my manager's office and asked if I could bring my child to work with me. I would not be able to bring the food home if I was home taking care of my child. . . . I shed tears. A few noticed and asked me why I was sad. I told them about my child's condition and wasn't sure who to send him to. We would both die of starvation if I was home taking care of my child. They told me to bring my child in to work after they heard my story.

While she was fortunate to be able to take her child to work—many employers would not have allowed her to do so—this arrangement was still far worse for her son than being able to attend a childcare center. And the work-related arrangement was completely unnecessary. It was not too hazardous for Toan to attend childcare; the staff there would have been able to attend more closely to his needs than Phuong Khanh (or any other parent) could while working. Phuong Khanh sobbed while describing her life as "extremely hard" and explaining what it was like to simultaneously work and care for her son. During the day, Toan's chance for early education and development consisted of lying next to her table while she worked.

The barriers that Phuong Khanh and Toan faced were preventable. As recounted earlier in this chapter, Pham Dieu Hien's son, Liep, had severe health problems, involving both refractory seizures and developmental delays. Even though Hien's son's developmental delays made him more challenging to care for, a childcare center had accepted him. And Hien, her husband, and his parents could readily see the difference it was making in the child's basic life skills. Hien explained:

> My son is learning to be independent. The teachers teach the children to be independent. My son, when he was at home, I had to spoon feed him. It was very difficult. He was very lazy at eating. Each time when he ate, his grandfather and then his grandmother had to entice him every way. But since he has entered childcare, he has learned to sit at the table and feed himself.

Hien was grateful to have found a childcare center that would take her son. Even though it took half her pay, some money remained from her wages to pay for his medicine.

But the childcare center continued to be unprepared. While Liep's childcare providers accepted and cared for him, they were sometimes overwhelmed by his behavioral problems and frightened when he had seizures. Also, his special needs required extra teaching time and expertise. In Mexico City and Milan, in Houston and Ho Chi Minh City, it remains the case that most childcare centers and schools are poorly prepared to deal with even the most common chronic children's health conditions—whether asthma or epilepsy. Whether or not Liep had a fever with his seizures, his teachers panicked because they had received no training on what to do and were frightened by witnessing the unfamiliar. As a result, their response, no matter how many times it happened, was always to call Hien. Describing a recent incident, Hien recounted: "All of a sudden, he had a seizure. His eyes rolled up. His teacher was scared. She had to call home. I was working at the company; my family had to call me to go pick up my son." A little education and training in the straightforward measures needed to deal with the seizures—in fact, they are far more straightforward than the measures appropriate to the developmental problems accompanying the brain injury—would have gone a long way. In addition, the teachers needed to be told that Liep (like most children who are already being treated for epilepsy) needed to see a doctor if he had concurrent illnesses but that he did not need to go to a doctor or to go home with every seizure. With adequate training, the childcare providers could have readily and safely cared for Liep and other children with similar needs.

The great benefits that Liep gained through early childhood care and education when he was able to attend the childcare center were clear. All children—regardless of what conditions they are born with—should have similar opportunities. To achieve this, childcare providers will need training and support.

Impact on Parents

Wage and Job Loss

Ngo Van Cuong of Vietnam worked in home construction. He and his wife had an infant son, Kinh. Cuong explained that on one occasion his wife "bought some prawns from the market that she thought were good. She cooked them for Kinh. He developed some allergic reaction the next morning. His face and body turned red all over after he ate them." Their infant had the allergic reaction on a weekend when his mother was selling pots and pans in an open market; Saturday and Sunday were her busiest days. Because the family needed the money she would earn on those days to get by, Cuong went to his workplace to explain that he needed to take the day off to care for his son. "I asked my boss to take that day off. But he insisted that I couldn't take that day off or else he would fire me, so I had to listen to him." Cuong stayed at work in the morning, but when he returned home from the midday break, he saw how sick Kinh was. "When I saw my poor child after I came home in the afternoon, I stayed home to take care of my child and didn't return to work."

Cuong described how he took the afternoon off and then returned to work on Monday to find that his employer had fired him. Cuong had a simple desire: "My dream job is to be a regular corporate employee so I still get paid when I'm sick or my child is sick." In the absence of paid leave, he was always torn between meeting his family's financial needs and meeting his child's need for direct care. It was obvious why a one-year-old—especially one covered with hives and experiencing a serious allergic reaction—could not be left home alone or in poor-quality care. But Cuong's need for earnings was equally marked, as he noted:

> My child, he just recently got sick. We borrowed the money so that
> we could pay the hospital. The hospital expense was just little, about
> 100,000 Vietnamese dong. But we spent more money purchasing
> meals, paying transportation, and other miscellaneous items. The
> cost of transportation from the hospital to home and vice versa was
> many times as much as the hospital expense. And I only make
> 200,000 dong each week, so we didn't have enough money.

He explained that that month he had needed to borrow "shared money" from people in the neighborhood. The 20 percent interest rate on this shared money made it hard to repay. He commented:

> It affected the family a lot, especially when all of the bills—the elec-
> tric, the water, and the energy—came due at the end of the month.
> They all pile up at the end. I put the money I earn in the piggy bank
> at the end of each day so that I can pay for those expenses. I break
> the bank at a specific time each month to pay for the expenses. I
> won't be able to put the money in the bank if I'm unemployed.

Like so many other aspects of the experiences of working parents and their children, we heard the stories of suffering across borders. Refilwe Keetetswe of Botswana risked losing both her pay and her work. In the end, she lost any chance at promotion. A mother of two, Refilwe worked at a bank. She explained:

> At times, my child would get sick and I couldn't afford a caretaker, so
> I had to stay home. If you stay home for three days, it appears on
> your record. At the end of the year, you don't get an increment for
> that. At times I had to stay for three to four days, or I'd take my son
> to Molepolole until I'd find someone to look after my child in

Gaborone. At times he was sick, the caretaker had left, and there was no one to look after him. They'd ask me if I still needed a job or did I need to go and look after my child. That's what they'd say. . . . It was so difficult. They would maybe ask how my child was, and then they'd leave me. They needed me at work. They said to me, "We need your services or we will employ someone else while you take care of your child."

Even when parents weren't fired from their jobs, the risk of being fired weighed heavily on the choices they made. In Moscow, we spoke with fifty-two-year-old Viktoriya Daniilovna Kozlova, who was working as a dispatcher for transportation and raising her two sons. She never felt she could take time off to provide care when they were sick, since she feared losing her job in a setting where there was no support for working parents and in an economy where jobs were scarce. "We need money. My child is sick and I would be happy to stay home, but I need money," she explained. "I cannot even take one day a week because I'm afraid I will be fired." The experiences of the families we interviewed around the world made clear that it was, in fact, the poor who were most likely to lose pay, to lose promotions, and to lose jobs while meeting their caregiving responsibilities.

Around the world, parents reported to us the costly impact that caring for sick children had on their ability to earn a living. The parents not only lost wages, but they also lost chances for advancement in jobs. Overall, 40 percent of the parents we interviewed about this lost pay when they missed work to care for a sick child (21 percent in Botswana, 45 percent in Mexico, and 58 percent in Vietnam). Eleven percent lost job promotions or had difficulty retaining their jobs because of their need to care for sick children (14 percent in Botswana, 11 percent in Mexico, and 8 percent in Vietnam). Almost half (46 percent) had lost pay or job promotions or had difficulty retaining their jobs because of their need to care for sick children (28 percent in Botswana, 48 percent in Mexico, and 62 percent in Vietnam). The impact was particularly marked for families in which a child had a chronic condition. In three out of four families where a child had a chronic condition, caring for the child's health problems led to difficulties at work, including loss of pay, loss of promotion, or loss of the job itself (see figure 4-11).

Caretakers suffer a great deal when they have no options for decent care and work opportunities, and in turn, their entire families suffer along with

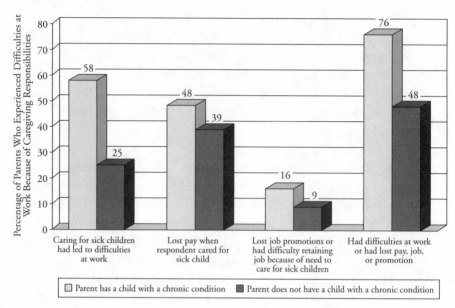

Figure 4-11
**Parents of Children with Chronic Conditions Are More Likely
to Experience Difficulties at Work as a Result of Caregiving.**
Note: Data from Project on Global Working Families' in-depth interviews with working care-givers. Analyses in the above figure are based on households with a zero- to fourteen-year-old child.

them. Because of the far worse working conditions frequently faced, and be-cause their families were economically on the margin to begin with, parents living in poverty and their children often endure the gravest impact.

Health and Personal Toll

When options for care are inadequate, parents' mental and physical health suffer along with their children's. Twenty-five-year-old Nguyen Le Thi of Vietnam worked seven days a week in a garment factory. Her twenty-one-month-old son had been sick often. Whenever Thi missed work to care for him, she lost pay. Thi took off two weeks to care for her son when he was hospitalized with hemorrhagic fever, which can be life threatening. Thi's employer let her take the leave, but without income. "When I work, I have income. When I don't work, I don't earn money," she succinctly told us, leaving the toll it took largely unspoken. As with many other families, the cost of the lost pay cut into essentials. Only when asked the consequences did Thi explain:

> We have to reduce the portions. The family doesn't eat the full
> amount of nutrition. For example, before, we bought four portions
> of meat a day [for the entire extended family]. Now, we only buy
> three portions. We spend the money we have on food, not buying
> furnishings for the house or personal things.

Thi went on to describe how they cut back on the quality of formula they bought for their infant son. Her mother-in-law told us: "[When Thi's son came home] from the hospital, [Thi] was hospitalized. It is because she doesn't have her health. She doesn't eat much." The poor health of her son had led to wage loss for Thi. Having lost essential income, Thi's family had less for food and other essentials. The health of Thi and other family members went downhill. The cycle of poor health leading to income loss and greater poverty in turn leading to worsening health was sickening everyone in many families.

Irene Echeverria Perez grew up poor in Mexico. Irene knew a lot about needing to be absent from her work washing dishes in a hotel to care for sick children. While her daughter had not been sick often, her son had been born with a serious heart condition. Before he died, at the age of only nine months, she was always torn between taking leave to care for him directly and earning money to pay for his medical care. She explained: "They don't pay. No, they don't pay. If you don't work, they don't pay you. . . . [It is] 1,000 pesos every two weeks that I receive. If I work a day less, it's less money." She went on to describe how missing a day of work without permission meant losing three days' pay, instead of one day's. Irene's son died on a day when she was at work. She often wondered if he would have survived longer had she been at home, but with three days' lost wages for each day missed without permission, there was no way to feed her children if she missed more days. The doctors had to give her tranquilizers when she learned of her son's death. Six years later, her mental health was still fragile; she sadly summarized, "I suffer."

The cycle is vicious for families with sick children living in poverty. A child becomes sick. He has frequent illnesses or is born with or develops a chronic condition. The child needs his parent to provide care. The parent has no paid leave or job flexibility and so loses wages each time she provides care. Often the penalties are even greater than lost daily wages. The parent pays triple "damages" for each day missed or risks job loss. Already living in poverty, the income loss means that the parents can't pay for enough food, fuel, or other essentials. More family members grow sick. Alternatively, knowing the very real threats to survival that missing work will present, the parent goes to work and the sick child is left alone or in lesser care, and the child's health deteriorates.

But none of this has to be. If parents only had a basic amount of paid leave and flexibility to care for sick children, 90 percent of the problem would be addressed. If work and social conditions were constructed with the understanding that caring for sick family members is one of the most common dilemmas those working face the world over, children would not be home alone sick when it places them at risk nor sent to school sick when it spreads infections to others, and parents' health and welfare would not be threatened by unconscionable conflicts.

Bridging the Gap

Meeting Preventive and Curative Health Needs

There is little mystery in what needs to be done to enable families to meet the health needs of their children. As detailed in this chapter, far too many parents are currently forced to make devastating choices between having a job they need to feed their children and being able to get their children's basic health-care needs met. As a result, we spoke with families whose children went unvaccinated, families in which serious diagnoses for life-threatening diseases were delayed, and families in which children had been left alone so sick that they later had to be hospitalized. What makes these risks to children's health and the near-tragedies that resulted so abhorrent is how utterly preventable they are.

The conflicts that parents faced between being able to support their family economically and being able to care for their children when they were sick were *not* inevitable. In the final analysis, these conflicts resulted from working conditions that prevented parents from being able to take even modest amounts of leave to attend to the health needs of their sons and daughters. Working conditions that allowed parents to take leave from work—either due to paid leave or flexibility—halved the risk of parents having to leave children home alone sick. Families who had both paid leave and flexibility rarely needed to leave sick children home alone. In fact, they were less than one-quarter as likely to leave their children home alone sick as families that did not have both of these workplace benefits (see figure 4-12). The ability to get paid leave from work or flexibility on the job also significantly reduced—by one-half—the risk that parents would have to send a child to school or day care sick (15 percent versus 29 percent).

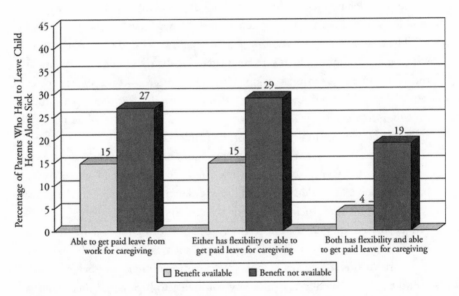

Figure 4-12
**When Parents Have Decent Working Conditions, They Are
Less Likely to Have to Leave Children Home Alone Sick.**
Note: Data from Project on Global Working Families' in-depth interviews with working caregivers. Analyses in the above figure are based on households with a zero- to fourteen-year-old child.

Worldwide, when parents receive leave from and flexibility at work to address their children's health needs, they do. Caring for children's health was a top priority for the overwhelming majority of parents in every city, town, and village we visited. The question was whether they had the leave to do so. When that leave or flexibility was available, their children fared well. In rural and urban areas, in informal and formal sector work, parents were willing to help do what their employer needed to "get the job done." The parents just wanted to be able to care for their children's health at the same time.

While paid leave and flexibility at work are critical in determining whether parents can address sick children's care needs, the availability of high-quality childcare plays an equally important role. Parents who had access to formal childcare were the least likely to have left a child home alone sick. Six percent of those who used formal childcare had left their child home alone sick compared to 22 percent of those who only used informal care. Parents who used an unpaid child were at highest risk of having to leave a sick child home alone. Thirty-seven percent of families who used an unpaid child as a care provider had left a child home alone sick compared to 11 percent of families who did not use unpaid care by a child (see figure 4-13).

The vast majority of working parents we interviewed faced conditions which made it impossible to care adequately for their children's health and at the same time succeed on the job. However, scattered stories of employers who did provide leave and flexibility demonstrate the feasibility of running private businesses, government offices, or informal work sites while not ravaging the employee's health or that of the employee's family.

In Vietnam, Lam Thi Suong was fortunate, because her childcare center was right at her workplace. "They pick a few workers of the company who have experience in childcare to work at the daycare center so that the other workers can focus on their work. Only the children of the company's workers can be placed in that daycare center." Because the childcare was located nearby and was coordinated by her employer, she was able to take breaks during work to breast-feed her infant. "When my children were below twelve months old, I came out of work every two hours to breast-feed them. When they grew up and could eat rice soup, I did not come out to breast-feed them. I only came out to visit them in the afternoon." Suong's children were healthier as a result of the quality care they received at the center and her ability to breast-feed. Suong's employer benefited from providing decent care options

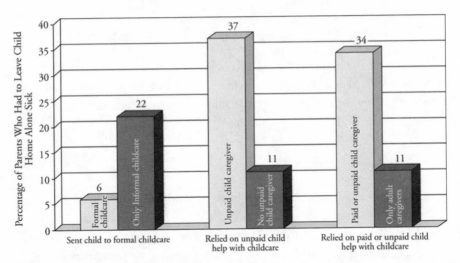

Figure 4-13
**When Parents Have Good Childcare Choices, They Are
Less Likely to Have to Leave Children Home Alone Sick.**
Note: Data from Project on Global Working Families' in-depth interviews with working care-
givers. Analyses in the above figure are based on households with a zero- to fourteen-year-old
child.

because it resulted in less turnover among the workforce and less unpredictable absenteeism.

While breast-feeding breaks are only important to mothers, leave and
flexibility to meet all other needs is equally important for men and women.
Ntoto Ramasoloko, the father of two children, worked as an electrician in
Botswana:

> It was last year, around March, and I was working at the lodge. My
> mother was not at home and my son was in the house by himself. He
> saw a root, or a plant, or something, and put it into his mouth. At
> the time, you see, there was no one around—my mother and father
> were gone and the only one who was there was someone who was
> renting a house in the yard. That man had to take him to the hospi-
> tal. . . . I told [my boss] that my son was sick and I had to rush to

see him at the hospital. I said I would call and that was it. . . . My employers understand as long as they feel it's the right thing to do.

As was the case for Suong, having a basic foundation of decent working conditions meant that Ntoto could provide essential care for his children while working. They could address unpredictable and urgent health needs as well as provide essentials for health promotion.

Coordinated Policies

Regarding sick children, one critical question is whether workplaces' policies and childcare centers' policies are coordinated—that is, if childcare centers will not allow a child to attend, can working parents stay home to care for the children? As it turns out, all too often, the policies are not coordinated: rules require that a parent keep his son or daughter home from childcare or school for a particular health problem, but do not allow the parent to stay home from work. This begs the obvious: Who is supposed to care for the sick child?

Few parents are fortunate in the coordinated options they have; these exceptions demonstrate the feasibility of solutions. For example, Paulina Vasquez described what happened when her son got sick at day care while she was working for an employer covered by Mexican social security:

> When he's been sick, [the daycare staff have] called me right away at my work. They would tell me that the baby was sick. I would ask for permission at my work—we can ask for permission in these cases—and go to the daycare center. The doctor would tell me what was wrong and give me a referral sheet for medical consultation. With that sheet I would go to the clinic the same day, since there they would get his fever under control or stop his diarrhea. They would suspend the baby from the daycare center for several days, but they would do the same thing to me. Thus, both of us were protected. They would give me a three-day permission not to go to work, which is usually the time it takes for the child to get better. When he was stable again, he would go back to his school and I would go to work.

The same social security that provided her childcare also provided her health care and governed the rules of when she could receive paid leave. Sensibly, the rules were in sync. Having both benefits come from one source by no means guarantees coordination; frequently, employers who provide childcare will simultaneously set incongruent leave policies for employees. But good public policies can ensure coordination even when childcare is provided by someone other than the employer.

Solutions exist. Yet, the evidence is clear: Children's short-term survival is being placed at risk and their long-term health and development undermined by the fact that millions of working-poor parents have no option but to leave their children home alone or in dangerously poor-quality care. Children without any adequate care face far higher rates of illness and injury and far lower rates of receiving the preventive health care they need. Moreover, when they do become sick or injured, their chances of receiving adequate diagnostic or therapeutic care are dramatically diminished. When parents cannot take leave from work without losing their jobs, often no one is available to bring a child to a clinic or a hospital. When workplaces threaten the poor with an unaffordable loss of income if they change their schedule or miss work, sick children are often left home alone and unable to administer prescribed treatments or otherwise care for themselves. What the global community decides to do in terms of making it feasible for families to address children's health needs will reflect on our fundamental values. Do we really believe that all children should be given their best chance at a healthy life? Do adults have not only an obligation to economically support themselves, but a right to care for others? Are we willing to create a world that embodies this? To do so, we will need societal rules that respect the ability to care for children and other vulnerable family members.

5

Economic and

Gender Inequalities

Clearly, the dramatic changes in adult work lives are transforming the lives of children around the world. As earlier chapters of this book have documented, the impact on the lives of preschool and school-age children, on their health, development, and education, has been profound. But what effect has the labor force transformation, the rise of urbanization, and an increasingly globalized economy had on the economic well-being of families?

At times, the goal of having both men and women in the family in the formal labor force was to increase economic security. At other times, the goal was to increase gender equality. It remains to be demonstrated whether these benefits are being reaped. Likewise, for many, the chance to move to a city or town offered the hope of exiting poverty. Living without basic infrastructures and subject to the unpredictable vicissitudes of weather and disease, those working-poor families in rural areas who were also land-poor rarely had any economic security. Yet the question remains whether those families are now more secure as they seek to balance earning a living and raising children in urban areas.

This chapter will address these crucial issues and will seek to answer the following. First, as parents have moved from trading their labor in kind to being paid in cash, from controlling their own hours to answering to an employer, from working with their children right by their sides to working far from home, what has happened to their economic security? Are parents able to succeed in formal and informal workplaces, in cities and towns transformed by the global economy, at the same time as rearing their children? Do low- and middle-income families have the same chance of succeeding? What about women and men?

Finding Paid Work

Across diverse geographic, social, and economic settings, adults explained to us how childbearing and -rearing affected their ability to find work. Women described discrimination when they were pregnant and when employers knew they were raising children. Men delineated the discrimination they faced when they were deeply involved in their children's care. For men, the discrimination more often began when they lost a job because they stayed home to provide essential care for a family member. For women, the discrimination arose as soon as employers anticipated they would be rearing children as well as working. One mother after another told us of parallel experiences, across the world, of how raising children impeded their ability to find and keep decent jobs.

Twenty-two-year-old Evangelina Alvarez Guzman had a nine-month-old son when we interviewed her in Mexico. She worked as a secretary for 180 U.S. dollars a month. Evangelina described what looking for work had been like:

> I filled out an application at Banamex as a teller, and they asked me if I had children. I said, "Yes," and they interviewed me and they asked how old my son was. . . . They didn't hire me just because I had a son.

In Russia, thirty-seven-year-old Anastasiya Rodionovna Uvarova was raising two children, aged sixteen and eleven, while working as a cleaner and a classroom assistant. She was clear about employers' attitudes toward hiring parents who needed to care for children while working:

> If you were trying to find a job, children are regarded as a burden and hindrance, and it appears that I have children only to create hardships for myself. Because everybody around starts to say, "And what if [he] gets sick? . . . Who is going to watch him? What are you going to do? We don't need such people." So if you are trying to find a job, it's impossible to get something.

At times, employers were more flexible about the qualifications needed for a job than they were about a parent's ability to give care. Thirty-nine-year-old Olga Mikhailovna Shukina, for example, told of her experience: "When I looked for a job, I found two places where I had an interview. Even though they required a higher education, they were lenient and ready to hire me. But when they found out that I have children, they did not offer me the job."

The only thing more likely to prevent one from being hired than being a parent was being pregnant. Evangelina explained that the employers she had spoken to thought pregnant women were "useless":

> I think that [the employers] must see our presence as an imposition. Regardless of our dizziness and our nausea, our minds and our hands work the same way with or without children, don't they?

We heard many times and in many countries how those caring for children felt they had to lie in order to get a job. Thirty-four-year-old Mmapula Sikalame had five children, aged six months to thirteen years. Though Mmapula lived in Botswana, the words she chose to describe her experience while looking for work could just as well have come from women we interviewed in Latin America, Asia, and Europe:

> I experienced problems. When they hire you, they ask questions in the interview like "Do you have children?" and "When you are working, who will take care of the kids?" Since we are desperate for the job, we always say we have a caregiver around or our mother is around—that when we go to work, somebody is around.

Often the statements were not true, but the women, who faced far more discrimination than men, knew that making such statements was often their only way to obtain work upon which their ability to feed their children depended.

Having to Settle for Poor Jobs

Across national borders, we also repeatedly found that even when parents living in poverty were able to get jobs, they all too often had to settle for jobs with meager pay and grossly inadequate working conditions in order to be allowed to care for their children.

The income of the family of thirty-eight-year-old Faina Sergeievna Demidova fell when she lost a decently paying job and settled for substandard pay in order to be able to care for her children:

> I used to have a very nice job. I was a manager of personnel at a prestigious supermarket. One day my daughter broke her collarbone, and I had to stay with her. But I was told that was not a solution, that I must choose: I had to keep on working or be fired. . . . That really was an ultimatum: I continue my job without any interruption or I am fired.

She chose to care for her injured child. When she looked for a new job, she faced discrimination:

> I left my previous job and then started seeking a new job. I wanted to apply for posts as an administrator. I was asked whether I have children. I try to convince them that we've got a granny in our family (in fact, there was not any granny, of course). I never got a phone call from the personnel offices of those companies. If you have two children, this is a bad thing for anyone applying for a job. It is a kind of stigma even.

Faina finally found a government job as a packer in a refrigerator factory. But while this job protected Faina from being fired for providing essential care for her family, the conditions were poor. When she needed to take time off from work to care for her children, she had to compensate by working an additional two hours for every one hour of leave she took. Moreover, she often had to work night shifts:

> When there is a shorter day in our kindergarten, I have to ask for permission to leave my workplace earlier, and I always must compensate these working hours, by working during the night shift. I do not like it at all, but there is no other way. This is the rule in my company.

Faina described how, when the kindergartens closed early, she would leave work four hours early but then have to compensate by working an additional eight hours. When she had to work the night shift to compensate, her children were home alone. She knew this situation affected their safety and education since they never did schoolwork when they were home alone. But she could not afford the $2 an hour for a baby-sitter.

In many countries, we interviewed primary caregivers who ended up working in the informal sector—in spite of its frequently lower pay, inadequate or nonexistent job benefits, and often riskier work conditions—because it provided the only jobs in which parents who had limited education could work while also caring for their children. In Vietnam, thirty-year-old Bui Thi Diem was working as a clerk in a government office when her daughter, Mai, was born. But it was impossible for Diem to pay for adequate childcare for Mai on the salary she earned. Mai was growing progressively weaker in the poor-quality childcare center that Diem and her husband could afford:

> She was three. She was suffering so severely from malnutrition. It hurt me when I looked at her. I did not want to focus on my work any more. So I had to give up my work. . . . First of all, the [place where she was in childcare] was built in such a way that it was not well ventilated. There were many children but few teachers. The rooms were crowded. . . . My child had to suffer the difference between our home and the stinky smell there. . . . She would often throw up during meals. She would get a fever or a continuous cold or flu. If one child was infected, the disease would spread to the whole group. So my child was continuously sick.

The inadequate nutrition had profoundly affected her daughter's health and their daily lives:

> My daughter's leg, it was like she was having a handicap problem. But in fact, she was just weak due to malnutrition. She would cry every night to such an extent that I could not sleep because she lacked calcium. At that time, each night, she took her bottle for about five times. She urinated five times, too. So I would be very tired and would only be able to bring her to the bathroom the first three times. The next two times she would piss in the bed.

Diem explained that, eventually, "One of us had to sacrifice our work. I took leave from work." It was hard for Diem to leave her formal sector job. She explained:

When I live [or work] in the community, a rapport builds up that holds everybody together. Suddenly, when I wanted to leave, I felt distanced from the people who had been close to me for so long, so many years. I was very sad. But it was for my child. I considered her more important. She was more important than my job. I tied her life to mine. I had to do it for her. It was a sacrifice for my child.

When Diem moved back home to do informal sector work, she was able to care for Mai at the same time. Her daughter's nutrition improved, but Diem's new work, which involved printing on silk, provided a less-steady income. Moreover, she had no occupational safety protections. "I am afraid that in doing silk printing, I am exposed to chemicals a great deal. I am afraid that in the future, I may suffer from some side effect, because they are all hazardous chemicals." Mai was being exposed to the toxins as well.

Losing Pay

Even after settling into jobs, we found that parents repeatedly lost essential pay in order to care for children. In Mexico, 54 percent of low-income parents had lost pay in order to care for a sick child. Thirty-five percent of low-income parents in Botswana and 62 percent in Vietnam had lost pay to care for a sick child (see figures 5-1, 5-2, and 5-3). When parents were barely making ends meet, losing several days' wages in a month to care for a sick child could be the difference between being able to pay a food or housing bill and being destitute.

Lost Income in the Formal Sector

Some parents lost more than a day's pay for every day they missed to care for a child. Twenty-seven-year-old Bui Kim Tram had a five-year-old son and a three-year-old daughter. She worked in Ho Chi Minh City, Vietnam, for a Korean bag-production factory, where she faced a catch-22. In order to get leave, even when a worker or a worker's child was sick, the worker still had to dress in the regular uniform and go to the factory on the day of the requested leave. If the worker did not do so, higher penalties would be deducted from her or his earnings. But going to work first did not make sense when the

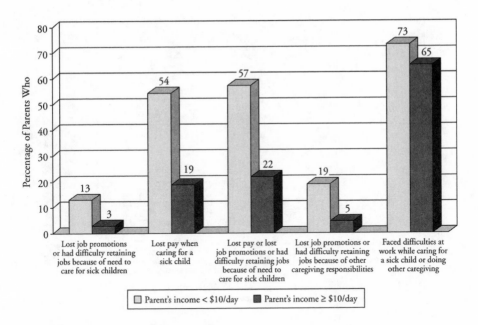

Figure 5-1

**Mexico: Low-Income Families Are More Likely
to Experience Penalties at Work as a Result of Caregiving.**

Note: Data from Project on Global Working Families' in-depth interviews with working caregivers. Analyses in the above figure are based on households with a zero- to fourteen-year-old
child. Income data from each survey have been converted to a common currency using the
World Bank's purchasing power parity (PPP) conversion factors.

worker was seriously ill or caring for a seriously ill child. At best, it meant significant delays in attending to health needs; at worst, the requirement made it
impossible to care for sick children. Tram explained what happened when she
attended to her children's health needs first:

> They didn't believe me. . . . They said that I was home doing
> something else. I submitted the doctor's document, and they knew
> they were sick. But I don't understand [why they deducted such a
> high penalty]. For example, on a day that has overtime, I would work
> from 7:30 in the morning until eight o'clock in the evening. I would
> make 30-something thousand—36,000 or 37,000 dong. I would sew
> for that whole day. So if I had to be absent for a day, 40,000 or

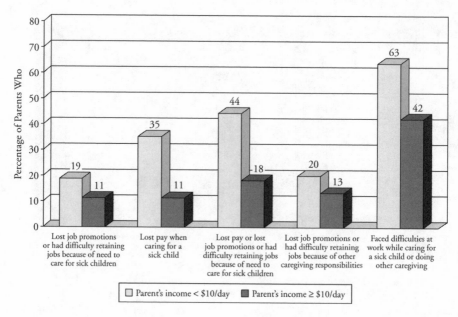

Figure 5-2
**Botswana: Low-Income Families Are More Likely
to Experience Penalties at Work as a Result of Caregiving.**
Note: Data from Project on Global Working Families' in-depth interviews with working caregivers. Analyses in the above figure are based on households with a zero- to fourteen-year-old
child. Income data from each survey have been converted to a common currency using the
World Bank's purchasing power parity (PPP) conversion factors.

41,000 dong would be subtracted from my salary so that I would not
take leave. They subtract a higher amount like that so that in the
future I would not take leave.

Lost Income in the Informal Sector

Many parents, particularly women, ended up in the informal sector because
they couldn't get or keep formal sector jobs while caring for their children.
Yet, while only some formal sector jobs provided limited paid leave, the informal sector offered no protections when their children were sick. In Vietnam,

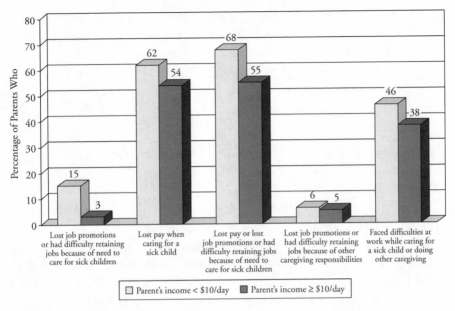

Figure 5-3
Vietnam: Low-Income Families Are More Likely
to Experience Penalties at Work as a Result of Caregiving.
Note: Data from Project on Global Working Families' in-depth interviews with working care-givers. Analyses in the above figure are based on households with a zero- to fourteen-year-old child. Income data from each survey have been converted to a common currency using the World Bank's purchasing power parity (PPP) conversion factors.

forty-four-year-old Ngo Hoang Dung was working as a seamstress in the informal sector while also raising a three-year-old daughter with Down's syndrome and caring for an elderly mother with diabetes. To pay for her mother's and daughter's hospital bills, doctors' fees, and medications required a higher income than Dung was earning. Yet, far from being able to earn the additional income that her mother's and daughter's care demanded, Dung's family income actually declined because attending to her daughter and mother prevented her from working the necessary hours. Dung described what it was like trying to earn money while caring for her daughter:

> [My daughter] has been hospitalized five times. . . . I had to stop [my business] until I came back and continued to make clothes. So

there had been an embarrassing moment that I had to endure. Some people would understand and still leave the fabric for me to make clothes and give back to them. Some do not, which I have to accept. . . . Yes, many times when the order has been kept a while, when the customer came, I would have to talk to them so they would understand. If they didn't, I would lose the customer. There would be many lost cases.

Dung explained that when she took leave from work to care for her daughter, "There is no income possible. I have to spend very tightly and save up to care for her."

In the absence of any social insurance providing paid leave for parents caring for sick children, those in the informal sector lost essential income and lost the ability to buy food and medicine when they took time off, like Ngo Hoang Dung. Others tried to continue to work while caring for a sick child, like Uyapo Mbulawa. Uyapo, a twenty-one-year-old mother of two children in Botswana, had a small stand in the compound next to her house from which she sold food and basic goods. Her four-year-old daughter, Thumisang, was sick often, but caring for her at all costs was central to who Uyapo was. Uyapo told us, "If I am lying in bed sick and I see that my children are hungry, I just lift my head and go and build the fire to cook." When her daughter was sick while Uyapo was at work, she took her into the store:

I called Thumisang next to me. She can sit next to me while I'm serving the customers. . . . Sometimes the customers they feel angry and they go away. They see that I'm serving them and caring for Thumisang. They become angry because Thumisang will vomit inside the shop. I'll be busy tending it and then they come saying, "I want sugar, I want this, I want that." Sometimes it's hard to get water quickly to wash my hands and they say, "No, this is not clean."

But in the absence of any preschool care for her daughter on a routine basis and lacking any program to help care for her daughter when she was sick, Uyapo had little other option but to take Thumisang to work every day or miss work. Either way, though, she lost wages.

Disproportionately, women we met had ended up with informal sector jobs because they either could never get or could not keep formal sector jobs when trying to care for their children. If they were self-employed in the informal sector, these women were frequently able to take leave to care for children without "losing their jobs" or were able to bring their sons and daughters to work. Women paid a high price for working in the informal sector, however: meager wages and stark working conditions. Moreover, they lost any chance of receiving the paid leave to care for their children that the formal sector sometimes provides.

Losing Jobs

Job loss and pay loss were two different strands intertwined on the same rope, which tugged working parents down as they tried to care for their children. In Mexico, 13 percent of low-income parents had lost job promotions or placed their very job at risk when they tried to care for their children, while 19 percent of low-income parents in Botswana and 15 percent in Vietnam put their jobs or progress at work at risk by caring for their family (see figures 5-1, 5-2, and 5-3). Twenty-four-year-old Naome Gasegale worked as a salesperson through most of her first pregnancy in Botswana. But when she delivered prematurely, she was fired for not having given adequate notice—an impossibility, since she had had no way of knowing that she would go into labor early. She had done all she could to work throughout the pregnancy:

> My employment has me carrying big boxes of shoes, and the work
> was really heavy. I used to work overtime, and sometimes I would get
> off at ten o'clock at night. I was very tired. I delivered early because
> of that. The nurses said that working too hard made me deliver early.

When she had reported pains to her employer while she was doing heavy lifting late in her pregnancy, he told her, "You said you wanted work. Go on working." When she went into labor prematurely, she lost her job:

> I expected to deliver in February. But as I was going for a routine
> check-up at the clinic, they told me I should stop working because I
> would deliver too early. I delivered too soon [thereafter]. . . . When
> I got back to [the store], they had found somebody else. They said
> that I should have told them I would be gone.

The only job she was able to get after giving birth was working as a maid in someone's home earning half as much—only 320 pula a month, or 2 U.S. dollars a day.

Parents also risked job loss when they stayed at home to care for a sick or injured child, left work to be with a dying family member, or attended a funeral. Twenty-three-year-old Sekgwana Lebala worked as a maid in various homes throughout Molepolole and Gaborone in Botswana. Recalling her entry into the labor force, Sekgwana explained: "Poverty pushed me into the street. I had no choice. We were going days without food or water. My mother and father weren't working, and it was obvious that it was going to be me that had to work." At the time of our interviews, she was using her wages as a maid to support not only herself but her younger sister and her own four-year-old. She noted:

> Since I started working, I've confronted a lot of problems. But the main one is when I ask for leave. I've asked for leave in the past, especially when one of my relatives had died, but I was never allowed to attend funerals. I was never entitled to a day of leave.

On most days, while Sekgwana worked, she left her young daughter with her mother. But her mother's poor health limited the amount of care she was able to provide for the child. Sekgwana's mother was able to keep her granddaughter away from fires and other dangers when she was well, but Sekgwana's mother could not provide adequate care when her grandchild was sick. Sekgwana explained:

> My child usually gets sick during the summer. Once when I was at work and I was told that she was really sick that day, I took a radical step—I told my employer that she was sick. It was a Monday, and [my employer] said I could leave on Thursday or Friday. I left immediately. I just came back home until my child got better. This happened in 1997, and when I went back to work, my employer told me to take everything that belonged to me and leave.

She was fired without notice or severance pay. Sekgwana was unemployed for four months before she was able to find another job in a neighboring town.

While men less commonly faced discrimination in getting jobs and job loss, they did experience it when they were balancing significant caretaking responsibilities with work. The story of a father we interviewed in Honduras, Humberto Aguayo, illustrates this well. All one had to do was watch Humberto Aguayo hold his young son, Humbertocito, to recognize how involved he was as a father. He had none of the awkwardness that fathers who rarely care for their infants often do—none of the uncertainty about how to hold a child, how to reassure him, or how to make him content. Nor was Humbertocito ill at ease in his father's arms. Clearly, they were completely accustomed to being together. In a neighborhood in Tegucigalpa where many fathers abandon their children—spending neither money to help support them nor time to care for them or their mothers—Humberto was at home because he had lost his job while caring for Humbertocito. Like his wife, Julia, Humberto had been working ten-hour shifts for six days a week in a factory.

At age twenty-one, Humberto's wife, Julia, had had barely six weeks off after Humbertocito's birth before having to return to work. At forty-two days postpartum, she had returned to work and stopped breast-feeding. Bottle-fed from that moment on, Humbertocito had been placed at risk for infections, which exact a costly toll in developing countries. At age six months, he had developed pneumonia. The infection was serious enough that Humbertocito was hospitalized for fifteen days. Humberto had been allowed to take one day off to be with Humbertocito. When he'd asked for a second day, his supervisor had reported him. Upon his return to work on the third day, Humberto had found that he had been fired, in spite of the fact that he was supposed to have a right under the employment rules to take leave to care for his son.

When I met Humberto, he had been looking for a new job for four months full time since he had been fired. But he had been blacklisted. He had been going from one factory to another searching for a job, but the owners, while hiring other men, just kept telling him to "come back another day" or "call us later."

There is nothing random about who faces such degrading or devastating choices. Less likely to have paid leave at work and less likely to have any kind of flexibility, parents living in poverty far more frequently find themselves having to sacrifice either their children's health and education or their family's source of income. Thirty-one-year-old Victoria Ibarra Sabaleto of Mexico was direct when she described why she had to miss so many of the meetings at school for her three children: "I miss most of them because I don't have permission at work for that. I haven't gone to any of them because of my job. If I went to the meetings, I would be fired from my job." It wasn't just helping with their education she missed; she was unable to care for herself or her children when they became sick. She described what happened when her children were sick: "Yes, they've had to stay by themselves at home. . . . That's what we've had to do, so that I don't lose my job."

The Burden of Gender

Gender and Economic Loss

While men and boys are clearly affected by the economic insecurity of trying to be a parent, the burden is disproportionately carried by women and girls. In our research, far more women than men lost their jobs due to conflicts between work and caregiving. Women were one and a half times as likely as men to lose pay to care for a sick child. Women were six times as likely to lose job promotions or have difficulty retaining a job because of the need to care for sick children (see figure 5-4). Women were at increased risk of job loss both because they provided more of the care at home and because even when caregiving did not disrupt their work, employers were more likely to assume that it would disrupt the work of mothers than of fathers.

At times, women lost income and lost their jobs because inadequate working conditions and social supports created real—though preventable—conflicts between their paid work and caregiving roles. These conflicts were made more frequent by the fact that women had worse working conditions, less paid leave, and less flexibility than men. Thirty-six percent of women had no access to paid leave compared to 25 percent of men. Twenty-four percent of women lacked both paid leave and flexibility compared to 19 percent of men. But, equally often, they lost jobs because employers feared there might someday be conflicts.

While women were at greater risk for job loss throughout their children's lives, they faced particular risks during pregnancy and delivery. Twenty-six-year-old Duong Thi Y Lan worked in the marketing department of a company that had a policy of hiring only single people. Women were routinely fired when they became pregnant. So when she became pregnant, her fellow employees tried to help her hide the pregnancy. She would go off to a back room when she needed to lie down momentarily or vomit. Whenever there was a check, her colleagues would "run and call" her and warn her.

Thirty-six-year-old Huynh Thi Phuong Chau, mother of a four-and-a-half-month-old child, was caught in a bind by a rule that was meant to protect women. She worked in the billing department of an outpatient clinic. Phuong Chau had worked the night shift, but national labor laws prohibited women with infants from working at night. In practice, the law provided her with little protection. Since she was not offered a day job, she lost her employment.

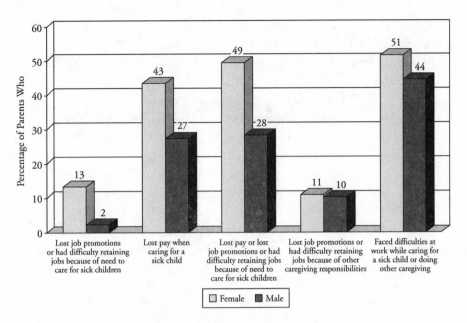

Figure 5-4
**Women Are More Likely to Experience Penalties
at Work as a Result of Caregiving.**
Note: Data from Project on Global Working Families' in-depth interviews with working caregivers. Analyses in the above figure are based on households with a zero- to fourteen-year-old
child.

The Double Workload: A Global Phenomenon

Even when both parents were working for pay and their earnings were similar
or equal, more often than not, women carried the larger burden of both the
paid and unpaid work, while most men escaped the demands at home. Faina
Sergeievna Demidova worked full time as a packer in a Russian refrigerator
factory. She explained:

> Unfortunately, my husband does not want to take part in solving our
> everyday problems. He works so hard and his working hours are so
> long that the weekend is not enough for him to get a good rest. . . .
> I cannot say that I am not working as hard as him, but the fact is that
> he is the breadwinner.

In addition, Faina's hours were extraordinarily long. As she described, "I come back home at nine, and I go to bed at least at three in the morning. . . . I am busy cooking and cleaning." Despite her full-time work, extremely long hours, and contribution of nearly half of the family income, Faina's experiences reflected a social context in which women clearly did not have an equal chance: Men were perceived as the first "breadwinner"; women carried the overwhelming share of unpaid work; and women faced far greater barriers to success at their paid jobs because of the lack of support.

Even in the households where men did help with housework or child-rearing, the balance was usually uneven, and women commonly bore the responsibility of caring for the children and the home. In Botswana, thirty-two-year-old Refilwe Ntshese's experience was emblematic. Refilwe worked eleven-hour days as a typist and then went home for a second shift that lasted late into the night and began early the next morning:

> I cook soft porridge for the youngest kids to eat before they go to
> school. Then I wash and go to work. In the evening when I come
> home, I prepare supper for the small kids. I don't have the money to
> pay for household help, so I cook for them, wash them, and then go
> to bed. I'm feeling very tired because after typing [all day], my fingers
> become painful. [Still] I prepare my bed, I prepare my children's bed,
> I sweep my house, take care of my stove, and then I go.

Refilwe did all of the housework early in the morning before going to a job that began at 7:00 a.m. because her husband would arrive home from his shorter day before her return. "My husband will not be happy," explained Refilwe, "if he comes home and finds that the house is dirty and the blankets are not prepared." At the end of the day, there was more to be done. "I come home, clean the whole yard, do the washing, clean all the utensils we use at home for cooking, clean my house."

Even with her disproportionate burden, Refilwe felt lucky. When she worked into the evening at her secretarial job, her husband at least would cook if he arrived home first:

> If there is something to cook, he cooks it. My husband is good. He's
> unlike other men. Others say, "She will cook when she comes home."
> But he doesn't think that. He cooks for himself and the kids—he
> knows that he has to take care of his kids.

Still, when Refilwe was home, all of the work fell to her. "If I am there, he won't stand up and do the cooking. If I am there, it is different because then he'll need me to prepare the water so he can wash, and he needs food from me."

In addition to conducting interviews in six countries, we examined the workload of women and men in five countries using national household data. When we only considered paid work hours, it looked, at first glance, as if men are more likely than women to be working more than sixty hours a week (see figures 5-5 and 5-6). However, when we analyzed those national surveys where information on unpaid household and caregiving work had been collected, a completely different picture emerged: Women are far more likely than men to be working more than sixty hours a week (see figures 5-7 and 5-8).

In single working-parent households in Mexico, 76 percent of women work more than sixty hours a week compared to 64 percent of men. In dual-

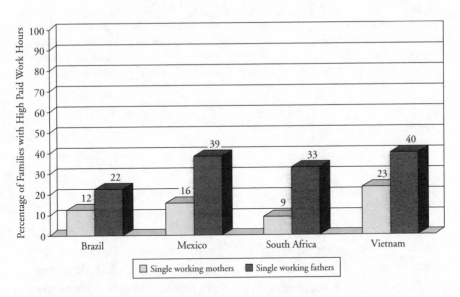

Figure 5-5
Single Working Fathers Are More Likely to Average Sixty or More Hours of Paid Employment Weekly.
Note: Data from national living standards surveys. Analyses in the above figure are based on households with a zero- to fourteen-year-old child. Sample size of single working parents was not sufficient to conduct parallel analyses for Russia.

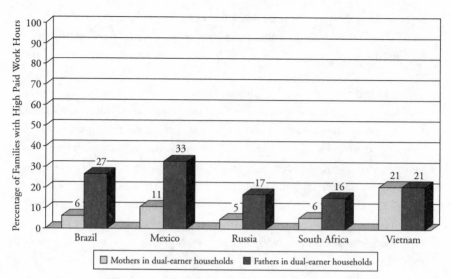

Figure 5-6
Fathers in Dual-Earner Households Are More Likely to Average Sixty or More Hours of Paid Employment Weekly.
Note: Data from national living standards surveys. Analyses in the above figure are based on households with a zero- to fourteen-year-old child. Height of bars reflects percentage rounded to the nearest whole number. In the case of Vietnam, 20.7 percent of mothers in dual-earner households averaged sixty or more hours of paid employment weekly, compared to 21.4 percent of fathers in dual-earner households.

earner households in Mexico, 87 percent of women work more than sixty hours compared to 52 percent of men. While it was not possible to make gender comparisons in single-parent households in Russia because of the small number of single-father households, in dual-earner households women worked disproportionately longer hours than men. In Russian dual-earner households, 83 percent of women work more than sixty hours compared to 44 percent of men. The comparable figures for dual-earner households in Brazil are 69 percent of women and 36 percent of men. The pattern holds for single working-parent households in Brazil as well: 65 percent of women in single-parent households worked more than sixty hours a week, compared to 43 percent of men.

We also examined extended-family households in which all adults worked. In every country, employed men in these extended-family households were more likely than women to work more than sixty hours of paid work a week. However, the fraction of men working these long hours was small; Mexico was the country with the highest fraction at 25 percent. When it comes to total work hours—paid and unpaid work combined—another story unfolds. In every country we examined, women in extended-family households were far more likely to work more than sixty hours per week of combined paid and unpaid work. Moreover, the percentage of women working these long hours was high. Eighty percent of women in extended-family households in Mexico labored for more than sixty total hours, including paid and unpaid work, 52 percent in Brazil, and 91 percent in Russia.

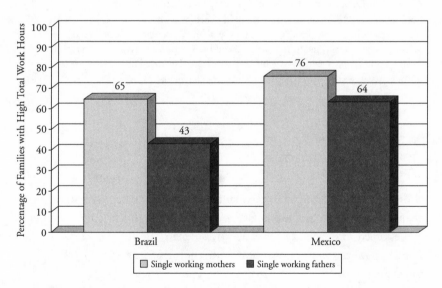

Figure 5-7
Single Working Mothers Are More Likely to Average
Sixty or More Hours of Paid and Unpaid Work Weekly.
Note: Data from national living standards surveys. Analyses in the above figure are based on households with a zero- to fourteen-year-old child. *Total work hours* equals the sum of hours spent on paid employment, housework, and caregiving. The Brazil figures are underestimates because no data were available specifically on caregiving hours.

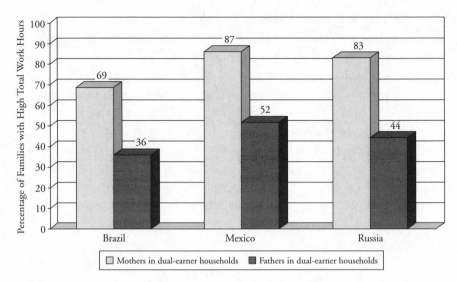

Figure 5-8
**Mothers in Dual-Earner Households Are More Likely to Average
Sixty or More Hours of Paid and Unpaid Work Weekly.**
Note: Data from national living standards surveys. Analyses in the above figure are based on
households with a zero- to fourteen-year-old child. *Total work hours* equals the sum of hours
spent on paid employment, housework, and caregiving. The Brazil figures are underestimates
because no data were available specifically on caregiving hours.

A Downward Spiral

Women are more likely than men and lower-income parents are more likely
than higher-income parents to face a downward spiral. They are more likely
to be forced to give up or lose a job in order to care for children and other
family members, only to replace it with a job that pays less, provides fewer
safeguards, and offers fewer benefits.

Anastasiya Rodionovna Uvarova's experience in Russia provides an important example of the downward economic spiral that parents face. While
working two jobs, Anastasiya also cared for her sixteen-year-old daughter,
Mariya; her eleven-year-old son, Sergei; and her mother and aunt. Sergei was
chronically ill and needed both her time and what money she made to go toward hospital and doctors' bills.

Anastasiya took a lower-paying job in order to get the leave she needed to care for her sick child. But as a result of the lower pay, in the end, Anastasiya had to work at two jobs to get by—one as a classroom assistant at a school and another as a janitor. With her wages and her husband's factory earnings, Anastasiya and her family could barely afford to live in a communal apartment where multiple families shared a single apartment and kitchen. Even having accepted a poorly paying job in order to be able to take leave to care for her son when he was sick, she worried about her ability to stay employed. Many of the safeguards that had been in place in the old Soviet Union had been eliminated with the economic changes accompanying *perestroika*, as Anastasiya noted:

> Before *perestroika*, they did not have such disorder. They could not fire me. I would bring a sick note, and whether they wanted to or not, they put up with it. And now . . . if you are trying to find a job, it's impossible to get something. If, on top of that, your child is sick—God forbid. And my child gets sick. And I have to take him to the doctor.

Her meager earnings meant that her son was often home alone when he was healthy. She explained:

> You see, if the parents are well-off, they can send their children to a school or an activity. That is, if the children are well-off, they have an activity. They don't go to the street. They are busy. And if there is no money, it is impossible to send your children somewhere, and he goes to the street.

The negative impact on Anastasiya, Sergei, and the rest of her family of her being forced into the lower-paying job in order to be able to care for her children was common among the other parents with whom we spoke in Russia. A vicious cycle of gender inequalities had evolved as well. First, she had fewer job opportunities than did her husband because the initial caregiving burden had fallen solely on her. Then, the fact that she had a poorly paying job reinforced the notion that she should carry more of the caregiving burden. "With us, because the children were sick a lot, I took up a lower-paying job because my husband provides [more] money. So all responsibilities, including putting a nail in or fixing an outlet, are mine."

Ill-Fated First Steps

The first step in the downward spiral often occurred when the nearly impossible conditions that middle- and low-income parents encountered as they sought to care for their family members led to them losing needed pay or their jobs.

Prior to our interviews, thirty-nine-year-old Hoang Thi Ngoc held a job as a middle-school teacher in Vietnam. With few extended family members nearby, Ngoc was largely on her own when it came to meeting her children's needs. She was able to scrape by until they got sick, and then things fell apart:

> When I was teaching, I was home half a day, and the other half I was teaching. . . . When I was teaching, my son was often sick. He had a kidney disease—*nhiem mo*. He is still sick right now. Local and district doctors could not diagnose his illness. He was always in discomfort. I had my teaching. I couldn't take time off all the time. . . . [But] when he was sick, I did not teach. I was close to my son's whereabouts. Each night he slept near me. If he became sick, I knew and did not work.

Ngoc went on to explain how in this poverty-stricken community there were no supports for working or caring for a child:

> There was no place at school to bring the children in for breastfeeding. The commune is generally very poor. . . . [There are] not any childcare places in my village. If there were childcare places, I would not have quit teaching.

While there were problems in keeping her job even when her children were not sick, the starkest problems arose when they were. Ngoc simply summarized, "When my children were sick, I couldn't be near them." Each time Ngoc had to take leave from work to care for her children, the principal took "points" off her record and made deductions from her salary. In the end, there was no way for her to keep the job while meeting her children's basic needs. Like many others who were unable to keep a job in the formal sector, Ngoc landed in the informal sector. Like others we interviewed who ended up in the informal sector and those who ended up in lousy jobs in the formal sector, Ngoc now earned lower wages and experienced worse working conditions. As of our interview time, Ngoc was working seven days a week, from morning until night, both farming and selling rice and pigs' feed in a stall next to her home.

When adults lost jobs in order to care for a sick child or a dying family member, they often experienced months without any reliable income before they were able to find another steady job. In Botswana, thirty-two-year-old Dipogiso Motlhagomile was working in construction. She needed the work to support her three children and her cousin, who was sick with AIDS. Three weeks after she took maternity leave for the birth of her third child, her infant died suddenly for unknown reasons—described in the West as Sudden Infant Death Syndrome (SIDS).

After this tragedy, a grieving Dipogiso tried to return to her old job, but the employers would not hire her back. This was the beginning of a downward free-fall. For nine months, Dipogiso was without any formal work. She cut and sold thatching grass to earn what money she could, but the maximum possible income from that source was not enough for a family to survive on.

At first, Dipogiso's mother used money from her old-age pension to help her daughter buy food. When that wasn't enough, Dipogiso had to leave her children with her older sister while searching for any job. Dipogiso finally found some work nine months later as a laborer. But her wage was half of what it had been: it dropped from 600 pula prior to her having given birth to 300 pula, or not quite $60 a month. The conditions were worse as well. As a result of the dangerous conditions while cutting bricks, she injured her back so severely that she could no longer go to work. While it was a work-related injury, the company would not pay her. She found herself back at home, trying to figure out how to get a job as a household servant, which would involve still lower pay. But even to get that job, she had to recover physically from her injury to be able once again to do such basic household tasks as fetching water and sweeping. "I cannot do the daily chores," she explained. "I can't go to fetch water each day. . . . I can't sweep because I can't bend, and I can't wash my clothes."

For each of these women, a new job with worse pay and worse working conditions had replaced the first untenable job.

Replicating Disadvantage

On nearly every measure, from the availability of paid leave to adequate flexibility at work, the parents living in poverty we interviewed were facing worse working conditions. While the poor were less likely to be able to get any leave from work for caregiving, they were at the greatest disadvantage when it came to paid leave—the kind of leave they needed the most. Only fifty percent of the poor received paid leave compared to 81 percent of parents who were not poor (see figure 5-9).

Consequently, parents living in poverty were more likely than other parents to face difficulty caring for their sick children because of work responsibilities (58 percent versus 48 percent). Parents living in poverty also were more

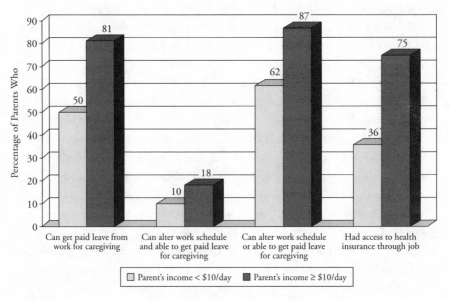

Figure 5-9
Low-Income Families Are Less Likely to Have
Decent Work Family Conditions.
Note: Data from Project on Global Working Families' in-depth interviews with working caregivers. Analyses in the above figure are based on households with a zero- to fourteen-year-old child. Income data from each survey have been converted to a common currency using the World Bank's purchasing power parity (PPP) conversion factors.

likely to leave their sick children home alone (22 percent versus 11 percent) and to describe the negative impact that their own working conditions had on their children's health (35 percent versus 23 percent).[1]

Poor families also had the fewest options when it came to routine care for their children. They were significantly less likely to be able to place their children in formal childcare centers (27 percent versus 52 percent). Not only were the children less likely to be cared for in formal childcare centers, but they were markedly less likely to be taken care of by a paid adult in informal settings (22 percent versus 45 percent) and were far more likely to be cared for in an informal setting by another child, who was unpaid (21 percent versus 13 percent). As a result, children in poor families face wide-ranging disadvantages. They start school behind their peers and face threats to their health and development.

When parents had limited schooling, their children started out life with limited early educational opportunities. Parents who did not have the chance to get a formal education were not able to get jobs with decent wages and, as a result, were more likely to have to rely on an unpaid child as a care provider than were parents with more education. They were less likely to be able to send their children to formal daycare centers or to pay an adult to care for them in an informal setting. Thirty-two percent of the parents we interviewed who had a middle school education or less left their children home alone, 22 percent relied on informal care provided by an unpaid child, 27 percent relied on informal care of a paid adult, and only 28 percent sent their children to a formal center (see figure 5-10).

In an effort to assuage collective guilt for doing so little to make it feasible for indigent families to succeed at work while meeting their children's essential needs, most societies promote myths about the availability of extended family to fill the gaping holes in services and decent working conditions that the poor face. However, the evidence does not support these myths. In fact, families living in poverty are the most likely to find themselves at multiple jeopardy—that is, with the fewest social supports and the worst working conditions. Parents earning less than $10 per day were more than twice as likely to lack paid leave, lack regular help from extended family, and lack other caregivers in the household (see figure 5-11). The consequences of these combined disadvantages for the ability of parents living in poverty to earn a living and care for their children adequately are devastating. They simultaneously damn children's and parents' futures.

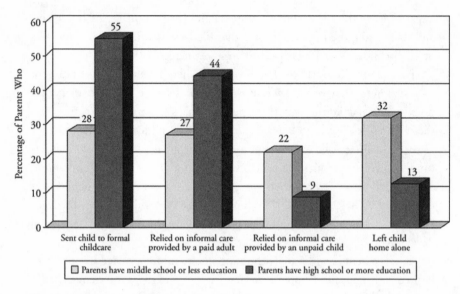

Figure 5-10
**Parents with Limited Education Are More Likely
to Have Poor Childcare Options.**
Note: Data from Project on Global Working Families' in-depth interviews with working caregivers. Analyses in the above figure are based on households with a zero- to five-year-old child.

Countries' policies can make a difference in terms of decreasing the disparities across social class and thus improving the chances for the next generation (see figure 5-12). Of the countries we studied, Vietnam had more families overall with access to formal childcare, and the differences across income groups were smallest due to the higher availability of public childcare services. Fifty-seven percent of lower-income families in Ho Chi Minh City were able to send a child to formal childcare, as were 62 percent of higher-income families. While disparities in access to formal childcare by income were also marked in Mexico, these disparities were narrowed in the formal sector by the Mexican social security system mandate to provide social insurance that includes childcare for children between the ages of six weeks and four years old[2] (see figure 5-13). Overall in Mexico, 22 percent of low-income workers had access to formal childcare compared to 58 percent of higher-income workers, but in the formal sector, 39 percent of low-income workers used formal childcare compared to 58 percent of higher-income workers.

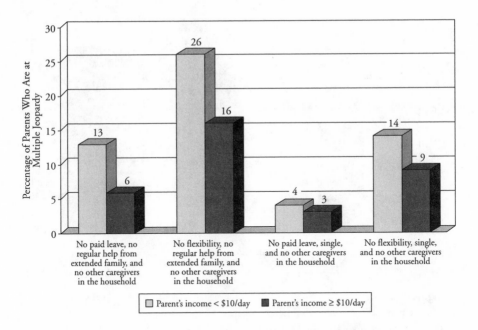

Figure 5-11
Low-Income Parents Are More Likely to Be at Multiple Jeopardy.
Note: Data from Project on Global Working Families' in-depth interviews with working care-givers. Analyses in the above figure are based on households with a zero- to fourteen-year-old child. The category "no other caregivers in the household" includes one- and two-parent households for which there is no extended family and no other caregivers besides the parents living in the household. Income data from each survey have been converted to a common currency using the World Bank's purchasing power parity (PPP) conversion factors.

Keystone to Reducing Poverty and Gender Inequality

Without a doubt, being able to get and keep well-paid work is the most common and reliable route out of poverty for those who make it. Yet, too few men—and far fewer women and parents with young children at home—find a steady ladder they can climb. In every country we studied, we met parents who could not get a job they needed because they faced discrimination or impassable barriers around caring for their children. We met men and women who had to take jobs with miserable pay because those were the only ones

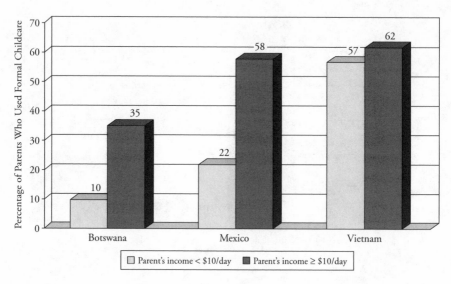

Figure 5-12
**More Universally Available Public Childcare
in Vietnam Narrows Income Disparities.**
Note: Data from Project on Global Working Families' in-depth interviews with working care-
givers. Analyses in the above figure are based on households with a zero- to five-year-old child.
Income data from each survey have been converted to a common currency using the World
Bank's purchasing power parity (PPP) conversion factors.

that would allow them to care for a sick child or attend to an elderly parent
while working. We sat in the small one-room shacks with adults who had lost
pay or jobs because, when forced to make an unimaginable choice between
acquiring desperately needed income and providing essential care for their
children, they had chosen the latter. While this affected both women and
men who were primary caregivers, women disproportionately bore the burden. In every nation, we also met parents who chose earning essential income
over caring for their children. These mothers and fathers thought their families would be worse off if they did not keep working for the meager earnings,
which covered basic food and shelter. However, that decision often came at
great cost to their children's future because their children had to be left home
alone at young ages, suffered serious injuries, had health crises that were left
unattended, or were pulled permanently out of school in order to care for

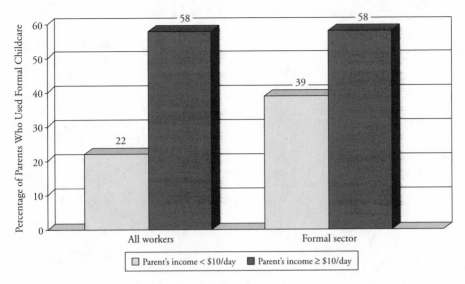

Figure 5-13
**Mexico's Mandate to Provide Childcare for Employees
in the Formal Sector Helps to Narrow Income Disparities in That Sector.**
Note: Data from Project on Global Working Families' in-depth interviews with working caregivers. Analyses in the above figure are based on households with a zero- to five-year-old child.

younger children in the family—thus damning their future chances. Witnessing the inconceivable alternatives among which parents in poverty are forced to select hammered home the critical importance of addressing working families' needs.

The individuals with whom we spoke made devastatingly clear that to successfully keep families from being destitute, to address intergenerational poverty, and to decrease gender inequalities, we need to reduce the nearly insurmountable obstacles that parents in poverty currently face as they try to thrive at work and to care for their children. There is no other way. Adults living in poverty absolutely need work to survive, let alone prosper, and children dearly need adults to raise them.

6

Families That Work
in Times of Crisis

Outsiders and insiders have utterly different views of crises. Like most outsiders, I began with the mistaken assumption that the importance of the
dilemmas that working families face fades during crises. As profound as the
problems many families face on a daily basis are, I assumed they would somehow pale next to problems raised by economic and health crises, natural and
manmade disasters.

As part of the Project on Global Working Families, we examined the experience of families facing different types of crises over different time frames.
We spoke with families about their experiences in the midst of epidemics,
after natural disasters, and after war. Over time, parents and children taught
me that what changes in times of crises is not how important caring for
family and work are, but how completely central and enormously difficult
these essential tasks often become. For those living through a crisis, the first
questions are: How do you keep yourself and those you love alive? How do
you find a way to pay for necessities? How can you eke out a living that will
provide for food, housing, and health care while caring for those you love?

Throughout short- and long-term crises, caring for family remains central
among the concerns of most adults. Moreover, while some may cease to work
for a brief period during an acute crisis, most crises last months or longer, and

as a result, most adults must work while simultaneously coping with the effects of the crisis. During these extended periods, families and communities struggle to survive—to find a way to pay for food and other essentials while caring for children, the elderly, and the disabled.

This chapter, which examines what matters and what does not in times of crisis and afterward, begins with families in Botswana, where the AIDS pandemic has led to a reduction in life expectancy measured in decades. The chapter next examines the lives of families in Honduras, two years after massive mudslides displaced more than a million people. Third, we spoke with families in Vietnam a quarter-century after a war that led to several million deaths. Even in the midst of these tragedies and their aftermaths, there are glimpses of hope—programs that are truly making a difference in the lives of children, not just for a moment, but for a generation. The chapter will end by describing these programs and the chance they provide for profound change.

In the Midst of Crisis: The AIDS Pandemic

The AIDS pandemic has transformed the childhood, youth, and adulthood of tens of millions worldwide. In 2003, nearly 3 million children and between 31 and 43 million adults were infected with HIV worldwide.[1] A staggering 20 million people died of AIDS in the 1980s and 1990s.[2] Moreover, the number dying each year is rising as the epidemic spreads and as people long infected grow sicker. In 2003 alone, the number of deaths was between 2.5 and 3.5 million.[3]

Recently, attention has been focused on the rapid rise of infection rates in Asia and in Central and Eastern Europe. In Eastern Europe and Central Asia, 1.2 million adults and children were living with HIV/AIDS in 2002, and 1.5 million in 2003. India has 4 million infected adults and children, a total second only to South Africa.[4] By 2010, if current trends continue, 10 million Chinese could be infected with HIV/AIDS.[5]

While the footprint of the HIV/AIDS pandemic is felt globally, the impact is currently greatest in Africa: The southern cone of Africa is in the midst of an expanding crisis. In 2002 alone, there were 3.5 million new HIV infections among adults and children in sub-Saharan Africa and another 3.2 million new infections in 2003.[6] The statistics on life expectancy too dryly recount the ravaging of family lives brought about by HIV/AIDS. AIDS has already led to a drop in life expectancy from sixty-eight to forty years in Botswana, from fifty-nine to thirty-five years in Lesotho, from fifty-five to thirty-eight years in Malawi, from sixty-seven to forty-eight years in South Africa, from fifty-three to thirty-two years in Zambia, and from sixty-eight to thirty-three years in Zimbabwe. By 2010, life expectancy will have dropped even further—down to thirty-two years in Botswana.[7]

One of the most important challenges for those nations that already have high infection rates is how adults can simultaneously work and raise healthy children while addressing the needs of those adults and children who are already infected. For a number of countries, this challenge is particularly urgent. In South Africa, an estimated 20 percent of adults are infected, in Zimbabwe 34 percent, in Botswana 39 percent, in Swaziland 33 percent, in Lesotho 31 percent, in Namibia 23 percent, in Zambia 22 percent, and in Malawi 15 percent.[8] The calculus is almost unfathomable: When 15–40 percent of reproductive- and working-age adults in a country are infected with HIV, nearly every family has a member who is infected, has grown sick, or has died. The majority of extended families has many members who have become HIV infected. Thus, daily life changes indelibly for everyone.

Pandemic Permeates Lives of Children and Their Caregivers

Even though treatment existed for HIV in the United States and Europe, HIV infection was rarely treated in Africa before 2004. Without treatment, AIDS was uniformly deadly—it was only a question of time. While new global initiatives in 2004 began to bring hope for greater availability of treatment, they are too late for the 12 million children already orphaned.[9]

To Lorato Kambewa, her boyfriend, Baruti Mmati, had seemed healthy. Lorato had not realized he was sick until it was too late. She recounted simply but poignantly, "He wasn't the kind of person you'd expect to die so soon." But in retrospect, the signs of his compromised immune system had been evident. Even minor infections had become intractable. His major complaint had been a finger that had a sore on it and was swelling. Lorato explained: "The sore wouldn't heal."

Soon, Baruti became terminally ill with AIDS. Baruti's time went quickly. On a Monday, he took his first day of sick leave from work. On Tuesday, he was vomiting a great deal. "When he threw up, he said he was nauseous," explained Lorato. "When he walked a little, he said he was nauseous." On the third day, he grew weaker. "On the fourth day, they took him back to his home village. On the fifth day, they took him to the hospital, and on the sixth day he died." Lorato had tried to take care of him. "Those days when I'd visit him [in the hut where he lay 100 meters away], I'd just clean his house, pour him some water to bathe—he bathed himself—and then I'd give him water to drink. He would throw up so often, so I'd have to change the clothing and clean it."

After Baruti's death, though she was grieving, Lorato had many practical details to worry about. Each month, when he was working, Baruti had given Lorato 600 pula (approximately 120 U.S. dollars) from his earnings to help with the living expenses for her three children: a one-year-old daughter, Unity; a three-year-old son, Masilo; and a seven-year-old daughter, Ontibile. His contribution had been essential in helping Lorato and the children make ends meet. Lorato explained to us how little cushion she had for feeding and clothing her children, even with Baruti's contribution:

> With the money, I always made sure I paid the rent first. If we didn't have accommodation, it would be extra difficult. We make sure we pay the rent and with the money that is left we buy food and try to live off piece jobs. I used to get my money from piece jobs and buy some used clothing for my baby—the shawls, vest, socks—that's what I needed to get. There was another lady we knew who worked at the clinic. Because other children were getting food from the government and were picking it up at the clinic, we usually asked her to give us some cooking oil. She'd take some for us if she could manage it. Sometimes it was *paleche* [corn porridge], beans, or milk. She would help us in that way.

After Baruti died of AIDS, there was less money for food or clothing—as even her young children noticed:

> After he passed away, I think my children noticed a change in my care. My ability to provide food for them and other needs had changed. [Before he died,] there were times when there was a favorite meal—meat with beans. Very soon, it wasn't there, and they started asking for it. I'd just tell them, "Look, I have only porridge today, so you'll just have to eat it."

Lorato and her children survived on her meager earnings from doing housework for other families. Lorato was relieved that working as a maid allowed her to keep Unity in her own care, instead of leaving her infant home all day alone. She couldn't afford private childcare centers, and no public ones were available to her. Nor could she afford adequate informal care. In the past, when she had left her children in informal care, they had been left alone or neglected. She described one instance: "I came back after a very long time, and my baby had the same diaper on as when I left. Even now, my child is being treated for her diaper rash. The baby still has it." Lorato went on to describe another occasion:

> [The care provider] had taken her [own] baby and left my children
> hungry and with no one to take care of them. When I came home,
> my youngest son had eaten a *chongololo* [a type of centipede]. They
> have many, many legs. He swallowed one, and its legs were all over
> his throat. The legs had to be taken out at the hospital.

So, at the time of the interview, Lorato only worked jobs where she could take Unity with her. Still, that too often meant that her seven- and three-year-olds were home alone. Moreover, when Lorato described what it was like to try to work and care for her infant simultaneously, it was clear that the care of Unity was still compromised:

> So I'd have to bring my child to my workplace. As you can imagine, I
> have to fetch water sometimes. Having the baby on me and fetching
> water, doing laundry—it's not easy. Sometimes I'd put her in the
> shade and do the laundry without her. Sometimes when she'd cry, I'd
> just have to ignore her so I could finish the work. . . . Sometimes
> I'll get a piece job and they'll ask me to thoroughly clean the house. If
> I have the baby on my back, it becomes difficult because the baby
> will become sick from the dust in the house while I am dusting and
> moving around the house. Sometimes, because [of] washing the
> dishes, standing up with the baby on my back will also feel heavy for
> me so I have to leave [her] when I get home—my back will hurt so
> much.

Lorato wanted to be an attentive mother. She knew that infants needed adults' attention to develop well. But she simply could not give Unity that attention and keep her job. In fact, she couldn't even take enough time out from her workday to feed Unity regularly.

Back at home, her seven-year-old daughter, Ontibile, cared for her three-year-old son, Masilo, because Lorato could not afford childcare for them on her low wages. Lorato tried to give them reminders of when to eat while she was at work, but she had to rely on Ontibile to ask the toddler if he was hungry. Lorato explained how she would tell Ontibile as she left her children alone, "Later on, if I'm still not back, if you see children coming home from school, take the food and eat it."

But even the precarious balance that Lorato and her children had achieved after Baruti's death was threatened when Unity, the one child Baruti had fathered, became ill and Lorato's work situation became even more perilous. Lorato explained:

> My baby started to get sick in the beginning of December. Toward the middle of December, maybe around the 13th, that's when she looked weak. Although I was breast-feeding her and she ate and fed well, she started vomiting after eating. I watched her, thinking she would be okay—giving her porridge often during the day so that she would still have her strength. I gave her some water and she got better. On the 16th, I decided to bring her to the hospital because she had started to have diarrhea now. She was throwing up and having a runny stomach. She was admitted that same day in the hospital, and on December 25th she was getting better. On the 29th, it started again. That's when she didn't want to eat anything—she didn't take any food. Only recently, one of the doctors here asked me if people ever visited me who were my guardians and who were close to me. I started getting worried. What if something serious were to happen? What if I have the world's worst problems?

When Lorato was in the hospital caring for Unity, she lost her sole income. Paid only on a contingency basis, she received no paid leave and no wages or salary of any kind when she had to be in the hospital herself or had to be with one of her hospitalized children. Lorato described what she and her family were left to live on:

> I really can't afford anything because I'm not working and there really isn't anyone who is helping me with anything. None of my relations have come to visit me except my sister. . . . When we were first here at the hospital, she gave me 50 pula from the money [her boyfriend] had given her. In that sense, that's all I can live on. Some-

times the people who are in the hospital as well send me to go to a tuck shop [a small, informal stand or stall close to a roadside which sells basic provisions] and then on the way I meet somebody I know. They'll say to me, "Here's 5 pula, go and buy yourself a drink." "Here's 2 pula, go and get yourself a drink." I don't use that money for drinks; I make sure that I buy soap.

She was trying to do everything she could to improve her child's health and hoped that cleanliness would decrease the risk of infection.

Lorato increasingly suspected that Unity was infected with HIV. When she finally asked the doctor to test Unity, he said, "What if you and your baby or one of you comes out positive?" She tried to respond, "Look, I wouldn't be surprised. We're living in a time when it's affecting all of us here in Botswana. I wouldn't be so surprised if either one of us has it." But, at the same time, she was desperately hoping that although Unity's father had been infected, their infant had somehow been spared. Even though she had asked for the HIV test and acknowledged that the results might turn out positive, Lorato tried to convince herself that Unity was not infected:

I don't think my baby has [AIDS] because you know when a baby has it. Even some of the mothers in here have confided in me that their babies are sick with HIV. My baby is different than theirs. Her skin is more elastic. Others, if you pull it, it just stays pulled. The skin on their head is too tight, it's like they don't have any meat on them. Sometimes they lose weight in a way that's really awkward. My baby has lost weight only gradually because she's sick.

Lorato knew that if both Baruti and Unity were infected, she undoubtedly was, too. She wanted to be tested—despite the extensive discrimination against those who were known to be infected—because doing so was her only chance of getting some help for her children, should she die. Lorato explained: "If I'm positive—actually, one of the doctors asked me that—I really don't know what I'd do. I guess I'd immediately go and register with one of the social workers here so that when I die they can buy a coffin for me and help with the things that my kids need at home." Even though she wasn't sure what she could do, she wanted desperately to find some way to provide for Ontibile and Masilo, who seemed healthy but would be left orphaned, as well as for Unity, if Unity were to outlive her.

Ultimately, Lorato wanted the same thing for her children's future that any other parent would want: "I wish that my children will one day be better off than I am right now. . . . I want them to be educated and have a life for themselves that is healthy and independent." But in the absence of help, the odds are almost insurmountable. AIDS had stripped her of her partner's health and income, had led to the loss of her work, and now threatened her and her children's health.

Perhaps because AIDS is sexually transmitted or perhaps because its most widely publicized early victims were largely single, the image that many people carry with them of who is affected by AIDS—single adults—is grossly inaccurate. While too many single men and women have suffered and continue to suffer the ravages of HIV infection, for the majority of the millions infected worldwide, AIDS is a family disease. Husbands become infected and unknowingly—or knowingly—bring the virus home to their wives. In a Zambian study, only 11 percent of women thought they could ask their husbands to use a condom.[10] If infected mothers do not receive treatment, more than a third of the children born to these women begin life themselves infected.[11] As a result, 3 million children have become infected with HIV.

The epidemic affects all of childhood both through the illness and death of children and through the illness and death of parents, teachers, and other caretakers. Those children who are not infected themselves still struggle through being reared by parents who are often too sick to provide care or too weak to earn a living. Even for children whose parents are uninfected, their families' meager resources—in terms of both time and money—often must be shared with sick and dying aunts and uncles or orphaned cousins. Finally, there are fewer teachers and caregivers in the communities. Children attend schools where the turnover rate for teachers has risen geometrically as a high percentage of teachers have become sick. It is estimated that in 1999 alone, 860,000 children in sub-Saharan Africa lost their teachers to AIDS.[12] In Kenya, AIDS-related teacher deaths more than tripled from 1995 to 1999. South Africa could lose 133,000 teachers in the current decade, and Tanzania could lose 14,460 by 2010.[13]

While the virus's impact on children is too vast to summarize succinctly, the nature and extent of the effects become clearer if we look at three types of families caring for children: those in which children are orphaned, those in which children are infected with HIV, and those in which caregivers are HIV infected.

Reverberations throughout Families, across Generations

Just as there is no doubt that adults who are caring for their children, grand-children, parents, sisters, brothers, neighbors, and other family members and friends who are infected are providing care that is essential—both to the individuals who are sick and to the communities that need to survive the AIDS epidemic—it is clear that providing this care takes a toll on their own families.

In a series of in-depth ethnographic and large-scale quantitative studies, we have documented the impact of AIDS care on working families. To begin with, after providing essential HIV care, adults inevitably have less time left for their own children and parents. Parents who were HIV/AIDS caregivers at the time of our studies or who had recently provided this care and who had children zero to five years old spent an average of seventy-four hours per month caring for their children. This was markedly less than the ninety-six hours per month spent by parents who had not been HIV/AIDS caregivers.

Not only did parents have less time to care for their families, but they had less flexibility. When the small amount of flexibility in their work and family lives had to be devoted to HIV caregiving, parents had less ability to meet the educational needs of their own children. Because of this, parents who were HIV caregivers were more likely to face barriers to helping children with homework and participating in school activities (see figure 6-1).

Accidents and injuries serve as sentinel indicators of families at risk. While any child can experience an accident or injury, when injury and accident rates rise substantially, it is invariably an indicator of children being left home alone or receiving inadequate care. Our in-depth interviews found that the rates of accidents and other emergencies rose substantially in households with HIV caregiving responsibilities. Sixty-eight percent of parents who were serving as HIV caregivers had children who had experienced accidents or other emergencies while the parent was working, compared to only 41 percent when the parents were not HIV caregivers (see figure 6-2). In in-depth interviews, parents revealed why this was true. Parents often had no option but to leave their young children home alone or in the care of other children when they cared for family members who were sick or dying. Supporting their sick family members economically as well as by providing personal care, these parents had no resources left to pay for childcare for their own children. In fact, when parents had HIV caregiving responsibilities, their children were more likely to be left home alone, more likely to be left home alone sick, and more

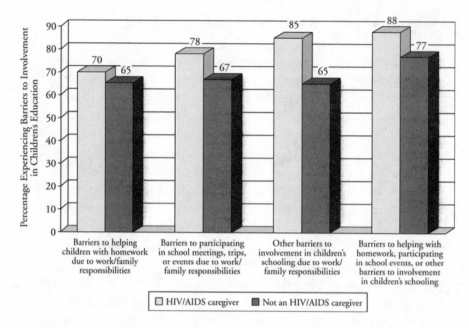

Figure 6-1
**HIV/AIDS Caregivers Face Greater Barriers
to Meeting Children's Educational Needs.**
Note: Data from Project on Global Working Families' in-depth interviews with working caregivers in Botswana. Analyses in the above figure are based on households with a six- to fourteen-year-old child. *HIV/AIDS caregivers* are those individuals who reported that they cared for
an HIV-positive person while working.

likely to have to forgo school in order to serve as childcare providers for
younger children. The children of HIV/AIDS caregivers were nearly twice as
likely to be left home alone, and more than one and a half times as likely to
have to forgo school or other age-appropriate activities in order to provide
childcare.

The multiple caregiving responsibilities that parents carried would have
been feasible had they received support—whether in the form of childcare,
home care, respite services, or hospice help. But since they were living on the
margin economically before the AIDS epidemic, trying to address the health
crisis brought on by HIV/AIDS had pushed them over the edge.

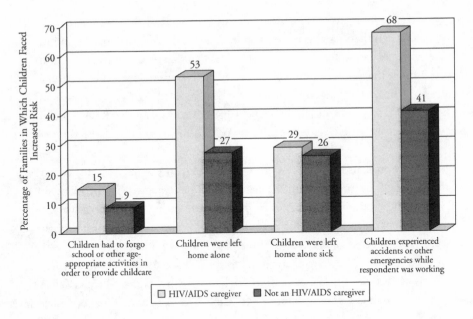

Figure 6-2
Children of HIV/AIDS Caregivers Face
Heightened Health and Developmental Risks.
Note: Data from Project on Global Working Families' in-depth interviews with working care-givers in Botswana. Analysis of parents whose children had to forgo school to provide childcare is based on households with a six- to fourteen-year-old child. Analysis of parents whose children had been left home alone is based on households with a zero- to five-year-old child. All other analyses are based on households with a zero- to fourteen-year-old child.

Higher Caregiving Burden

Like many acute crises, AIDS has tragically raised the caregiving burden. In many cases, individuals are caring not only for their own families but also for several sick and dying extended-family members and friends, as well as the or-phaned children of family members who have died.

RAISING AIDS ORPHANS

In sub-Saharan Africa, more than 12 million children have already lost a mother, father, or both parents to AIDS.[14] When orphaned, these children often lost both their source of care and the sole source of income available to provide for basic necessities.[15] Millions more have landed in complete destitution when their parents either became too sick to work or lost jobs and income while caring for close family members who grew ill. In twelve African countries, the devastation of families by AIDS is so prevalent that, by 2010, 15 percent or more of all children under fifteen are likely to be AIDS orphans. By 2010, 22 percent of children under fifteen in Botswana will be orphans. There will be an estimated 25 million AIDS orphans worldwide by the year 2010.[16]

Most orphans in southern Africa are cared for by extended family, not institutions.[17] Rearing orphans means not only that extended-family members are raising additional children, but that they are caring for children who are more likely to have critical mental and physical health needs.[18] Some orphans are HIV infected themselves. Even among those who are not infected, orphaned children are more likely to suffer from both acute and chronic malnutrition.[19] Studies throughout Africa, including in Botswana, Ghana, Kenya, Niger, Tanzania, Uganda, Zambia, and Zimbabwe, have found that orphaned children are more likely to have had their education halted or delayed.[20] In Uganda, 49 percent of orphans studied were depressed.[21] In Tanzania, 34 percent of orphans had contemplated suicide in the year prior to being interviewed.[22]

When we surveyed adults at health centers in Botswana, 37 percent were already caring for orphans.[23] The majority (59 percent) of the currently or recently working adults we interviewed who were caring for orphans were caring for nieces and nephews. Six percent of those caring for orphans were caring for siblings, 5 percent for grandchildren, 4 percent for a friend's or neighbor's child, and the remainder for other relatives. Many of these working adults were providing comprehensive support to orphans living outside their households, acting *in loco parentis*. Sixty-seven percent provided financial assistance, 58 percent helped to meet basic needs, 47 percent helped with educational and personal development, 27 percent with health care, and 21 percent with childcare (see figure 6-3). In 2002, when we conducted the interviews, adults were providing this care for orphans largely on their own or with the help only of family members. While the government had begun to provide some food assistance to orphans, all other services were largely unavailable—including childcare for preschool children, after-school care, and general assistance with the education, health care, and financial needs of orphaned children. Religious and community-based volunteer programs had

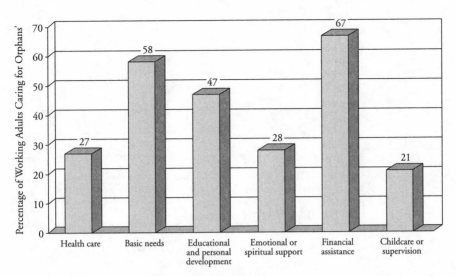

Figure 6-3
Types of Care That Working Adults Provide for Orphans
They Are Supporting beyond Their Household.
Note: Data from Project on Global Working Families' survey of HIV and family health
in Botswana. Analyses in the above figure are based on working adults providing care for or-
phans residing outside their household.

arisen to provide childcare during the day and after school as well as financial
assistance, but these services were available only to the most destitute families
caring for orphans, and thus served only a fraction of those in need. What little help most caregivers received was primarily from other family members.
Forty-three percent received help from other household members, 39 percent
received help from relatives outside their home, 34 percent from the council
or government, and 2 percent or fewer from friends, neighbors, and community volunteers (see figure 6-4).

The cost to working parents of caring for the orphaned children of
extended-family members was, at times, enormously high. Overburdened
parents who cared for orphans faced substantial barriers to meeting their own
children's needs. The majority of families we interviewed who took orphans
into their home experienced material hardship (see figures 6-5 and 6-6).
Nearly half of all orphans' caregivers faced financial difficulties. For 18 per-

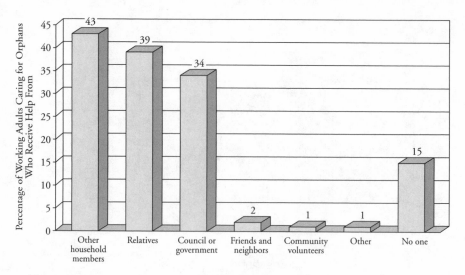

Figure 6-4
Working Adults' Sources of Help in Caring for Orphans.
Note: Data from Project on Global Working Families' survey of HIV and family health in Botswana. Analyses in the above figure are based on working adults providing care for orphans.

cent, the economic problems that resulted were severe enough to lead to difficulties in paying for or obtaining such essentials as food, water, shelter, and transportation to meet daily needs. While the greatest frequency of material hardship was experienced by caregivers with only a primary-school education, significant hardships were experienced across social class.

CARING FOR HIV-INFECTED CHILDREN

The problems that all working adults face are magnified for those who are caring for HIV-infected children. Seventy-two percent of working adults we surveyed in Botswana who were caring for an HIV-infected child were worried about the quality of the care the child received (compared to only 33 percent of those who were not AIDS caregivers). When children became sick, respondents' worries were heightened. Eighty-nine percent of those caring for an HIV-infected child worried that their children did not receive adequate care when ill.

Adults caring for children who were HIV infected were also more than

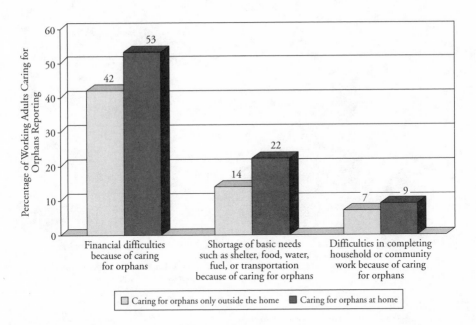

Figure 6-5
Orphans' Caregivers Face Economic Problems.
Note: Data from Project on Global Working Families' survey of HIV and family health in Botswana. Analyses in the above figure are based on working adults providing care for orphans.

twice as likely to need to take leave from work at least once a month to care for the sick child. Of the working adults we surveyed in Botswana, 36 percent of those caring for a child with HIV/AIDS took leave at least once a month to care for a sick child (compared to only 16 percent who were not caring for an HIV-infected child). These caregivers did not take different amounts of leave from work for children's routine needs. The higher illness burden faced by their HIV-infected children, their children's critical need for care when they were sick, and the caregivers' commitment to providing as good care as possible markedly affected their work.

BEING AN HIV-INFECTED CAREGIVER

When parents are HIV infected themselves, their children often need greater support to deal with their parents' illness and possible loss. As a result of the heightened needs of the parents and their children alike in conjunction with

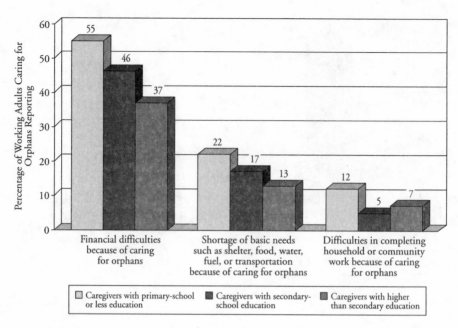

Figure 6-6
Orphans' Caregivers with Less Education
Face Greater Economic Problems.
Note: Data from Project on Global Working Families' survey of HIV and family health in Botswana. Analyses in the above figures are based on working adults providing care for orphans.

the greater constraints on family resources that HIV/AIDS often brings, HIV-infected parents are more likely to worry about their children receiving adequate educational, developmental, and emotional support. These greater concerns arise when parents are HIV infected even when their children are not infected with HIV perinatally. The problems are further heightened when the children have been infected with HIV from parent-to-child transmission or when the children have grown sick with other infectious diseases, such as tuberculosis or diarrhea, which their parents are at greater risk of having due to AIDS. In our study, 48 percent of HIV-infected parents worried about the quality of their children's childcare, 58 percent worried about the adequacy of childcare when children were sick, 39 percent about the adequacy of educational and developmental support, and 39 percent about the level of emotional support their children received (see figure 6-7).

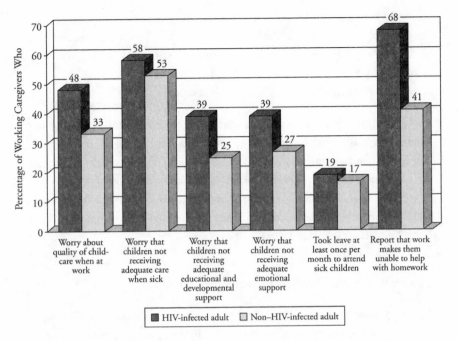

Figure 6-7
HIV-Infected Adults Have Greater Worries
in Balancing Work and Caring for Children.
Note: Data from Project on Global Working Families' survey of HIV and family health in Botswana. Analyses in the above figure are based on working caregivers. An *HIV-infected adult* is someone who reports having HIV/AIDS or meets the World Health Organization's clinical diagnosis of HIV/AIDS based on the symptoms they report.

FAMILY UNAVAILABLE

At the height of crises, the demands on adults to provide increased care for children and adults alike at the same time as they need to earn enough money to survive is heightened. Yet, at this time, when their need to balance both roles is greatest, they often have the least help available from family members. Twenty-four-year-old Matshwenyego Moiketsi, who had a four-year-old daughter, was not yet infected with HIV. Matshwenyego had been working as a salesperson in a produce store while her mother provided care for Matshwenyego's daughter. But when Matshwenyego's sister grew sick with AIDS, their mother needed to split her time between caring for her dying daughter and caring for her granddaughter. Matshwenyego explained:

Every time [my sister] needs my mother's help, my mother has to go to her place to help out. She leaves my daughter alone. In the house, it is my mother, my daughter, and some kids who go to school. [The older children] would be at school and my mother would go to attend to my sister [and leave my youngest daughter alone].

Constraints on the ability of extended family to help occur not only at the height of a crisis but in the months and years that follow. The extended-family members themselves may have grown sick, been injured or killed in the epidemic, war, or disaster, or forced to live in another part of the country or world. Those extended-family members who live close enough to potentially help parents care for children may have no choice but to work long hours themselves to rebuild their own lives.

Greater Material Needs and Declining Resources

Among the poorest households in Botswana, per capita income has fallen by 13 percent, and every earner is supporting an additional four people because of illnesses and deaths due to AIDS.[24] There is considerable consensus that many families throughout southern Africa are currently stretched to the breaking point and desperately need support from services and public programs if they are to manage the herculean caregiving tasks they face.[25] At the same time that the caregiving burden is exploding, work and economic issues are becoming more, rather than less, critical. Research in Cameroon, Kenya, Tanzania, Swaziland, and Zambia has shown that the AIDS pandemic may reduce economic growth rates by 25 percent over twenty years.[26] Countries and companies face increased labor costs and declining productivity due to illness, grieving, and loss.[27] The costs are chilling. By 2010, families' income will have fallen by 8 percent in Botswana.[28] Where between one in six and one in three adults are afflicted with AIDS, the need for those who can work to continue working—to support their families and their nations economically—grows even more critical.

After devastating epidemics, just as after natural disasters and wars, children's and adults' need for care increases and the availability of extended-family support declines while at the same time families also face their greatest economic struggles. Kereng Seetasewa was forty-five when we spoke with her, and her surviving children ranged in age from five to twenty-three years old.

Kereng found herself caring for a daughter disabled with cerebral palsy and a daughter with AIDS at the same time:

> It was very difficult because I was taking care of two people, and again I wasn't working and we were without food. I once came to the clinic to ask for gloves, and they came to our house to assess the situation. They themselves were really shocked. They asked me how we could survive, and I told them there were times we went without food. They told me to always go to the clinic to collect food. I was given maize meal, beans, and cooking oil whenever our food ran out.

It was not until after her HIV-infected daughter died that Kereng could try to return to work. When she did, her old job was gone.

During the time of our interviews, the number of adults in Botswana who had lost work to care for children and adults who were sick was climbing. As more families grew impoverished in the wake of the pandemic, signs of the heavy toll were popping up everywhere. Children began increasingly to stand outside the markets and beg for food.

When parents are infected with HIV, families are torn by how to earn enough money to survive and simultaneously to care for both the sick parent and the growing children in the family. The experience of twenty-nine-year-old Motheo Matswenyego was emblematic of this struggle. Like other parents in extended families, Motheo needed to earn enough to support his two children as well as his own parents. Making an adequate living by selling construction supplies in a store had been difficult enough when he was well, but when we spoke to Motheo, he had already been sick for three years, and his body was covered with painful sores. AIDS was not only decreasing how often he could go to work and what he could earn but was also increasing his need for money to cover health-care costs that were not covered by either public services or private insurance. Motheo explained what happened when sores broke out all over his body:

> I start concentrating on my illness. It makes everything heavy and difficult. I can't even learn the names of the items we are selling well. When I am supposed to be there, I keep thinking about the illness. . . . Whenever the rash develops, it becomes so difficult that I can't concentrate. I keep on thinking about where to go and borrow money and see if someone can help me. . . . It's really difficult

when you have to buy things for your children who are still growing. They need new uniforms every year. When they grow, the other uniforms will be too small for them. You have to buy a new uniform . . . and pay private doctors.

Motheo detailed how he was cycling into increasingly deeper debt as he tried to meet his family's basic needs and get any health care:

You give 50 pula to your parents; 100 pula goes to rent; another 100 pula goes to the kids. Then you have to pay back the loans from your friends. And then there might remain 20 pula for your family to buy food. That's not really enough for the family. That means you have to go and ask for another loan from another friend. The loans keep on adding up. When they come back to you, you can't even pay. For a sick person like me, you have to chase after other people and tell them that at the end of the month you'll give them money. At the end of the month you find that you have a shortage, a serious one. At times they will tell you that there is a traditional doctor you should see. You can go and see him and he will help you. So you rush to that person. But you also need money for that. Whenever you get to the hospital, they tell you that you have to go to Gaborone [the capital] and you have to see a doctor there. Then you need money for transport to Gaborone. That would mean that you have to go to a friend and ask for a loan again. I have been to the private doctor four times. That means that I don't have enough money to keep my family going. . . . Always when you get to the hospital you are told that you have to eat particular foods. For this, you need money. With the salary that I'm getting, I can't afford these foods. I have to see that my children have got clothes.

Motheo also described the number of years it had been since he had new clothes, his difficulty in paying for shoes when any of his children needed a new pair, his inability to afford following any of the health-care providers' recommendations while also paying his children's fees for school meals, and his parents' upset reaction when he couldn't provide them with any support for months. "At times," he said, "I have to live on short porridge for the whole month because I can't afford better food." The choices he had to make between covering expenses that might lengthen his survival and meeting his children's basic needs were tearing him apart:

The impact that this illness has on my family is that I have to divide the money that I have. Part of the money that I've been using to take care of my children, to buy clothes for them, and take care of what they need, I've been using for medical attention. . . . At times we find during midmonth I have no money, but I'm really sick and I have to go to the hospital.

Motheo's children began to have mounting difficulties in school, as he explained:

One of them failed. She was the last in the class. She used to be number ten, but that term, she was last. The elder one also—she used to be number one. Last year, first term, she was number twelve. Her work has dropped. . . . They couldn't learn very well because they were not eating very well.

Economic shortages threatened Motheo's family, as they did the families of other HIV-infected parents. Being HIV infected led to greater material hardship than did other major illnesses. Forty-eight percent of adults who were HIV infected reported experiencing financial difficulties due to their health condition compared to 31 percent of adults with other health conditions. Twice as many adults who were HIV infected as adults with other health conditions reported profound financial difficulties in obtaining shelter, food, water, fuel, or transportation because of their medical condition (23 percent versus 11 percent).

The economic burden extended beyond HIV-infected adults to family members who cared for them. Dipogiso Motlhagomile was one of many people with whom we spoke who took on the care of extended family at substantial personal cost. Dipogiso was thirty-two years old when we spoke with her. She was working in construction when her cousin was fired from his job as a driver because he had become progressively ill with HIV. Her cousin Thabo and his wife came to live with Dipogiso and her eleven- and six-year-old children. "If I wasn't doing this heavy kind of job," Dipogiso explained, "I'd be able to help his wife wash his clothes. And I'd make sure that the people from the clinics visit him. When they came, I'd make sure I was there so that I could learn exactly what we are expected to handle."

Because Dipogiso's job had become the sole source of income for her now-extended household, she couldn't afford to risk those earnings by taking time off. Her income was inadequate even without any loss of wages from taking what would have been unpaid leave. She explained:

> I run short of food. The reason that I run short of food is because whatever I buy for me and my children, I end up sharing with [my cousin and his wife]. He's been laid off and he's not getting an income. His wife isn't working either [because she's caring for him]. So that means there is literally no money coming in. They depend on me for food and soaps and that sort of thing. I always share with them, though this has had a negative effect on my family.

It became clear during our interview that Dipogiso's reference to "a negative effect" merely hinted at the depth of the deprivation they were facing together. She was far from alone in facing financial hardship due to HIV caregiving. Sixty-four percent of HIV/AIDS caregivers that we interviewed reported financial difficulties. For twenty-seven percent of HIV/AIDS caregivers, these financial difficulties were severe enough to lead to shortages in paying for such basic needs as food, shelter, water, fuel, and transportation (see figure 6-8).

Months and Years after a Crisis: Natural Disasters and War

The caregiving needs of families following crises that range from natural disasters to war are often elevated for years and decades afterward. Because families have fewer adults on whom to rely for an income at the very moment when they typically have far greater economic needs for rebuilding, the pressures not to have any wage loss are magnified many times.

The Devastation of Hurricane Mitch in Honduras Years Later

At first sight, it is immediately obvious why Tegucigalpa, the capital of Honduras, is so vulnerable to landslides after hurricanes. The city is built amid mountains, and its poorest communities are built on the edge of steep escarpments. In 1998, more than a million people were displaced due to Hurricane Mitch and the associated flooding and mudslides.[29] When the river that divides Tegucigalpa from its twin city of Comayagüela rose to previously unseen heights, it flooded streets and covered the tops of nearby buildings. Lo-

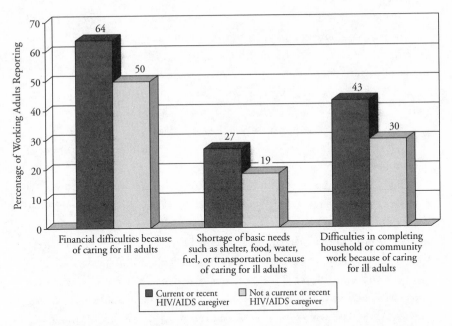

Figure 6-8
HIV/AIDS Caregivers Are More Likely
to Face Economic Problems.
Note: Data from Project on Global Working Families' survey of HIV and family health in
Botswana. Analyses in the above figure are based on working adults who report that they
currently provide or recently provided care for an ill adult. *HIV/AIDS caregivers* are those
individuals who report being current or recent caregivers for someone who has HIV/AIDS or
who meets the World Health Organization's clinical diagnosis of HIV/AIDS based on the
symptoms they report.

cation determined which neighborhoods were hit hardest by Hurricane
Mitch: Those buildings located halfway or farther down the city mountainsides were flooded with mud and rocks sliding from above.

As with many other natural disasters that wreak havoc in a short time, it is
the pace of the floods that never left the minds of those community members
whose mental health was most disturbed. At the beginning of the day on September 30, 1998, everything was normal. When the rains came, however, the
floods rose at an alarming rate. In a matter of hours, the river rose not only
above its banks but past the first avenue, higher than the second avenue
on the steep incline, past the third avenue, and up the hill to the fifth ave-

nue above the river. Within hours, the water line covered five stories of nearby buildings. The popular mayor, Cesar Castellanos, who was nicknamed Gordito, traveled around the city to try and convince people at risk to leave their homes for safety. In one working-class neighborhood, Barrio Abajo near Puente Chile, it was 11:00 p.m. before he could convince people to leave. By midnight, the whole neighborhood had been flooded. Gordito went from one hard-hit area to the next by way of helicopter, the only possible means of travel during the storm. Tragically, the helicopter crashed amid the torrential rains, and he died instantly.

Olivia Perez had a home without the tiled floors, interior brick walls, or exterior cement retaining wall which the middle class used to protect their homes during storms. Instead of a retaining wall, Olivia had only stones laid one on top of the other on the escarpment. Olivia's living and kitchen areas were separated from the bedrooms by only a plywood wall. During the hurricane, the wall of piled stones had been decimated, and Olivia had been awakened in the middle of the night when one of her younger children had called out that the house was coming down on top of them. After everything was destroyed, she spent months in a nervous depression and was barely able to get out of bed.

Vicki Querpis had a three-year-old son born before Hurricane Mitch devastated the Honduran capital and an infant born afterward. The hurricane destroyed both Vicki's and her sister's homes. After the hurricane, Vicki's sister, Inés, who had previously cared for Vicki's son, returned to work to earn enough money to rebuild her own home. As a result of being left without any childcare, Vicki had to stop working in the factory. Her husband continued to work selling soda at a refreshment stand, but on his small earnings they could not afford to repair their house, which had been destroyed by the hurricane. Two years later, they still did not have a house of their own.

The rapidity and extremity of the trauma that people experienced were what led Dr. Marcelo Javaloyas to speak of the walking dead—the survivors who could think only of getting themselves through the day. They could think of getting dressed or getting food, but they were completely unable to consider the future any more. This was particularly true among poor families who had sacrificed what little they had to build toward a slightly better future, only to see it all taken away by one storm. They were the ones who had no savings to fall back on. They were also the ones most likely to lose their daily jobs in the wake of the hurricane—just when they could least afford that additional loss and desperately needed to find resources to rebuild. In the areas with the most cataclysmic flooding, all of the homes were swept away, regardless of their owners' social class. But on the mountainsides, it was the poor who were at the greatest risk, because their houses had no foundations and no retaining walls, and they were on hillsides that were denuded of any trees that could have held the clay soil in place.

There is no doubt that for families with scarce resources, work-family conflicts both magnified and prolonged the hurricane's impact. Because they had less money, the poor were the most likely to be living in dirt, old wood, or cardboard-coated houses, which were destroyed by the hurricane. Furthermore, they were the least able to afford to rebuild, and this remained true more than two years after the hurricane. Those were the same families who couldn't afford to pay for childcare centers to help them care for their children while the parents worked, and therefore, they were the families most likely to leave children by themselves.

AFTERWARD: PICKING UP THE PIECES OF A BROKEN LIFE

The extreme economic toll of disasters affects families for years. The destruction of homes and dislocation of families leave many needing to rebuild homes from scratch. Whether the immediate cause is flooding, landslides, tornadoes, or bombs, families find themselves having to start with little or nothing—with no clothes, no tables, no dishes, no place to store food, no walls to keep out the wind, and no roof to keep out the rain. Getting and keeping a job that pays enough to rebuild becomes central to survival.

Nicole and Marco Labiosa's house, with its walls of wood, was completely destroyed by Hurricane Mitch. It had stood far down on the embankment and had received a great flood of wood and mud from above. Nicole had felt and looked so terrible after the hurricane that her neighbors had sent her to the hospital. But the hospitals had been overflowing with people, and the staff had done nothing except diagnose Nicole as having a case of *nervios*. When we interviewed her, Nicole's eyes still filled with tears as she described those first days after the devastation. Nicole, Marco, and their three children had gone to live in a shelter since their house had been completely destroyed. Nicole had gone from having two full-time jobs—working for wages and caring for her children—to having three full-time jobs: working, caring for her children, and rebuilding their home late at night. She would leave the shelter early in the morning to go to work in other people's houses; she washed their clothes and did whatever else she was asked so she could earn the money necessary to send her children back to school and to pay for the repairs to her home. She would come back from work in time to cook dinner—her children's sole real meal of the day—in the shelter. Then, at night, she would take her children to the rubble where their house had once stood. While the children slept on the ground, she would work with Marco, who was a carpenter, late into the night to reconstruct their home. It was always at least 11:00 p.m. and sometimes as late as 2:00 a.m. before they finished for the day, cleaning the mud from the rubble of their home and beginning to rebuild. Late at night, they would put their sleeping children on their backs and carry them back to the shelter.

After the hurricane, when Nicole and Marco had to work multiple jobs while rebuilding their home and their children had to be left to care for one another, the children's grades began to drop precipitously, until they were failing school. There were no waking hours left for Nicole and Marco to help their children study. They needed all of the paid work they could get to rebuild their home and to help their siblings and parents survive the hurricane's aftermath. Nicole's mother and father lived in the mountains, and all of their crops had been destroyed by the hurricane. Nicole had been buying them food, which she sent as care packages into the mountains in the arms and on the backs of youths. When her children's grades sank to a failing level, Nicole stopped working outside the home. As she worked with them on their schoolwork, their grades rose back into the nineties, but her family's income fell, and the extended family's income sank even lower.

Vietnam: Decades Later, Reverberations Continue to Rock the Fault Line

Years, even decades, after the peak of human disasters, their reverberations continue to shake the lives of families. This is devastatingly true in the case of wars. After almost all wars, the "losers" face economic ruin, and often even the "winners" must rebuild their basic infrastructures. After World War I, unemployment was high and inflation spiraled out of control in Europe—a result of food and fuel shortages that increased prices.[30] After World War II, the infrastructures of European nations were severely damaged. Power delivery systems, roads, bridges, canals, harbors, and railways had been destroyed. In 1945, coal production in Europe, which was critically important to the redevelopment of industry, was only two-fifths of its total before the war.[31] Adding to the economic strains caused by the infrastructure loss were the waves of migration which had taken place during the war. It is estimated that 50 million Europeans had been forced to leave their home regions during the war, and 16 million were unable to return after the war was over.[32] Food and housing shortages persisted, and there were fuel crises in the winters of 1945–1946, 1946–1947, and 1947–1948.[33]

In some wars, more civilians die from the devastating aftermath than from the violence of the conflict itself. An estimated 111,000 Iraqis died from "adverse health effects" of the 1991 Gulf War. Seventy-four thousand children died in that year alone.[34] Economic and health consequences of the war accounted for an estimated 227,000 excess child deaths between 1991 and 1998.[35] Increases were seen between 1991 and 1996 in the percentages of children with chronic malnutrition (19 percent to 32 percent) and acute malnutrition (3 percent to 11 percent) and those who were underweight (9 percent to 23 percent). Diarrhea and typhoid fever were far more prevalent in 1996 than they had been in 1990, and infant mortality also increased.[36] In addition to economic sanctions, Iraq was crippled by its damaged infrastructure, which was unable to produce the electricity and clean water that was needed. While economic sanctions exacerbated a fiscal depression after the Gulf War, lives have been ravaged by postwar economic depressions in the absence of sanctions as well.

War-related hazards undermine the lives of children and families decades after the wars themselves end. Land mines provide just one visible example. More than 110 million land mines that were laid during wars remain in unmarked locations in more than sixty countries.[37] Years after their wartime placement, these land mines continue to be triggered at unpredictable times by adults and children walking across apparently peaceful fields. Delayed time bombs, they continue to shatter the limbs and lives of adults who inadvertently set them off on their way to work. Children who wander across or play in fields that were once at the center of conflicts are disproportionately afflicted: Hundreds of thousands of children have been killed or maimed.[38] Each year, an additional 8,000 to 10,000 children are killed or maimed by land mines.[39]

During the decade from 1993 to 2003, more than 6 million children were seriously injured or became permanently disabled in wars.[40] Over the course of the same decade, a million children were orphaned or separated from their families due to war.[41] At the same time that wars and conflicts dramatically increase children's need for care, they often destroy what sources of care and education are available to them. During the war in Angola, an estimated 5,000 schools were destroyed and 1 million children remained out of school.[42] In Mozambique, nearly half of all primary schools were destroyed. Rwanda lost more than two-thirds of its schoolteachers due to death or flight.[43] Increased caregiving burdens arise as well when adults suffer severe physical and mental-health injuries and disabilities, and, as a result, the few unscathed adults find themselves caring for their traumatized husbands, wives, sisters, brothers, mothers, fathers, and children.[44]

The Vietnamese-American War was no exception to the pattern of severe economic consequences from infrastructure loss, dislocation of families, and other long-term consequences. The herbicides sprayed by the United States destroyed crops that were meant for export and for raw materials' production as well as those meant for domestic food supplies.[45] The defoliating chemicals removed all vegetation on sprayed land and thus led to erosion of the rich topsoil. Even after the war's end, land mines continued to kill civilians attempting to work the land. The situation in the cities was no better. Urbanization increased rapidly as refugees fleeing battles in the countryside poured into Saigon and other southern cities. It is estimated that there were 3 million unemployed Vietnamese in the cities of South Vietnam at the end of the war. This migration stressed the already-limited supplies of food, housing, and fuel.[46]

REPERCUSSIONS ACROSS GENERATIONS

For Troung Thi Thanh Ha's family, like many of the families we interviewed, the crisis of the war and its aftermath profoundly affected their ability to work and care for each other for more than a generation. Thanh Ha was in the early years of elementary school at the end of the Vietnam War. The agricultural basin of the south had been ruined by napalm, and the infrastructure for transporting agricultural and manufactured goods had been decimated. Many of those who survived the war were struggling to have enough to eat. Thanh Ha explained why her father had not been able to find work:

> Before the fall of Saigon, my father worked as an electrician. After that . . . he was not able to work. There was not really any economic development. No one needed electrical work that much. Besides, he was scared of the new government. He spoke up a lot and made some difficulties. My family was somehow labeled as siding

with the former government. He was not. But that was what they
said. So we were restricted from opening up [a] business.

Thanh Ha's father had come under suspicion at a time when heightened political insecurity and repression meant that suspicion alone was grounds for being blacklisted.[47]

The economic vulnerability of Thanh Ha's family was multiplied enormously by the deaths her family had suffered during the war. The same war that had left Vietnam's economy in shreds had also torn apart the safety net that family members could provide one another. Many in Thanh Ha's father's family had died or fled during the decades of war in Vietnam.

Because of her country's festering economic and political wounds, Thanh Ha and her siblings spent as much time working to obtain minimal food supplies as they did going to school:

> During the time when I grew up, it was difficult there, as it was difficult throughout the country. At that time in Bien Hoa, it was difficult just like in Saigon. . . . My mother, from the time of the fall of Saigon on, when the economy was difficult, sold rice at the market. As for my siblings and I, while going to school we weaved baskets for exports. It was during the time of government subsidies—if you work, then you have food. Therefore, it was determined for each family the number of baskets that they had to produce each month in order to be supplied with an amount of rice. I don't remember exactly. For my family, each month we were able to receive two to three bags of rice. Each day, returning home from school, my siblings and I would weave the baskets and give them to the government. We were paid money which was used to buy the government's rice. It cost about 50 cents. If we didn't weave, then buying the rice from the market would cost us $2.50.

Her family had no option; they could not have afforded to pay $2.50 for the food. For Thanh Ha's husband, the political and economic aftermath of the war contributed to the death of one of his siblings, as Thanh Ha rued:

> In my husband's family there are six children. One died after the fall of Saigon—at about four or five years old. . . . A general illness, but during that time, just after the fall of Saigon, there was no medicine, and his family had hardships. His family was busy trying to

make a living; they did not have time to care for him. . . . After the fall of Saigon, one couldn't make a living. . . . After the fall of Saigon, the family went to Ca Mau to live. There they made a living by catching crabs and snails; that's what he told me. His mother sold half-hatched eggs, all kinds of things to earn a living. Often, they did not make money.

One of the ways that wars take a toll across generations is children more frequently must be pulled out of school to meet essential survival needs. As a result of the dramatically increased caregiving and economic demands and diminished sources of support during crises, many parents have no choice but to rely on their young children to help—either to earn enough money to get by or to care for the youngest and sickest in the family. The repercussions continue for generations.

Vo Thi Ai Van had to drop out of school because of the economic crisis that followed the war in Vietnam. Ai Van's mother was working as a street sweeper and raising her and her sisters alone. Her earnings were far too meager to feed her daughters and keep them in school:

> I was born in 1971. As you know, in 1975 Vietnam was liberated and the following years were very hard times—no food; lack of food; staple food was a mixture of rice and sweet potatoes. . . . Mom said, "I could bring you up in that moment only," and she gave us the same job. We had no choice because we are limited in education. We were not skilled people. I started to work first, to have a stable salary, second to help my mom. . . . My sisters helped with plowing, growing rice. But that work did not give you high income. Then my mom applied for us to sweep streets. It was easy to apply for this job in the 1970s and 1980s. At that time you could get a job though you had only finished third or fourth grades.

Ai Van needed the job if she and her sisters were going to eat, but taking that job forced her to leave school at a very young age and, in turn, condemned her to having severely restricted work choices for the rest of her life. As a result, Ai Van would feel the economic and personal reverberations of the aftermath of the war for the rest of her life. Unable to compete for different jobs as she grew up because of her limited education, Ai Van remained a street sweeper. Street sweeping was not an easy way to make a living and raise children, either for Ai Van's mother or, in turn, for Ai Van. When the government switched her job to a night one, Ai Van had little choice but to work nights while trying to raise her son. She explained:

> From 1997, all workers shifted to working at night, because this is
> a state company and the government just issued an order to sweep
> the streets at night to avoid dust. . . . I start to work at 4:00 p.m.
> and come home at 2:00 a.m. . . . No more time to spend with
> my child. During the day, if I have someone at home to help, I
> can sleep from 4:00 a.m. until 8:00 to 9:00 a.m. If nobody's at
> home, I would have to get up early to take my son to school. With-
> out any help, it is more difficult without anybody to manage the
> child.

Had Ai Van had the chance to finish school herself, she might have gotten a better job. Any job which did not require her to work from four in the afternoon through the evening and into the night would have allowed her to spend more time raising her son.

CAREGIVING AFFECTED FOR THE LONG TERM

After the war in Vietnam, millions of families had higher caregiving burdens. Adults were caring for family members who had been wounded in the war, those who had become physically disabled, and those for whom the trauma had left an indelible mark on their mental health—all in addition to caring for their own children. While millions of adults had more caregiving responsibilities, most had less support available to them in the aftermath of the war than they had in the years which led up to the war. As a result of the high fraction of the population that had been killed, some parents were raising children without grandparents, who had traditionally been able to help; others had lost husbands and wives, aunts, uncles, brothers, sisters, and other extended-family members.

Duong Thi Y Lan's childhood was forever changed when she found out her mother had brain cancer seventeen years after the end of the war. While there is no way to know for sure what causes an individual case of cancer, it is clear that for the population as a whole, exposure to toxic chemicals during the war led to devastating increases in cancer rates and birth defects for the next two generations. In Vietnam, carcinogens were still found in the soil in high doses twenty-five years after chemical defoliants had blanketed the south during the war. Regardless of what caused the cancer that Y Lan's mother faced, there was no question that the economic and political aftermath of the war contributed to the devastating impact the disease had on Y Lan's life chances.

Before her mother developed cancer, Y Lan began, "We relied more on Mother emotionally; we seldom depended on my dad. When we were sick or something, it was only my mom who cared for us. She would ask what we wanted to eat, or how tired we felt inside, and she would care for everything." But when Y Lan's mother was diagnosed with cancer, Y Lan had to quit school. She became responsible for both raising her younger brother and caring for her dying mother:

> At the time, I went to school. But when [my mother] got sick, there was only me. My youngest brother was only seven years old then, so I had to stop going to school immediately. I stayed home to care for my mother because my father had to go to work.

All of Y Lan's family members who could work needed to do so, since the economy had been destroyed to such a point that millions were left in hunger. At home, Y Lan was very much on her own. When Y Lan was sixteen, her mother's cancer led to a severe stroke and, in its wake, a coma. Y Lan mourned:

> Right at that time, the doctor informed me that she required an emergency operation. Since then, she was unconscious, even after the operation. She did not know anything. She simply lay motionless and was supported by tubes providing food. In general, in the morning I got up and washed the clothes for my mom because she had been lying in the same place and went to the bathroom there. Then I would feed her every meal with that food [through a tube]. Apart from that, I also mixed in milk for her, to give her more nutrition, with medication. . . . We were no longer in the hospital then. At that time, after lying for too long, my mother suffered from rashes, so I had to care for everything. I was not used to it at first because I was still very small. I made mistakes. . . . I was tiny and my mom was huge. Each time I tried to lift her up, it was very hard. It was very hard to move her from one place to another. Caring for Mother at that time, she was very weak. Every now and then, she would scream. Each time she screamed, I was afraid that she would die. I was so

afraid. . . . The most difficult thing at that time was the fact that I
was all by myself at home. . . . Each time there was something like
an emergency, I did not know who to call. I only ran over to the
neighbors and asked them to help, that's all—until when [my
mother] really breathed out and passed away. It was in the empty
house with only me around. That time, I was very afraid. I ran over
to the neighbors, asked them to call a pedicab to bring her to see if
she could still somehow function, to save her. When reaching the
hospital, the doctors said, "She has really died." At that time, I felt
lost and panicked. I could not think that only in the morning [my
mother was alive and] I was still caring for her.

While postwar Vietnam's national economy was plummeting, Y Lan's family
was depleting the limited financial resources they had been able to save, as Y
Lan regretted:

[My mother] had already made plans for us. . . . Though we were
small, she did put an amount of money in the bank to give us when
we grew up. But when she was ill, we had to take all the money to
care for her. In general, she had already made plans for our future.
But then she got ill, and we were forced to care for everything. So
after she died, our lives were broken in many ways.

Y Lan's family could no more escape the war's political fallout than they could
its health or economic fallout. Y Lan told us:

Initially, it was possible to care for her. After a while, what we had in
the home started to be gone. On the day of her funeral, it was necessary to sell some housewares to pay, because the illness had been prolonged so long. With many expenses by the time she died, there was
nothing left in the house. . . . After she died, my father's needs
were complicated in many ways. About two months after she died,
my dad was imprisoned in a reeducation camp. . . . The government took the house away. From then on, we, brothers and sister,
were separated. My big brother lived with an uncle. I went down to
an aunt. Only my youngest brother lived with the stepmother. . . .
I did not have time to study, only to help the aunt to make [artificial]
flowers to live on . . . and wait until my dad came home.

Care needs skyrocketed in Vietnam because of the war. At the same time, earning a living while providing care for family members became immeasurably harder. The social support which was available declined not only because of deaths, but also because of the large number of families who were displaced or relocated after the war. Moreover, economically in tatters, like other countries after a war, the Vietnamese government was in less of a position to provide families with social supports than it had been before. The desperate economic struggles that many Vietnamese families faced after the war resulted in parents having to pull children out of school. Lacking any chance to finish school, those children faced few job choices when they grew up and became parents themselves and, as a result, ended up with particularly bad working conditions when it came to balancing work and caring for their own children.

Duong Le Thu's husband, Vinh, was injured during the war. Vinh had the misfortune of not only being injured while in the military but also being a veteran of the side that lost the war. As a disabled veteran from the wrong side, he had less access to medical services in the immediate aftermath of the war. A quarter-century later, he still had a bullet lodged in his back. The effects of Vinh's injury reverberated throughout Thu's life. She noted: "There was a long, long time when he was sick. So it took a toll on us. A lot of expenses. That time was pretty difficult. . . . Whatever money and savings we did have were all spent toward caring for the injury."

Thu tried to balance caring for her husband, raising their two sons, and earning enough to meet her husband's health needs and her family's necessities:

> Right now, I'm the only one in the family who can work. The most
> important matter is for [our youngest son] to go to school. The hope
> is that I can continue working for at least a few more years. . . . To
> be honest, with my salary, it is very difficult to live in this city.

The fatigue Thu experienced after working and caring for her disabled husband limited the support she could give her younger son. "Teaching my child, I'm too tired. There's the economic part of it, and then there's the influence of my work. I'm so exhausted that I can't make it a reality." Her younger son's grades had begun to drop, but Thu had neither spare time nor spare resources to try to address the problem. Her older son had recently died in an automobile accident and her widowed daughter-in-law found out she had throat cancer, so she was coming to Thu's house for care.

Deeply depressed, Vinh could not work or fully care for other family members. In addition to the readily apparent physical scars of war, psychological wounds are common in postwar periods.[48] Civilian war refugees as well as combatants have high rates of posttraumatic stress disorder and depression.[49] Nonrefugee civilians who experience war or large-scale violence also have high rates of posttraumatic stress disorder.[50] Children are particularly vulnerable to psychological trauma with haunting long-term effects.[51] In speaking about her injured husband, Vinh, Dong Le Thu told us, "His spirit has declined a great deal, which then creates a personality that's not normal." Vinh's level of mental and physical disability was common. In addition to the 3 million Vietnamese civilian and military deaths between 1965 and 1975, there were 360,000 to 500,000 physically disabled, including 83,000 amputees in South Vietnam alone.[52] Few resources were available in the postwar period to rehabilitate the wounded and injured. Families like Thu's were left to endure the problems alone with little assistance.

The high death toll decimated the functioning of extended families. Families like Kim's felt the profound impact for generations. Quach Thi Kim lost family members through both death and divisions during the war. As a result, as she began to raise her own daughter a quarter-century later, she explained:

> I only have my mother. My dad passed away. . . . He died around 1970 or 1971. . . . It was during the wartime. He was sacrificed. . . . There were six siblings. Two older sisters died. . . . One died due to sickness. The other was killed by a bullet. . . . I was too little then—just a few months old.

Kim had lived in My Tho in the Mekong River delta, where the fighting had been fierce and prolonged. Kim was left with only one sister who could help her in caring for Hoa, her daughter: "Friends? Family? No one has helped me, because I don't have a lot of family. I only have that sister to help me." When Kim's sister was able to help, Hoa flourished, but because there was no affordable decent childcare and no family when Kim's sister needed to return to the countryside, Hoa began to do poorly. Hoa grew thinner and sicker as she was fed on scraps off the floor.

Finding Support in the Midst of Crisis and Afterward

Our interviews in Botswana at the height of the AIDS pandemic, in Honduras in the aftermath of Hurricane Mitch, and in Vietnam decades after the end of the war document how catastrophes place long-term strains on families' ability to survive economically while caring for children. At the same time, these interviews reinforced how critical it is for parents to continue working for economic survival and caring for children throughout tumultuous times. The families' experiences powerfully refuted any misconceptions that work and family matter less in times of crises. Nevertheless, the question remains: Can anything of value be done for working families in the midst of a calamity? There are powerful examples of how great a difference the right services can make for children and their working parents and guardians in catastrophic times.

Working and Raising Children in the Midst of Crisis: The Case of AIDS

In the case of AIDS, there has been an enormous amount of debate surrounding the question: Should the world focus on prevention or treatment? The debate is wasteful because the answer should be obvious: Both are urgently required. There is no doubt that the 42 million people who have been infected with HIV[53] would far prefer to never have been infected. They would have chosen an effective prevention program—one that completely eliminated all of their suffering—over any treatment program. Unarguably, if we are to prevent some of the estimated 100 million infections that may occur by the year 2010,[54] we will need vastly improved prevention programs. Yet, it is equally impossible to deny the importance of treatment when 42 million people are currently infected and effective medications are available. Without treatment in place, a whole generation in more than sixteen countries in Africa will be more than decimated. While we think of the term *decimation* as meaning "complete devastation," it literally means "one in ten dying." In the absence of adequate treatment, the numbers felled by the epidemic will far surpass the worst historical comparisons, including the plague in medieval Europe.

Since the late 1980s, I've worked on a wide range of efforts both to prevent the spread and to speed the treatment of HIV in poor countries. While I have been in many settings where people have debated prevention and treatment, in no cases have I found that the two approaches to reducing suffering had to be in conflict. Quite the contrary, prevention and treatment are often naturally complementary. I've worked with programs that provide prophylactic drugs to mothers to prevent the transmission of HIV infection to their newborns; when women know that prevention is available for their children, they are more likely to come in and receive treatment themselves. Tuberculosis is one of the leading killers of adults with HIV/AIDS in Africa. Treating tuberculosis infection not only can significantly increase the survival of men and women but can help prevent the spread of the disease to their families and friends.

Yet, disconcertingly absent from both the debates about prevention and treatment and the calls for action have been any substantial discussion about who will care for the 40 million people who are already infected, who will care for the children left behind by those who have died, and how they will manage to survive while providing that care. The ability of tens of millions of adults to provide this care at the same time as working is essential to the survival of their families, communities, and countries.

ADAPTING WORKPLACES

While people with AIDS are frequently receiving heroic care from family members, their workplaces have done little to adapt. At forty-two years old, Neo Gobopilwe was raising three children, including a daughter who had frequent seizures, while also providing daily care for her brother, who was growing progressively sicker with AIDS. She explained:

> [My brother] was sick for about two and a half years, so every day for two and a half years I went to my mother's house after work. . . . During the day, my mom was there looking after him. After work, until around nine o'clock, I'd be there. . . . I told [my employers] what was happening, but they said that I couldn't have a leave to just go and look after him. They'd say, "One day he's going to die. Where are you going to get the money to bury him? You should keep working. After working hours, you can go and help your mom at home. Tomorrow you should come back to work."

But no matter how much Neo did, she felt guilty about not doing more. "Working long hours made it difficult for me to look after him because I was always at work," she told us. At the same time that she grieved not being able to spend more time with her dying brother, the time she was dedicating to him threatened her work. "It made my work decline," she explained, "because I was always thinking, 'What am I going to do for my children? What am I going to do for my brother's children?' I was always thinking about that."

As her brother progressed into end-stage AIDS, his care grew more difficult, as Neo described:

He couldn't do anything for himself. He couldn't sit up. He couldn't eat. We had to take him to the toilet, put him in the bath, bathe him, put on his clothes, and so on. . . . He was always bleeding through his nose. The week before he died, he had a bloody nose from Monday to Friday.

After her brother died, Neo cared for his two- and five-year-old daughters. What little money she earned as a cleaner was divided to buy food and clothing for her children and her brother's. She didn't have enough money left over to pay someone to come and look after her own children after school. Consequently, her daughter had repeatedly been alone when she lost consciousness from seizures.

While adults in Botswana and other HIV-affected countries face an urgent need to be able to continue to work while providing essential care, few workplaces have developed policies to address these issues. Even in Botswana, which has been among the leading nations in publicly addressing HIV, only 25 percent of adults we interviewed reported that their workplaces had HIV policies. Among these, only 8 percent had any workplace policies which addressed the role of HIV caregivers (see figure 6-9). Many of their workplaces were slow to respond, if they responded at all.

Worldwide, among the first family policies that many workplaces adopted were ones that addressed the birth and care of a newborn, such as maternity and paternity leave. Yet, even in the absence of serious illnesses, the care of an infant represents only a small portion of a family's responsibilities. Children need care throughout preschool, elementary school, and adolescence. Adults whose health is threatened likewise need care from their family members. While adult care needs affect families on a routine basis around the world, the AIDS pandemic has made adult care needs particularly urgent throughout sub-Saharan Africa. They raise fundamental questions for workplaces that desperately need answers: How can adults get the time they need to care for sick family members at the same time as working? How can men and women accept additional caregiving responsibilities, such as

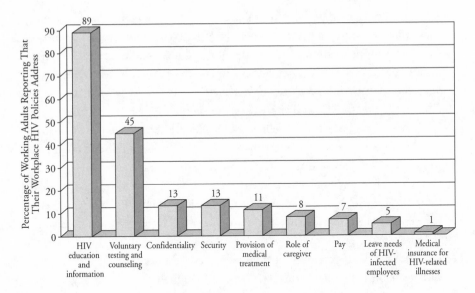

Figure 6-9
Areas Covered by Workplace HIV Policies.
Note: Data from Project on Global Working Families' survey of HIV and family health in Botswana. Analyses in the above figure are based on working adults who report that their workplaces have policies with respect to HIV issues.

raising orphans—and carry these responsibilities out well—at the same time as working?

Workplaces will need to adapt. Adults may need leave at the adoption of newly orphaned children as well as at the birth of their own children. Adults may need leave from or flexibility at work to care for infected family members, as well as to care for their own health. New work hours and schedules that allow adults to keep their jobs while balancing substantial caregiving responsibilities related to illness may need to be developed. All of these changes are readily realizable if we make the commitment. If we don't, not addressing the critical care needs of millions will tear HIV-affected communities apart.

CARING FOR CHILDREN

The Keletso counseling center takes a 360-degree approach to meeting the needs of those affected by HIV/AIDS. Their services range from educational outreach regarding prevention to pretest counseling, testing for HIV/AIDS, social support for those who are infected, and bereavement counseling for those who lose family members. When the Keletso counseling center opened, there were no plans for a childcare center or an after-school center, but the great need for such services rapidly became apparent. There were parents who were too gravely ill with AIDS to adequately care for their own children. There were orphans with nowhere to go during the day.

In 1998, the Keletso counseling center added a daycare center, Bana ba Keletso, to their range of services. Bana ba Keletso offers a full-day program to preschool children and after-school care for primary- and secondary-school children. The preschool children are cared for by nine dedicated adults known to the children as "center moms." For older siblings in larger families, the center plays a particularly important role. Many of these children not only lacked adequate adult care themselves, but had to fill the role of caregiver for their younger siblings before they attended the center. In addition to caring for orphaned and other HIV-affected children during the day, every week the center moms visit the homes in which the children live to offer counseling and to address additional needs that any HIV-infected family members may have. In the afternoons, orphans who have graduated from the program have begun to return to help the primary- and secondary-school children with their homework.

Many of the children are living with family members who are nearly destitute after having lost the income of adults who became sick, having to cover their medical costs, transportation, and all-too-often funeral expenses on exhausted incomes. In addition to providing care for the orphaned and HIV-affected children, the center helps to ensure that the family members caring for them get food baskets. Between the food the children receive at the childcare program and the food baskets the families receive from the government, the nutritional status of the children attending Bana ba Keletso has improved markedly.

In addition to addressing basic nutritional and care needs, Keletso provides counseling, health, and educational support to the children and their families as they deal with the devastation of the epidemic. Keletso offers camps, sponsored by UNICEF, that mix games with counseling during the school holidays. While the routine and holiday counseling is staffed primarily by laypeople, most have undergone special training on trauma and bereavement.

The Keletso center faced many of the challenges that any program would in the context of a crisis where the need rapidly outstrips the services available. It needed more staff, staff training, space, and secure finances. But it put together a remarkably successful model—a model that provided the most relevant types of help and support to all members of an HIV-affected family— and its organizers recognized that ensuring decent daily care and opportunities for education was essential to orphaned and HIV-affected children.

Men and women in extended families can provide the needed care for HIV-affected adults and children while working, but to provide that care, they will need help. Parents will need childcare for their own children while they have to travel to other towns to care for sick extended family members. They will need childcare available during the day for orphans that they foster. Those who are ill will need nursing care when immediate family members have to continue to work in order to eke out enough of an income to pay for food.

There are many ways to markedly reduce the devastating impact of HIV. Essential steps include ensuring that adequate health care *and childcare* are available to all, regardless of income; that people are allowed to work while infected and physically able and while caring for those who are infected; and that support is available for those unable to work.

Care in the Wake of Disaster: After the Hurricane

In Honduras, I visited a childcare center that was built at a Red Cross center serving families who had been left homeless in the wake of the hurricane and the subsequent mudslides. Erica Rosa de Sanchez, a clinical psychologist, ran the childcare center, which was staffed by a teacher, a psychologist, a nutritionist, and six youths who served as direct childcare providers. The center served children aged six months to five years from 7:30 a.m. until 3:30 p.m. Insufficient funds meant the center could not stay open later in the day, and as a result, children were often picked up before their parents returned home from work by brothers and sisters, cousins, or other young family members. In spite of this limitation, the center provided critical services to young children who otherwise would have been forced to spend the entire day home alone or in the care of older siblings who had been pulled out of school.

The center director introduced us to toddlers who had arrived with significant psychomotor retardation but had been rehabilitated through the general exercises they received in childcare. She spoke of the children whose development had lagged behind for lack of attention from parents who, at best, had been able to spend time with their children while they worked long hours in the informal sector and, at worst, had to leave children home alone. Other children arrived at the center malnourished.

Even children who were neither malnourished nor affected by gross developmental problems lagged behind in language and fine motor skills when they arrived at the center. Toddlers and preschool children who had been cared for by school-age children had developed large motor skills from running around after each other and running to safety. But their fine motor skills were nearly nonexistent. They had not had the chance to hold pencils and crayons or to cut and glue paper. Furthermore, few people had talked to them, and their language skills were poorly developed. It was clear that they lagged behind in all of the areas important for school. The opportunity they got to catch up at the childcare center would make the difference between having a chance to stay on track once they got to primary school or not.

Emotionally, many of the children had been severely traumatized by the destruction of their homes in the hurricane and mudslides, as well as by their living conditions during the aftermath. Erica, the center director, described how angry the children had been when they first came to the daycare center—angry about all they had lived through during the hurricane and after. When she took us around the single, large warehouse room that served as the childcare center, she explained why the walls were mostly bare. When the staff put up posters, the children tore them down. When the staff put up hammocks, some of the children ripped them apart. The same occurred with the beds in which children had the option to sleep at nap times. The children had been around a great deal of violence, including armed adolescents in the *albergues*, or shelters. One twelve-year-old girl had recently been found knifed to death, and many children who were left home alone had been raped.

It was in this context that the children's experience at the center was particularly remarkable. The children sat in a circle and sang together. Smiling and giggling, they then moved to small tables where they did artwork. Clearly, they were well nourished and relaxed, and they felt safe and happy to be there. Parents needed to pay only one lempira (seven U.S. cents) per child per day, and the only other requirements were that they bring their child on time and that the child be bathed. The main problem with the childcare center was that there were far fewer spaces than needed; it was filled beyond capacity. Fifty-eight children were actively attending, but the center had capacity for only forty.

At the end of the day, I spoke with family members picking up young children. Samantha Calderon picked up her niece and explained how much the safety of the childcare center meant to her. She described her fears after another child, left home alone, had been hit by a car while wandering around. Olivia Saenz, who worked washing clothes in various people's houses, went right to the point about what she thought the childcare center provided for her three-year-old daughter. She explained that before a space in the center had become available, her children had to be home alone. Since attending the center, she remarked, her daughter had become *más gorda, más vívida*—fatter, livelier. This parent and others clearly attested to the center's impact on their children's health, nutrition, and well-being.

From improving children's nutrition and physical health to their mental health and development, the center demonstrated what an enormous difference quality childcare services can make in the immediate aftermath of a disaster. Combined with temporary housing for families and physical and mental-health services for adults, the center was part of a well-integrated program which made it possible for families to have a chance at getting back on their feet. That was the good news. The bad news was that the center was not going to be funded for many more months after our visit, in spite of its demonstrated effectiveness. Without childcare, parents working to build new homes for their children and themselves were going to be forced to choose between leaving their children home alone at a time when violence was becoming increasingly common and with no one to look after their health and development—and keeping a job so they had a chance of pulling themselves out of homelessness.

What Fades Away in Importance and What Stands Out More Starkly

In short, children's and parents' basic needs are put in jeopardy not only during epidemics, wars, and other disasters, but for years afterward. In Botswana, caregiving burdens rose exponentially with the AIDS epidemic. In Honduras and Vietnam, the reverberations from natural and humanmade disasters continued to rock families years after the initial crises had occurred. Parents' challenge—being able to earn enough to survive at the same time as caring for their children and other dependent family members—is multiplied many times by the sequelae. These include the increased health needs of children; the increased injuries, illnesses, and disabilities of adults; the heightened economic needs in postcrisis rebuilding periods; and the dramatically diminished availability of extended family to help.

There are countless things that become less important in the wake of natural disasters, like epidemics and hurricanes, and humanmade disasters, like war, including what blue jeans to buy, the local gossip, and whose team won the soccer game. But while the importance of many things fades into the background, the urgent demand of core needs moves starkly to the foreground. Central among these, individuals by necessity focus on their own survival and the survival of those they love and those for whom they feel responsible.

It is because of this that the need for opportunities to find work, keep a job, earn an income that is sufficient to survive and rebuild essentials like roofs over one's family's heads, care for children, and care for vulnerable family members comes to the forefront. Yet, inevitably, the same tragedies which focus families on struggling to meet essential needs make meeting those needs far more difficult.

While humankind has little power to prevent hurricanes, tornadoes, earthquakes, and the like, people do have the potential to greatly limit the impact these disasters have. To do this, we will have to change disaster relief and postwar reconstruction efforts so that they can begin to address the many ways in which these tragedies have made it barely possible for some, and impossible for others, to work, economically survive, care for their children, and rebuild.

7

Addressing
the Burgeoning Problems

Unattended Global Transformations
and Their Unintended Consequences

The same demographic transformations that have brought work and family issues into the spotlight in North America and Europe are occurring globally. Throughout human history, both mothers and fathers, in addition to rearing children, have been engaged in productive activity. In recent history, what has markedly changed is not the fact that fathers and mothers work at multiple tasks but the location and nature of that work. The transformations that occurred in North America and Europe between the mid-1800s and the end of the 1900s, moving men's and women's work away from home and farm into a wage and salary labor force distant from childrearing, have occurred and are continuing to take place worldwide. The twin trends of urbanization and rising paid labor force participation occurring in most of the world's developing regions mean that fewer adults are near their children or other family members during the workday. Even in rural areas, the transformation of the agricultural economy is pulling the spheres of work and home apart and dramatically changing how children and other family members are cared for.

As a result of these demographic and labor force changes, hundreds of millions of working families in low-income countries are now facing work-family challenges similar in nature to those faced by families in high-income countries, but with two important differences: They are doing so with caregiving burdens that are significantly higher and with far fewer resources. Age dependency ratios—the ratio of children and elderly to working-age adults—tend to be from 50 percent to 100 percent higher in the developing world than they are in industrialized countries.[1] In addition, illness rates for both common and serious diseases are higher in low-income countries, further adding to the caring responsibilities of working adults. At the same time, working adults in these nations have fewer resources to help them meet family needs. Not only are family incomes far lower, but governments in the developing world invest less in social services than do those in Europe and North America, not just in absolute dollars but also as a percentage of total public expenditures, in part due to debt burdens.[2]

On their own, the growth of cities and the movement of mothers and fathers from farms into factories and burgeoning service-sector jobs need not have led to two-year-olds being left home alone nor to seven-year-olds being pulled out of school to care for them. Demographic and labor force changes alone did not lead to children facing poorer health conditions, having less of a chance at an education, or families having little or no way to exit poverty. In fact, the success stories of countries that were able to respond to the changes in work and family life make mincemeat of these myths.

A great rift has occurred between the experience of families in countries that adapted to the demographic and labor force transformations and the experiences of men, women, and children in those countries that failed to adapt. Countries which lagged behind in ensuring decent working conditions for families might have been able to catch up had it not been for the corrosive effects of a tremendously costly version of "free" trade.

At the same time as these marked shifts were taking place for working families around the world, the number of large multinational corporations and their influence over the rules of trade and over limits on governments to ensure decent working conditions was increasing. Corporations had recognized that it was in their financial self-interest to be able to produce goods in any country without being bound by tariffs or labor rules. While there was no strong evidence that most individual workers, their families, or their communities would gain from companies being free to move jobs to the location with the least costs (where wages and benefits were lowest and safeguards for workers were fewest), it was quite clear that influential corporations and their stockholders stood a great deal to gain economically. The era of so-called free trade was born, an era of global rules which protected the flow of wealth but offered no protections to the individuals who labor, their children, and their communities. Whatever legitimate questions existed at the outset, the consequences of the era of free trade have become increasingly clear.

There is now an unprecedented level of global competition for jobs—and global movement of jobs. First, the jobs began to leave high-income countries. The greatest job loss from the United States to other countries began with the manufacturing sector: The percentage of the U.S. workforce in this sector was cut in half between the mid-1970s and the early twenty-first century. However, the job loss is now widespread in the United States and includes jobs in the service sector, as well as low-skilled entry-level and high-skilled professional jobs. One estimate is that by 2015, 3.3 million American white-collar service sector jobs will have been lost overseas.[3]

A wide range of professional jobs is being lost by other high-income Organization for Economic Cooperation and Development (OECD) countries as well.[4] These jobs range from computer programmers to radiologists and pathologists.[5] But jobs are not only being lost now from Europe, the United States, Canada, and similar economies, jobs are also being lost from middle-income countries. While Mexico at first benefited from the North American Free Trade Agreement (NAFTA) in terms of job growth, many of those jobs have since gone to China and other nations with even lower wages and fewer job protections.[6]

If it were only about job loss, it could be readily argued that one nation's job loss is another's job gain. The problem is that the movement of jobs has spurred a downward spiral in working conditions. Employers have used the threat of relocating jobs to different countries as a basis for exacting lower wages and worse working conditions.[7] Half of the employers in a series of union-organizing drives used threats of plant movement and plant closings to oppose unionization.[8] This tactic results in worse job conditions and lower wages. In call centers in Great Britain, for example, the level of intensity of the work and productivity expectations have risen markedly. Flexibility and time off have declined substantially in order to compete with lower-wage countries. As globalization pressures have led service centers to require those working to reduce average call times to two minutes, an employee described not having time for lunch or going to the bathroom and feeling "out of control."9 Facing far worse working conditions from the start, the factory workers we interviewed in Honduras were not losing their chance to eat or go to the bathroom, they were losing their chance to spend any time at home. One factory worker we interviewed, who worked seven days a week, fifteen-hour and longer shifts, explained that when she and her coworkers asked to have any days off, they were told that the factory would close and move to China.

Around the world, families are increasingly living on the edge. Employed adults face working conditions that make it increasingly difficult or impossible to care for themselves and their families' health and well-being. Parents are being forced to make untenable choices between caring for their children adequately and earning the income they need for their families to survive and have a chance at thriving. This book has provided evidence that these experiences are devastatingly common, rather than remarkable for their rarity.

What are the costs to children and their families? There are many; a few will be highlighted here. Children are being left on their own, they are being left in the "care" of older children in the family, and in poor-quality care on a daily basis. The first situation leaves children to face potentially deadly, more-immediate consequences, and the latter two have long-term but equally devastating consequences—both for the care provider when that person is only a child and for the recipient.

Children on Their Own Too Young

As a result of the failure to adapt workplaces and societies adequately to the marked transitions, children in a wide range of countries are increasingly being left in dangerous conditions: left alone at too young an age, left unsupervised with young siblings, brought to unsafe work settings, and left without parental care when sick. No parents want to leave their preschool children home alone. Parents take that course of action only when they have no other choice. Some children are locked in one-room shacks or apartments for their own "safety"—or at least to lower their risk of injury compared to wandering outside alone—while others are brought to unsafe workplaces. Others are being left with very young brothers and sisters. It is euphemistic to say that these children are being "raised by" other children. It is equally misleading for anyone to say they are "in the care of their older sister" or, less commonly, "brother." Seven-year-olds simply cannot raise three-year-olds on their own, nor can four-year-olds adequately care for two-year-old twins. These trends are new and on the rise. While it has long been true that one could visit many parts of the world and see five-year-old children carrying swaddled infants on their backs, in the past, parents and extended-family members were nearby, working on a plot of land or cooking food at home. Now, this is far less commonly the case.

While the majority of families found some way to provide adult care for their children—even if it meant bringing their children to unsafe workplaces—a significant minority were forced to leave their children home alone or in the care of an unpaid child. Thirty-six percent of the families we interviewed had left a young child home alone. Thirty-nine percent had left a sick child home alone or had to send a child to school or day care sick, and 23 percent took children to work, often under unsafe conditions. Twenty-seven percent had left a child in the care of a paid or unpaid child.

It is not random which children suffer the devastating and sometimes deadly consequences of being left alone at very young ages. The thousands of families we have interviewed make several facts disturbingly clear about which children pay the highest price for the world's neglect of the enormous obstacles facing working families. The poorer a family is, the more likely the children are to be left alone or in the care of other children. When parents feel that they risk losing pay or a job which their family needs to stay out of poverty, they are more likely to have to leave a child home alone. When families are headed by a single parent, they are more likely to be poor and without social supports and more often are forced to leave their children to manage on their own. Finally, when families face additional risks and burdens—from health problems to wars to natural disasters—they are more likely to land in extreme poverty, and their children are more likely to be left facing these additional burdens alone.

In every country with limited access to formal childcare, children who are poor are more likely to be left home alone than children who are not poor. In Botswana, 56 percent of parents we interviewed who were living in poverty had been forced to leave their children home alone compared to 45 percent of parents who were not living in poverty. In Mexico, 40 percent of parents living in poverty had needed to leave their children home alone compared to 31 percent of parents not living in poverty. The gap was substantially narrowed where parents had the greatest access to formal childcare. The parallel numbers for Vietnamese parents leaving children home alone were 20 percent versus 19 percent.

When parents know that the price of caring for their children may be the loss of pay or a job which they cannot afford to forgo, they are often forced to leave a child home alone in grossly inadequate care. Sixty-one percent of parents who had lost a job or a promotion or who had difficulty retaining a job because of caring for a sick child ended up leaving their children home alone on their own or with another child. Sixty-six percent of parents who had experienced difficulties at work because of other caregiving responsibilities ended up having to leave a child home alone or with another child.

When parents had to care for family members' health problems—whether as a consequence of routine health needs, health problems linked to poverty, or those brought about by war or natural disasters—they were at greater risk of having to leave a child home alone. Parents of children five and under who had multiple caregiving responsibilities, such as those who had to care for a sick spouse or other sick family member, were twice as likely to leave children home alone as were parents caring for children only.

When parents have few social supports, because they are single with little extended family nearby, they either need to take leave from work to care for their children themselves or be able to rely on paid childcare providers. If they can do neither, they find themselves leaving their children without care. Nearly 78 percent of parents who were single with no other caregivers in the household had to leave children alone, compared to 30 percent of parents who had a spouse, partner, or other caregiver to help in the household.

Daily Erosion of Children's Health and Development

When young children are left home alone or in substandard care, the potential for tragedy is real. In half the families we interviewed in Botswana and Mexico and more than a third of the families we interviewed in Vietnam, children suffered accidents or emergencies while their parents were at work. In one family we interviewed, children had been trapped in a hovel that was burning down, while in another, a preschooler fell from an escarpment, resulting in a serious head injury. In still other families, young children had become victims of violence. But there is another, slower, but equally devastating type of tragedy that is transforming the lives of tens of millions of preschool children. Unable to find or afford decent care, needing to work and only finding jobs under the worst conditions, these parents are forced to leave their preschool children in care which jeopardizes their health and development as well as their safety. The quality of the care they receive is so poor that with each day that passes their health and development slowly deteriorate, and their life chances decline further.

A substantial number of parents had to bring their children to work regularly. This included 28 percent of the poor, 26 percent of those with middle-school education or less, and 49 percent of parents working in the informal sector. There should be no romanticizing what it meant to these children's lives to be brought to work regularly. One need only remember the experiences that parents in the informal sector shared with us of having to cook with infants near flames, sell goods in crowded marketplaces on busy streets where children repeatedly witnessed accidental injuries and death, or having to tie their children up during the day to avoid injury. The lack of decent options of care for their children, amid a desperate need for an income to survive, is dangerously eroding the health, education, and development of children and the welfare of families.

In one-third of the families in Botswana, one-quarter of the families in Vietnam, and one-fifth of the families in Mexico, the conflict between parents' working conditions had additional negative impacts on children's health, such as when parents were unable to get children to well-child checkups or were unable to stay with them when they were sick. The number of parents losing pay or job promotions or having difficulty keeping their jobs because of the need to care for sick children was large: 62 percent of parents faced these economic penalties in Vietnam, 48 percent in Mexico, and 28 percent in Botswana. Tragically, those who have the greatest need are affected most severely: 67 percent of parents with income under $10 a day faced a choice of either losing pay because of their need to care for sick children or having to leave sick children home alone. Seventy-six percent of parents of children with chronic conditions had difficulty at work or had lost pay, jobs, or promotions because of caring for them. Globally, the lack of support for working families not only dramatically affects the world's children, but it also exacerbates gender and income inequalities. Forty-nine percent of women in our study had lost pay or job promotions or had difficulty retaining jobs because of the need to care for sick children compared to 28 percent of men.

Just as their health is affected, so too are the development and education of children affected by working and social conditions. We found that too often the gap in care available to infants and toddlers was met by parents— who had little other choice—pulling their young daughters out of school and requiring them to provide care for their preschool siblings. When this occurred, the development and education of both the infants or toddlers and the school-age children were jeopardized. In families that had to leave children on their own, 49 percent had children who had experienced behavioral or developmental difficulties (double the figure of those who were able to send their children to formal childcare). Even when young school-age children got to attend school, the question of who would care for them during nonschool hours remained. The costs to young elementary-school children left alone were high; children's needs do not end when they turn five or start school. Even when they were able to find routine care for their children during the day, work conflicts affected the ability of the majority of parents to become involved in their children's education. Barriers to helping with homework, participating in school events, or other involvement in children's schooling because of work were reported by 51 percent of parents in Vietnam, 66 percent of parents in Mexico, and 82 percent of parents in Botswana. When parents had barriers to becoming involved in their children's education, their children were twice as likely to experience behavioral or academic difficulties in school. The most common reasons for work presenting barriers to parents helping with their children's education were extremely long work hours, lack of paid leave, and lack of any flexibility.

Do we ignore the price that children are paying, or do we do something about it? In the mid-nineteenth century, amid the waves of urbanization and industrialization that had hit Western Europe, Rudolph Virchow wrote in the weekly medical journal *Die Medizinische Reform*, "It is the curse of humanity that it learns to tolerate even the most horrible situations by habituation." The children we learned about in our interviews who had to leave school to care for younger siblings, whose parents' jobs prevented them from spending time together, and who became ill from preventable diseases because their parents were not able to take time off to get them vaccinated never habituated. Virchow's curse will come to pass only if all of us who have a chance to change the lives of children like these and those of more than 900 million other children fail to act.

If children continue to be left home alone at young ages or without adult care and support for their health and education, the lives of too many will continue to be either riddled with acute tragedies or reduced by chronic neglect. But our children do not need to be left in inadequate care. As a global community, we have a choice.

The Myths Feeding Inaction

Myth 1: We Don't Know What Works

In making excuses for our neglect of the world's children, people often claim that no one knows what can be done to help. In fact, there is extensive evidence regarding what would make a difference in the health, development, and education of the hundreds of millions of children growing up in working families.

Our comprehensive review of the evidence base conducted as part of the development of our policy index—the Work, Family, and Equity Index—demonstrates the breadth and depth of our understanding of what would help working caregivers, their children, and their elderly and disabled family members thrive.[10] With respect to the care of children (our first ten items in the index), our knowledge base is particularly deep. We know that providing paid maternity and paternity leave at the birth or adoption of a child is crucial for children and parents. We know that ensuring that children four to five years old have access to high-quality early education will make an enormous difference to their later educational and developmental outcomes. There is no doubt that providing an affordable level of short-term paid leave for parents to meet the health needs of their children would improve children's access to preventive care when they are healthy and to adequate diagnosis and treatment when they are sick.

Other policies and programs which could transform the lives of children and parents are not hard to find. Children need high-quality care during the first three years of life. The care needs not only to be available but affordable and accessible. Parents need to be able to earn a living by working fewer than sweatshop hours so that they have time with their preschool and school-age children. School-age children need to have access to high-quality educational or enrichment programs throughout the day and year. Parents of school-age children need to be able to take leave from work to address critical problems if they arise in school. Parents of school-age children need to be able to work hours that allow them to support their children's education and development when the children are not in school, on evenings and nights, on weekends, and holidays. Disabled children need full access to schools and community activities so that they can interact with their peers and develop fully and access to health supports such as health insurance and developmental assistance to support their ability to contribute and participate into the future, as well as enabling their parents to work. Below are details on just three of the policies and programs included in our index that we know will make a difference: (1) paid parental leave, (2) early childhood care and education, and (3) paid leave for children's health needs.

PAID PARENTAL LEAVE

Paid parental leave provides one example among many where the evidence on what works to support family health is extensive. In a study of more than sixteen countries, providing paid parental leave was shown to lead to significant decreases in child mortality.[11] Providing paid parental leave decreases mortality and improves the chances of healthy development of newborns and infants in a variety of ways. One of the important ways is through increasing the opportunities for working mothers to breast-feed. Breast-feeding has been shown to lower infant mortality between one and a half and five times in both industrialized and developing countries.[12] Infants who are breast-fed have substantially lower rates of gastrointestinal infections,[13] respiratory infections,[14] meningitis,[15] and other infections.[16] Although health benefits of breast-feeding are well documented in all countries, they play a particularly critical role in developing countries, where millions of infants currently die from malnutrition, diarrhea, and other infectious diseases. Yet, despite the importance of breast-feeding, working mothers can face great obstacles to breast-feeding.[17] Work itself does not necessarily make it more difficult for mothers to breast-feed. In fact, under varying conditions, work has been shown to have a positive as well as a negative effect on the frequency with which women breast-feed.[18] When job conditions support women breast-feeding, high percentages of women breast-feed their infants.[19] Two types of benefits have been shown to make the largest difference. The first is the provision of paid parental leave. When mothers receive paid parental leave for the first months of an infant's life, this facilitates their initiating breast-feeding and being able to breast-feed during the period when the infant will need to feed most frequently.[20] As infants mature, the frequency of their feedings decreases, making it more feasible for mothers to return to work while continuing to breast-feed. At this second stage, what is most important is the availability of infant care near the workplace and breaks that allow the mother to breast-feed one to two times during the workday. Breast-feeding is important to women's health as well as to children's health; it leads to declines in the extent of postpartum blood loss[21] and women's rates of later developing ovarian or breast cancer[22] or osteoporosis.[23]

Paid parental leave also provides important benefits to children's emotional development. Newborns require intensive care at a level that few child-care centers are equipped to provide. Moreover, the newborn period has been long documented to be a critical period for the development of attachment between parents and infants and of the emotional bonds that are essential for children's later development.[24]

Paid parental leave plays a critical role in the ability of many families to economically survive. Newborns bring with them new financial costs to a family, and the time of a birth is often the time when families can least afford an unpaid leave. Because of this and because of the importance of parents spending time with newborns, paid parental leave plays a particularly crucial role in the ability of young families in countries around the world to both provide quality care to their infants and to survive economically. Moreover, paid parental leave has long-term economic benefits: In companies and countries where it is provided, mothers are more likely to be able to stay in the workforce and more likely to receive wages equal to those of their peers. When children receive early childhood care and women are able to get their jobs back after taking parental leave, they are significantly more likely to stay employed after a child's birth.[25] In the long run, parental leave policies have been shown to increase family earnings by reducing the wage penalty that mothers otherwise incur[26] (in the absence of paid parental leave policies, women not only lose wages when they take time off to care for infants, but their lifetime earnings trajectory is changed such that they earn less for decades to come than women who have not had children). It is important to note that in many cases there are economic returns to employers as well for providing parental leave. When paid leave is provided, parents are more likely to return to the same job and the same employer, thus reducing the recruitment and retraining costs the employer would otherwise incur.[27]

EARLY CHILDHOOD CARE AND EDUCATION

There is no shortage of evidence demonstrating the importance of early childhood care and education. The research is remarkable in a number of ways. First, the long-term beneficial effects of early childhood education have been demonstrated in a wide range of countries around the world.[28] More than forty years of research in industrialized nations and more than a decade of research in developing and transitioning countries have demonstrated that children who participate in early education programs have higher rates of cognitive development and better educational outcomes.[29] Studies following children during their years in early education programs and subsequently in school have demonstrated that children who receive quality care and early educational opportunities perform substantially better academically, whether the children are being raised in Latin America, Africa, Asia, North America, or Europe.[30] Second, the improved educational outcomes that children experience have been demonstrated in a wide range of areas, including the larger vocabularies and better reading skills of children who participated in early education programs,[31] increased primary-school enrollment,[32] lower grade-repetition rates, higher reading and math achievement scores, and overall better educational outcomes in middle school and beyond.[33] Third, in both industrialized and developing nations, preschool and other early education programs have been shown to make an enormous difference in children's social, emotional, and cognitive development.[34] Positive social and behavioral outcomes have been demonstrated, as well as academic ones, in countries that range from Turkey[35] to India[36] to Chile.[37]

The importance of early childhood care and education to children and youths' long-term outcomes should not come as a surprise, given all that is known about brain development. Brain development during the preschool years, in the first three to five years of life, plays a particularly critical role in long-term outcomes.[38] It is during these first formative years that there is the greatest growth in brain development, which affects everything from sensory development and language skills to neurobehavioral organization and social development.

Similarly to paid parental leave, the availability of quality early childhood care affects parents' work and families' economic survival as well as their children's outcomes. The affordability and availability of childcare has been demonstrated to significantly affect women's opportunity to work in countries ranging from the United States to Mexico, from Colombia to Russia to the Philippines.[39] When parents have access to reliable childcare, the impact is felt by employers as well. Job turnover rates and absentee rates decline,[40] and overall productivity on the job increases.[41]

The availability of short-term leave from work to care for children's health makes a critical difference from infancy to adolescence. In the United States, we found that parents who had short-term paid leave from work were five times as likely to be able to care for their children when they were sick.[42] In the absence of the availability of leave to care for children's health, parents in a wide range of countries reported conflicts between meeting their children's essential health needs and keeping a job. For example, conflicts with work have been found to be a barrier to parents getting their children immunized in countries ranging from Haiti to Indonesia to the United States.[43] The availability of short-term leave makes a difference not only in parents' ability to get preventive health care for their children, like immunizations, but also to care for their children when they are sick with acute and chronic illnesses. The importance of parents being involved in the care of sick children has similarly been demonstrated from the United Kingdom to Canada to the United States to Australia.[44] Sick children recover more rapidly from illnesses and injuries, demonstrate better vital signs, and have fewer symptoms when their parents participate in their care.[45] The presence of parents has been shown to reduce hospital stays by 31 percent.[46] When parents are involved in children's care, children have been shown to recover more rapidly from outpatient procedures as well.[47] Receiving care from their parents is important for children's mental as well as physical health.[48]

While parents having leave from work to address children's health needs is important for all children, it is particularly crucial for children with chronic conditions and disabilities. The United Nations estimated that in 1999, there were already 150 million children who were living with a disability.[49] Of these, an estimated 120 million were living in developing countries in Asia, Africa, and Latin America.[50] While all chronic health conditions affect middle-income and affluent children as well as the poor, the poor face a disproportionate burden of health problems.[51] The majority of working parents can only care for their children's chronic health problems if they are able to get leave from work. Taking leave is untenable for the poor if the financial penalties are too high. Paid leave makes providing that care feasible.[52] It is not surprising that the availability of leave to care for children's health needs makes a particularly important difference for families who have children with special needs, given that research has shown that parents play particularly important roles in the care of children with chronic conditions.[53] The importance of parental involvement has been demonstrated for children with conditions ranging from asthma to epilepsy to diabetes.[54]

Myth 2: Improvements Can't Reach Workers in the Informal Sector

A related misconception is that there are no ways to improve the lives of the many parents working in the informal sector and their children. After all, the argument goes, by definition the informal sector is unregulated so it is impossible to guarantee minimum wages, adequate leave, and the other working conditions critical to enabling parents to care adequately for their children while working. But this argument omits the fact that parents who work in the informal sector—and who frequently have lower incomes than their formal sector counterparts—also have urgent needs for services, such as early childhood care and education and after-school programs. The example of the San Isidro Center in Tegulcigalpa, Honduras, shows that providing services for children of parents working in the informal sector is possible. However, this is only a first step. Improving the conditions that parents face when at work is as important, and it is a step that is not beyond reach. Many of the parents we interviewed in all five regions landed in the informal sector when they were unable to keep formal sector jobs while caring for their children. Ensuring that parents in the formal sector have such basic benefits as the ability to take leave to care for a sick child without losing their jobs will play an essential role in decreasing the number of parents who are forced into the informal sector only when they have lost a better-paid job in the formal sector because conditions made it impossible to hold the formal sector job while parenting.

Even within the informal sector, it is possible to improve working conditions. For example, workers in the informal sector can be insured and paid leave provided through cooperative arrangements. Insuring paid leave is no more complex than other insurance systems for health care and for microlending, which have already been successfully introduced into the informal sector. These could be developed both for parental leave for the birth of a child and for short-term leave. The cost and coverage could be scaled to the number of hours the parent works weekly. The first step is for nongovernmental organizations, governments, and intergovernmental organizations to make a commitment to improving the conditions that parents working in the informal sector face.

Myth 3: No Affordable Solution

Response to the needs of working families has been stymied by the powerful fallacy that there is no affordable solution—for countries, for companies, for consumers. Will it cost money to address the needs of working families globally? Yes. Is it affordable? Clearly. In fact, all the available evidence points in the opposite direction: It's *in*action that is unaffordable.

Dr. Marcelo Jabalyas spoke with us about the problems of getting children vaccinated in Honduras when parents cannot get off from work to bring their children to clinics. It would cost less than $3 to give many export sector workers in Honduras the hours needed from work to bring a child in for vaccination—far less than the dollar cost or human toll of the diseases and deaths preventable by vaccination.

The affordability of facilitating adults' roles in caring for their family members' health–and the great failure to make straightforward solutions happen in contrast to the intensive energy devoted to medicines—are striking. The children of Tshegofatso Walone were left home alone sick when their parents couldn't take leave from work. But it would have cost less than $7 a day to provide the paid leave so that these children could be cared for when they were ill. To provide Ngo Van Cuong with the sick leave he needed to care for his son would have cost only $3 a day. Kereng Seetasewa needed time to care for her daughter with AIDS, and Dipogiso Motlhagomile urgently needed to care for her cousin with AIDS.[55] In each of their cases, ensuring paid leave for the average length of their absences would have cost less than $32.

Just as there is a sharp contrast between what is spent on medicines and what is done to ensure that someone is available to care for those who are sick, there is an equally stark contrast between our investments as a global community in education and the lack of investments to ensure that parents can be involved in their children's education—an ingredient that has repeatedly been demonstrated to dramatically affect educational outcomes. Victoria Ibarra Sabaleto, like many parents, doesn't go to any school meetings for fear she will be fired. Yet providing her with paid leave to address her children's educational needs would cost less than $3 for a critical opportunity to meet with teachers, even if the leave were paid. Supporting her and finding hours that allowed her to attend school meetings unpaid and keep her job would cost even less.

That these programs are affordable is manifest not only by the fact that successful examples exist, but also by the nature of these programs. Most of the programs and policies that are needed to support children's healthy growth and development around the world have self-scaling costs, that is, their costs are lower in poor countries, which have fewer resources, than in affluent countries, which have more resources. Over 90 percent of the costs of providing quality early childhood care and education for children five and under comes from the salaries of the caregivers. In low-income countries, where salaries are lower, the cost of providing this care is scaled down compared to high-income countries. When wages in countries rise, as they need to, costs for the programs will increase, but so will the countries' ability to afford these programs. Likewise, the costs of providing essential paid leave to workers who need to care for sick children or paid maternity and paternity leave are automatically scaled to local wages. Ensuring a week of paid sick leave to care for family members will cost 2 percent of what a wage earner makes in a low-income country. While this is the same 2 percent that it would cost of an employee's wages in a high-income country, it is substantially less in absolute international dollars because of lower average wages. Likewise, parental leave, paid annual leave, and mandatory days of rest are all automatically scaled to the cost of living in a country. The poorest countries may need assistance when they first begin to offer early childhood care and education to all families, but they will not need more economic assistance than the West can afford.[56]

It is noteworthy that in a study of OECD countries examining national productivity, countries which had among the best benefits to working families also ranked among the highest in economic productivity.[57] This should not come as a complete surprise. When people are asked to routinely work fifteen-hour shifts, it not only affects them and their families but their productivity is also markedly lower per hour than when they are working fewer hours. The majority of countries around the world—both low and high income, from a wide range of political and economic systems—have already passed legislation guaranteeing basic labor standards. To provide just a few examples: 163 countries around the world have legally mandated that women should receive paid maternity leave; 139 countries have either required companies to provide or have themselves created social insurance systems that provide for paid sick leave; 96 countries mandate paid annual leave; and 98 countries require employers to provide a mandatory day of rest.

What prevents individual countries from guaranteeing that all working adults have access to essential paid leave to care for themselves and their children is not the cost but the race to the bottom—competing for global capital to bring jobs to their countries on the basis of having the lowest cost and poorest conditions. As will be discussed later in this chapter, this needs to be addressed by putting in a floor of decent working conditions across all countries. Unless we strive for a humane minimum, the conditions that children and their working parents face in all countries will needlessly spiral down.

CAN COMPANIES AFFORD THE CHANGES?

In many of the contested industries, labor costs in general—and in particular the costs of the lowest-paid workers with the least benefits in companies—are a remarkably small portion of total costs, according to both labor and corporate sources. For example, in the production of athletic shoes, multinational enterprises were asked: Out of a $65 retail-price shoe, how many dollars were spent on labor costs? They estimated this to be $4.50.[58] Even if workers were provided with five weeks of paid leave spread across parental leave, sick leave, and annual leave, this would be the equivalent of raising the cost of a $65 shoe by less than 45 cents using these corporate figures. Labor organizations like the National Labor Committee have examined expenditures in other clothing factories. Their own estimate, as reflected in the case of baseball caps, is that an even smaller percentage of cost comes from labor. In Bangladesh, garment workers are paid on average 1.6 cents per $17 baseball cap, with labor costs amounting to only a tenth of 1 percent of the cap's market price.[59] Either estimate, that of corporations or of labor organizations, indicates that improving local manufacturing labor conditions would cost less than 2 percent of the product's market price—even before taking into account gains from improved productivity and retention.

WILL CONSUMERS STAND FOR CHANGE?

While it is unclear whether consumers would be willing to pay twice as much for clothing manufactured under better conditions, such increases would not be necessary to dramatically improve the conditions faced by low-skilled workers and their families around the world. There is little doubt that consumers would be willing to pay the 2 percent increase that it would likely involve to improve working conditions. The real question is how to accomplish the transformation in workers' lives.

Myth 4: Bad Jobs Are Better than No Jobs, and Action Threatens Bad Jobs

Action to address global work conditions has also been thwarted by the proposition that the poor conditions that workers in developing countries face are an improvement over past conditions and that asking for more threatens bad jobs. Paul Krugman wrote an article for the online magazine *Slate*'s economics column, "The Dismal Science." *Slate* titled Krugman's article "In Praise of Cheap Labor: Bad Jobs at Bad Wages Are Better than No Jobs at All"; the title aptly summarized the points made in the article, which simply argued that while current working conditions in export industries are appalling, they are better than the previous rural poverty.[60]

Krugman is not alone in making the argument that the abysmal conditions faced by workers and their families in developing countries are an improvement over their previous economic plights and then urging readers not to press for better labor conditions. There are three fundamental fallacies within this line of argument. First, before answering whether people are better off than they had been, we need to answer the questions: who, what, when, where, and how? In many rapidly industrializing settings, some of the poor face better working conditions than they did in the past; others face worse. For many families, the critical question is the point of comparison. Compared to not having a job in the present, they are often better off with a poor quality job. But frequently that is because they have given up their previous plots of land, crafts, and other grounds of economic stability. Compared to the conditions that their parents and grandparents faced a generation or two generations ago, many of the same workers are worse off.

Second, there is a larger problem with the argument behind this myth: Being better off—if that "better off" still means living in misery—is not an adequate reason to stop fighting for improved conditions. Many historical examples demonstrate this point. We would never argue that in the slums of Dickensian England and the gritty mill towns of New England during the United States' industrial revolution, everything was fine because any jobs were better than no jobs. Workers organized, labor movements grew, and policy makers fought to improve working conditions for all affected. Likewise, in response to millions of children needlessly becoming sick or dying in countries with low immunization rates, there have been substantial movements and investments to ensure that all children have access to the vaccines that can prevent diseases and avoidable deaths. No one wasted their time saying, "Oh, isn't it great that 20 percent of children receive this vaccine; it used to be that none did." People appropriately became outraged by the inequities between countries where nearly 100 percent of children receive vaccines and other nations in which, for want of a shot that costs less than $1, children are disabled for life or die. It is clear to all involved that children have a right to be fully vaccinated—regardless of whether the current situation of some being better off is "better than it used to be." Similarly, adults deserve decent working conditions globally so they can care for their families.

Finally, the most fundamental fallacy in the argument regarding bad jobs rests in the fallacy's failure to address the fact that if we ignore bad jobs, the global economy will race to produce more. When it comes to children having a chance to grow up in safe settings and parents having a chance to earn a living in jobs with decent working conditions while also caring for their children, we need to act with a sense of urgency: All children and all families around the world have the same basic right.

Myth 5: Parents Can Solve the Problems Alone

Perhaps one of the most pernicious and pervasive myths is that parents can solve the problems alone. I hope that the first six chapters of this book have served to explain why this myth is not true. As a mother whose husband had died, Gabriela Saavedra had no choice but to work if her nineteen-month-old toddler, Ana Daniel, was to survive. Constrained neither by morality nor law enforcement, the sweatshop in which she manufactured apparel for export paid her so little that she could not afford care for her daughter and forced her to work hours that prevented her from spending any time at home.[61] Ramon Canez's parents had little choice but to work twelve-hour days if they were going to earn enough to rebuild after Hurricane Mitch. Even so, their children had been crowded into a one-room shelter for more than two years. But in the absence of affordable early childhood care and education, the only possibilities they had were either to leave their preschool children home alone at dangerously young ages or to pull their school-age son out of school.[62] If she was to earn enough so her children and grandchildren could eat, Nunuko Ndebele similarly had no choice but to leave them home alone with devastating consequences.[63] Because their stories are already recounted in detail in earlier chapters, along with those of scores of other parents and the statistics from our in-depth studies around the world, I will let this book stand as the rebuttal to this myth.

Myth 6: Individual Countries Have No Choice

Some people have argued that nothing can be done because individual countries will not improve the conditions that their citizens face unless all other countries around the world do the same. To bolster their argument, they have noted that the globalization of the economy provides strong incentives for nations to compete for jobs by having the lowest-paid laborers and the worst working conditions, for which companies pay the lowest price. While the current form of the globalized economy does pressure every nation to provide worse working conditions, examples of good policies still exist in a wide range of individual countries.

We have conducted an extensive survey of the public policies and programs in 180 countries (see appendix D on the Work, Family, and Equity Index). In actuality, individual countries have passed into law protections vital to the welfare of working parents in every region around the world. In some areas, such as paid maternity leave, enormous progress has been made over the last century.

This progress has been made one country at a time, with countries taking individual approaches. Armenian law, for instance, provides for paid maternity leave for both 70 days before and 70 days after the birth of a child. Throughout the paid maternity leave, the woman is supposed to receive 100 percent of her earnings. Moreover, if she has a medical complication or multiple births, the maternity leave is supposed to be extended.[64] Brazil provides for 120 days of maternity leave, during which the woman is paid at full salary.[65] Chile provides for six weeks of paid maternity leave before the birth and an additional twelve weeks of maternity leave after the birth.[66] As in Brazil, mothers in Mongolia are expected to receive 120 days of maternity leave.[67] Women in Thailand are due 90 days of paid maternity leave.[68] In fact, 163 countries around the world offer guaranteed paid leave to women in connection with childbirth.[69] While a critical first step, the existing laws are only that—first steps. In many countries, the legislation is far ahead of the implementation. Moreover, the laws that exist often cover only part of the population in need. Finally, the vast majority of policies fails to adequately address the needs of a growing informal sector. Notwithstanding these caveats, the marked overall progress when it comes to maternity leave around the world demonstrates the feasibility of changing the ground rules for parents globally.

While far more has been done to date to provide for maternity leave than for other basic working protections that parents need, legislation has been passed in a wide range of other areas, demonstrating the feasibility. For example, Estonia and Japan have passed legislation to ensure that caregivers can be available to children at night. In Estonia, parents of children younger than fourteen and adults who are caring for disabled family members do not have to work at night. They are only supposed to perform night work if they consent to it. Similarly, in Japan, parents of young children and adults caring for disabled family members do not have to work between 10:00 p.m. and 5:00 a.m.[70]

While Gabriela Saavedra's experience is emblematic of the plight that many workers who are not yet protected from extreme work weeks face, many countries do have rules mandating that employers provide days of rest.[71] In Chad[72] and Tanzania,[73] workers are entitled to at least twenty-four consecutive hours of leave each week. In Ecuador, Saturday and Sunday are both considered holidays.[74] In Japan,[75] Nepal,[76] and Nicaragua,[77] workers are expected to receive one day off per week. In Estonia, employees are due to receive at least two days off per week, with the specific days undesignated.[78] Working overtime and holidays in most of these countries is possible but invokes a wage premium. In Ecuador, the wage premium for weekend work is 100 percent—that is, people who are asked to work on weekends, considered holidays, are supposed to be paid twice the normal salary.[79] Similarly, overtime pay calls for a "100 percent premium," or doubling of wages, in Nicaragua,[80] and in Tanzania, there is a 50 percent premium. In Tanzania, if the overtime is conducted on a holiday, the employee is due 200 percent of normal wages.[81]

A small number of countries have taken important steps forward in the provision of services to children. While many countries lack services overall and other countries provide services that do not reach many of the poor, current programs do illustrate the possibility of providing such essential supports as early childhood education in a wide range of settings. More than two-thirds of children between the ages of three and five are enrolled in early education programs in Cuba, Denmark, Hungary, Japan, Mexico, the Netherlands, and Thailand, among other countries. In each of these countries, the majority of children are enrolled in public preschool. The national resources available—particularly in the absence of international assistance—clearly make a difference, and the student-to-staff ratio varies substantially across these countries. With the exception of Japan, the better student-to-staff ratios are in the more affluent European countries. Denmark has a student-to-staff ratio of five to one,[82] Hungary of twelve to one,[83] and the Netherlands of ten to one.[84] In contrast, Cuba has a student-to-staff ratio of thirty-four to one, Mexico of twenty-two to one, and Thailand of twenty-five to one.[85] Even considering these disparities, however, the extent of early childhood education that has been made available in countries across socioeconomic conditions documents well the possibilities of what can be done with minimal resources and what services can be built upon with additional resources.

Myth 7: There's No Way to Move Forward Globally

While action by individual nations is clearly feasible, collective action holds many advantages in the context of a global economy. Collective action would allow countries to set a humane floor on working conditions and prevent nations from competing for capital, factories, and jobs by guaranteeing inhumane conditions. Floors are feasible and already exist, but they are obscenely low. As an example, countries do not now compete by offering enslaved or bonded labor. Yet countries have competed by creating zones where companies can operate with next to no regulation, with no labor protections, few limits on toxic exposures, no effective limits on extreme work hours, no minimum pay to ensure that employees can feed their families, and laws against workers unionizing so that they can't collectively bargain to survive. The hideously low floors are resulting in countless tragedies. If these Faustian bargains were replaced with a universal guarantee of humane conditions, countries could still compete. But instead of competing on the basis of how brutally adults and children could be treated with impunity, they would compete on the basis of having the best-trained, most-talented, most-experienced, or most-committed workforce.

Those who argue against collective action often contend that cultural differences would prevent consensus about what basic rights to guarantee. However, the evidence contradicts this claim. Dozens of countries around the world have been able to reach widespread consensus both with regard to what decent labor conditions should include and with regard to the rights of children and their families. The agreement that has been reached across nations, political systems, economic conditions, and cultures is embodied in a series of both United Nations (UN) declarations and treaties and International Labor Organization (ILO) standards. While these declarations, treaties, and standards have received insufficient follow-up and enforcement, the process of their passage demonstrates the potential for obtaining consensus on meeting the needs of and respecting the rights of children and working parents.

The importance of paid maternity leave was stipulated in the UN Convention on the Elimination of All Forms of Discrimination against Women (CEDAW), which has been accepted by 177 countries. CEDAW specifies:

> In order to prevent discrimination against women on the grounds of marriage or maternity and to ensure their effective right to work, state parties shall take appropriate measures: (a) to prohibit, subject to the imposition of sanctions, dismissal on the grounds of pregnancy or of maternity leave and discrimination in dismissals on the basis of marital status; (b) to introduce maternity leave with pay or with comparable social benefits without loss of former employment, seniority, or social imbalances.[86]

Paid maternity leave is also protected under the International Covenant on Economic, Social and Cultural Rights (ICESCR), which has been accepted by 149 countries and specifies that:

> Special protection should be accorded to mothers during a reasonable period before and after childbirth. During such period, working mothers should be accorded paid leave, or leave with adequate social security benefits.[87]

The importance of providing childcare has been agreed to by 192 countries under the UN Convention on the Rights of the Child (CRC), which specifies the following:

> States parties should take all appropriate measures to ensure that children of working parents have the right to benefit from child-care services and facilities for which they are eligible.[88]

More broadly, the CRC includes this agreement:

> For the purpose of guaranteeing and promoting the rights set forth in the present convention, state parties shall render appropriate assistance to parents and legal guardians in the performance of their child-rearing responsibilities and shall ensure the development of institutions, facilities, and services for the care of children.[89]

CEDAW also underscores the importance of providing childcare in order to assure that the rights of children and women are met. It also supports

> [t]he provision of necessary supporting social services to enable parents to combine family obligations with work responsibilities and participation in public life, in particular through promoting the establishment and development of a network of child-care facilities.[90]

Agreement that working adults must be able to spend adequate time with their family members is embodied not only in the labor standards approved under the ILO, but in the fundamental UN human rights accords. The UN Universal Declaration of Human Rights, agreed to by 171 countries, specifies the following:

> Article 23: (1) Everyone has the right to work, to free choice of employment, to just and favorable conditions of work and to protection against unemployment. (2) Everyone, without any discrimination, has the right to equal pay for equal work. (3) Everyone who works has the right to just and favorable remuneration ensuring for himself and his family an existence worthy of human dignity. . . .

> Article 24: Everyone has the right to rest and leisure, including reasonable limitation of working hours and periodic holidays with pay.[91]

The Universal Declaration of Human Rights makes clear that women as well as men have an equal right to work. Moreover, it makes clear that both have the right to be able to work and earn enough to support their families in dignity while working hours that allow them to spend time with their families.

The International Labor Organization (ILO) is one of the oldest global organizations. Founded in 1919 right after the First World War, the mission of the ILO from the start was to improve working conditions and living standards around the world. With more than 180 conventions on working conditions, the ILO has invested more time in obtaining passage of conventions by its membership—which includes business and labor sectors, as well as governments—than on their ratification. Until the 1990s, when the ILO began an initiative to ensure that the majority of the world's countries ratified the ILO's core conventions, relatively little effort had been placed on ratification.[92] As a result, most of the conventions have far fewer signatories than do the UN treaties. Nevertheless, the conventions do represent the ability of business, labor, and government to achieve consensus on important issues.

ILO conventions cover many working conditions central to families, including:

- Conventions specific to meeting family needs

  - Convention 183, the Maternity Protection Convention, which provides for fourteen weeks of maternity leave with pay
  - Convention 156, the Workers with Family Responsibilities Convention, which assures equality of opportunity and treatment for workers with family responsibilities

- Conventions addressing the time available to working adults to spend outside of the workplace, including with family

  - Convention 1, which provides for a forty-eight-hour workweek
  - Convention 14, which mandates at least twenty-four consecutive hours of rest per week
  - Convention 132, the Holidays with Pay Convention, which provides for paid annual holidays of at least three weeks
  - Convention 175, the Part-Time Work Convention, which provides for part-time parity and benefits, such as paid leave, sick leave, and maternity leave

- Conventions covering what are adequate wages to sustain a family while working reasonable hours

  - Convention 131, the Minimum Wage Fixing Convention, which provides for minimum wages that take into account the needs of those working
  - Convention 100, which establishes the principle of equal pay for men and women for work of equal value[93]

Together, this wide range of UN and ILO conventions and accords makes clear that substantial consensus is achievable globally about basic human rights when it comes to caring for children and working.

Hurdles along the Path

At the same time that there is an impetus to address the needs of working families on a worldwide scale, because nation-states are far less able to address them alone, the opportunities for addressing them on a global scale are also increasing. While to date global trade agreements have largely been conducted in ways that protect the interests of those with substantial financial capital, if they were transformed to provide the mechanism for representing the interests of all citizens—not just the affluent—these agreements on trade could be used to ensure basic rights for working families around the world. Agreements that ensure decent working conditions could become as common as those that protect the free flow of capital.

There are two hurdles that currently stand in the way of success. The first is making sure that each of us is aware of the impact of our actions on others—some of whom live quite proximate and others who live quite distant. The second is creating more democratic international forums—ones that represent the interests and needs of people across all social classes.

Caring about Global Conditions

When you live on a small island, the impact of every decision you make and step you take is readily apparent. If you walk on the coral, it will break, and there will be less where you live. If you break too much coral, there will be fewer fish by the next year. If there is no fresh water and every ounce you drink needs to be desalinated, you realize how much work goes into making water potable. If you have to carry your own water from a well, it affects how often you wash and what you wash. Likewise, if garbage has to be personally carried to a disposal site, you'll likely be deliberate in choices about which resources to use, recycle, or save. From a human standpoint, if this island is a small community with only a few hundred people, you are likely to know everyone. You will know the person who, if you ask for a store to be open or services to be available in the middle of the night, has to stay awake and be away from their family. Simply stated, you can see the impact of many of your actions. You know who is affected. It's easy to predict how you in turn will be affected. You know that your actions count because the number of actors is small and you can frequently trace the line of impact of your own decisions. Finally, on a small island, there is less of a "problem of the commons." The fact that your own actions will affect not only the environment and other people but will also come home to roost and have an impact on your own family is often much more readily apparent.

The difficulty we face in engendering global action today and are likely to face well into the future is, in part, due to the fact that the scale and distance of the effect of everyday actions taken by the majority of people have changed dramatically over the centuries. In the seventeenth century, colonial powers were sending ships around the world, but the majority of people still made their own clothes at home. In the twenty-first century, walk into any home in the United States and look at the labels of where clothes were made, and it will read like a global atlas: Bangladesh, Honduras, Myanmar, and so on. In the first half of the twentieth century, when people needed help with something that was broken in their homes, they were often going to a neighbor or someone in their local community. They thought twice before asking that person to come help at two in the morning—it had to be important. In the twenty-first century, when an adult needs help with a problem on their computer or in their finances, they place a phone call with little idea as to whether it's being answered in the United States, Great Britain, India, or the Ivory Coast. And they have even less idea about what working conditions those who are answering the phone are facing. Yet, whether achieved through labor agreements linked to global trade agreements, through economic aid directed at improving labor conditions, or through mandates on and economic incentives to companies to improve conditions, only by raising standards globally will countries be able to sustain or increase decent working conditions for families within their own borders.

Yet even when the commitment is there to ensure that all people have decent working conditions, the practical challenges will be great. The problems include among others: there are many national and multinational enterprises that lack the interest and will to follow national labor laws; many governments lack the human resources and thus the capacity to enforce their labor codes; bribes and corruption further eat away at any likelihood of effective enforcement; and mechanisms are lacking for workers to be informed of their rights and, when their rights are denied, to have a chance to protest the abuse of rights or seek remedies without losing their jobs. While these barriers are real, many are already a focus of large nongovernmental organizations (NGOs) and intergovernmental organizations (IGOs), and none are insurmountable.

Democratic Global Governance

Currently, global governance structures are limited, both in the mechanisms they have available to govern and in the extent to which they are democratic. By definition, those who govern are supposed to "conduct the policy, action, and affairs" of a state or other body. Currently, global institutions have limited means for true governance. Most international institutions were not designed to govern. While the World Health Organization (WHO) can offer technical advice to countries when invited, it has no mechanism for mandating public health protections nor adequate funding to actually provide essential health measures. The United Nations Educational, Scientific and Cultural Organization (UNESCO) has a global voice about education but similarly limited abilities to implement programs. The International Labor Organization (ILO) has managed to obtain agreement in principle from labor, employers, and governments on a substantial number of policies—but it too has no mechanism to enforce these. Those countries which are signatories merely report on their own progress. If they fail to progress, the only option is for the ILO to stop them from being active members in the organization—hardly a significant consequence. At that, even this consequence has been saved for the rarest, most-egregious examples of slavery and forced labor.

Still, tools for governance are already in play. The financial institutions, including the World Bank, International Monetary Fund, and other multilateral funders, can influence policy both by the funds they make directly available and by the requirements they attach to receiving those funds. The World Trade Organization (WTO) can enforce its policies through trade sanctions. While infrequently used, the UN can also impose economic sanctions. For the most egregious crimes, including genocide and other crimes against humanity, the International Criminal Court can try citizens of states that are signatories. Those are the tools that are currently available—relatively blunt carrots and sticks.

While the current tools are few and used in limited ways, they could be far more effective. Funding for governance, instead of being completely abstracted from the global organizations like UNESCO and WHO, which are focused on what works, could be integrated. Findings from within UNESCO and WHO should be used to guide the funding policies of the World Bank and International Monetary Fund that affect education and health. Trade sanctions, instead of being used just to protect the economic interests of global capital, could also be used to protect the basic rights of workers. An example of this would be to link the agreements on protecting the basic rights of all people who work, as agreed to by many nations through the ILO, to trade policy being implemented through the WTO. Individual countries would have the responsibility for overseeing employers within their own borders and ensuring that they meet the basic rights of employees. The international governing bodies would then oversee countries—holding them responsible for making sure that companies within their borders did not violate workers' basic rights. Employees whose basic rights were denied would have both national and international governing boards they could inform of the violations. This type of system would keep most of governance in the hands of nation-states, at the same time ensuring that all people around the world had their basic human rights respected. By holding countries responsible for the oversight of employers within their borders, such a system would have the important characteristic of protecting those working in industries aimed at internal consumption as well as export.

At the same time that the democratic issues need to be addressed, so too do the governance bases for global institutions. Currently, global institutions are limited in their democratic bases both at the level of who represents individual states and at the level of the relationships among different states. This has limited the voice of the poor. Low-income countries have increasingly banded together within some of the large global institutions to increase their voice. The need for countries to sign most treaties and agreements in order to be covered by them also helps to ensure the rights of less-powerful states. Even with these protections, ensuring democratic representation both among and within individual states needs to be a priority. The same changes which are essential to increase representation and fairness in governance within countries will help ensure that the interests of the poor as well as the affluent are represented in international bodies.

Visions of the Possible

Visions of the possible change with time. The examples in the case of technology are endless. When Jules Verne wrote about flying machines or submarines in the mid-nineteenth century, they were science fiction. What was then seen as impossible is now part of our routine life and in the case of transportation has been an essential piece of making us a truly global community.

But it is not only our visions of what is technologically feasible that have changed. There are social problems that have in the past seemed insurmountable, solutions that seemed infeasible or unaffordable, evils that we knew were wrong but were ignored because no one thought there was a successful way out. Slavery and servitude in the Western world seemed inevitable when the Western democracies began. More recently, a peaceful solution to apartheid seemed impossible to find. Eliminating devastating diseases like smallpox, an undertaking that required global coordination, seemed to face insurmountable barriers, yet succeeded. Addressing the needs of working-poor families is no more insurmountable.

Giving working families a chance globally faces the same problems today that each of these visions did in the past. It is as clearly important to do something about the fact that children are born into poverty without a chance at a full life as it was important to do something about smallpox. It is clearly as wrong to allow one group of citizens to purchase cheap clothing because another group works up to twenty-two hours a day while their children are locked home alone as it was wrong to do nothing about economies built on forced labor.

What stops many people who care from doing something today is the same thing that has stopped many people who care from doing something in the past. It seems infeasible, insurmountable. But these problems are as addressable as were past problems.

Accepting Uncertainty

Can we begin if we don't know with 100 percent certainty what the right solution is?

There is no other way.

We should be realistic from the start that there will be setbacks. Wrong turns will be taken. Efforts attempted will not always be successful.

But clearly that should not stop us. When a business sets a goal of producing 1,000 pairs of blue jeans in the first year, despite uncertainty about whether it will be able to meet its goal, the business still tries. If only 500 pairs of pants are made, the managers figure out how to improve production.

Social enterprises should be held to neither higher nor lower standards. At times, people expect that we will only undertake to address social problems if we are 100 percent sure that the solution will work. When one fails or, more commonly, when it succeeds incompletely, then the argument is made that it is better to do nothing. If nothing else, I hope the stories of these families make clear that working families living in poverty cannot afford for the global community to ignore their needs.

Although we will never successfully solve these problems without trying, just trying is not enough. While social enterprises should not be expected to have a clairvoyance that private enterprise lacks, social enterprise should be held up to similar standards of ongoing evaluation and improvement. Businesses examine whether they are reaching their goals, and when they fail to do so, they work on ways to improve their methods. The problems of extreme poverty and inequity have to be addressed. The difficulties we face in addressing these issues cannot be an excuse for avoiding addressing them any more than the difficulties the past generations faced in addressing slavery would have been an adequate reason for not eliminating it. We have to agree as a global community on what we need to accomplish, then wrestle with the best way to get there.

First Steps

If we are going to work toward everyone in a global community having equal opportunities, we need to ensure that expanded opportunities for public education are available worldwide. If we are going to avoid exporting bad working conditions and follow through on international agreements, we need to hold employers to guaranteeing basic human rights at work globally. Both public education and basic job protections have had widespread support in democratic countries; ensuring they are available to all should be a global priority.

What would these look like in practice?

Globally, we have made a great deal of progress on primary-school education. But we have made far less on early education or secondary-school education. While some children receive the highest quality early education, which research and common experience has repeatedly demonstrated give children a substantial advantage in how they fare throughout the rest of their lives, others do not even receive the basic supervision that will guarantee their minimum safety. In too many places, there are two-year-olds who are left in the care of four-year-olds, young children who are locked in shacks so outsiders can't hurt them, preschool children who lack the supervision needed to prevent them from hurting themselves and who have no opportunity for any of the stimulation that brain researchers demonstrate is so critical in the early years of development. We need to expand the ages that public schooling covers to make the early education of three- and four-year-old children universally available.

In developing and industrialized countries alike, whether or not someone has completed secondary school has a dramatic effect on their ability to leave poverty. Right now, access to secondary school in developing countries is frequently nonexistent for the poor. Children are pulled out of school to be unpaid laborers at home when no one else is available to care for the youngest children of working parents. They are pulled out of school to engage in paid labor when their parents' incomes are not enough to support the family. And they are pulled out of school even when it is in theory free because the costs of transportation to school, uniforms, and supplies are higher than families can afford. We need to ensure that all children have a chance at secondary-school education by providing truly free and public education, ensuring that adults can earn a wage sufficient to support their children as well as themselves, and ensuring that basic care is available and affordable for infants and toddlers so school-age children don't have to sacrifice school and their futures to become childcare providers.

Finally, we need to expand the school day and year. In many nations, public education began at a time when the population was largely agricultural. The school day and year developed to accommodate children helping on farms in the afternoons and summers. The school schedule and calendar then spread to other nations. When the schedule was first adopted in many developing countries, they too had largely rural populations. However, with the rapid urbanization of industrialized and developing countries alike, it is far more common globally that schoolchildren are home alone in the after-school hours or in the summers than that they are performing agricultural work. We need to reshape the school day and year to match children's educational needs and the needs of working families.

Enacting Basic Job Protections

There are many working conditions that political parties on the Right and the Left disagree upon. Yet, in most democracies, there has been widespread agreement that it is reasonable to put some cap on total mandatory hours, some floor on the minimum amount of leave employees should have, some guarantees for basic health and safety conditions, and some assurance that employees won't lose jobs when they take leave to meet the most essential needs of sick family members and newborns. While there are disagreements between parties and differences across countries on the levels of each of these standards, there are few that recommend removing the standards altogether.

We need to guarantee these same categories of minimum standards for all people around the world. Right now, individual countries that seek to legally ensure or enforce minimum standards for their citizens risk losing jobs to other nations that don't have those standards. That leaves them with an impossible choice between a mad race to the bottom by allowing the worst working conditions or losing needed jobs. There is no reason that it needs to be that way. Global guarantees of minimum basic working conditions will prevent the flight of jobs from one country to another. And there is no evidence that widespread guarantees of minimum working conditions will lead to a loss overall in work.

Finally, we should be able to reach widespread agreement that the wage earned by one adult should be enough for a family to live on. Progressives have argued that two parents should have the chance to work and rear their children equally—each working two-thirds of the time and caring for their family the rest of the time.[94] For this to be possible, two times two-thirds, or four-thirds of a salary is needed to support a family. Conservatives in many countries have argued that one parent should be able to stay home to care for the children. If this is to be the case, then the salary of the other parent needs to be sufficient to support the family. Liberals in many countries have argued that we have to be concerned about the welfare of single-parent families. If single-parent families are to survive economically, that single parent too needs to earn a wage sufficient to support a family. Clearly, there is common ground for the notion that an adult should receive a livable family wage. Not only is this livable wage essential to one parent being able to stay home in two-parent families, to two parents sharing equally in work and caregiving, and to the welfare of single-parent families, but it also underlies any solution to the global problem of child labor. In regions where child labor is most prevalent, it is because adults do not earn a living family wage. This lack of an adequate wage guarantee enables employers to pay survival wages to children and vastly increases the need for families to rely on child labor.

Children and Families in a Globalized Economy

Often, journal articles and books reporting on research end with recommendations that can be summarized as "We need to do more research." At times, this is the best recommendation. The information gathered is so tentative, the findings so preliminary, that it is impossible to know what action, if any, is warranted.

There is a great deal more we need to learn about the conditions in which young children are being reared and the struggles that their working parents are facing worldwide. But the evidence is clear about many essential points:

- Young children are being left home alone, in the care of other young children, and in grossly inadequate care.
- The health and development of all of these children are placed at risk, as is the education of the only slightly older children pulled out of school to care for them.
- The lack of decent working conditions and social supports makes it nearly impossible for millions of parents to balance caring for children well with working and prevents millions of families from exiting poverty.

We also know important facts about what impact the availability of child-care and extended educational opportunities can have on whether young children in poverty survive and thrive, what impact the availability of paid leave can have on families, and the importance of enabling parents to care for their sick and hospitalized children.

There is a great deal more we need to learn—from which models of preschool childcare are most feasible in different settings to how best to provide care for young school-age children when all adults work far from home. But in addition to gathering more information, we need to do our best to care for families now. I hope this book has provided some preliminary answers. At the very least, I hope it will spark debates, generate deeper understandings, and lead to steps that will make a difference for the more than 900 million children affected. The costs of inaction are too high.

The tragedies of inaction are being spelled out in the uncounted deaths of children from preventable malnutrition, diarrhea, disease, and injuries. The tragedies are also being etched across the daily lives of preschool and school-age children around the world who have no chance to learn before entering school, who are left alone with no adults available, who are tied up with no chance to move in order to prevent injuries, who are pulled out of school to care for their younger siblings, who are without any care when they are sick—as well as the lives of adults who lose bad jobs when they seek to care for their children and end up in worse ones and in the experiences of families who have no chance of exiting poverty.

At present, the problem with globalization is not that people around the world are able to communicate more readily with each other nor that they can travel with greater speed and ease between their nations nor that economies are rapidly changing, but rather with how the gains are being divided up. To date, the global economy has freed the flow of capital far more than it has freed the movement of labor. Likewise, systems have been put in place to protect the rights of capital in ways that have far outpaced the protections for working parents and their children. World Trade Organization agreements that provide for substantial sanctions when countries violate agreements regarding the free flow of goods provide one example. In contrast, the accords ensuring decent working conditions for laborers are all voluntary, and the enforcement mechanisms for these accords have no teeth. What this imbalance—the absence of any protection for labor yet a well-protected system for free-flowing goods and capital—has created is a race to the bottom in which countries have been forced to compete with each other for capital and jobs by offering the cheapest labor. And there are only a few ways to ensure the cheapest labor, none of which are good: provide the lowest salaries, the fewest protections, no leave, and no possibility for unionizing to ensure decent conditions.

But there is nothing about the race to the bottom that is inherent in globalization. In fact, the results of globalization are up to us. Increased social and economic relations across countries can just as readily lead to widely shared economic gains as they can to a downward spiral toward worse work conditions. For this to happen, labor—something all people possess—has to be valued as highly as the capital needed to conduct international commerce, which is something only a few are fortunate enough to have. We need to put in place universal standards for minimum decent working conditions. These need to comprise the kind of conditions essential to humane survival both for adults and the children they care for, including a living wage, parental leave, leave and flexibility to care for sick family members, and humane hours. At the same time, we need to widen the educational opportunities that make it possible for all to gain from a global economy by ensuring that children in poor countries and poor children in affluent countries have access to early education and quality primary and secondary schools and that they are not forced to leave school at young ages because their parents' earnings are too low to survive on or because there is no care for their preschool siblings. Just as it is not too much to dream of a world where all children can eat, it is not too much to dream of a world where preschool children are not left alone, where school-age children's parents can support their education, where older children are not pulled out of school to act as childcare providers, and where all children have adults who can care for them when they are healthy and when they are sick.

Appendixes

Appendix A
Analysis of National Surveys of Individuals and Households in Five Regions

My research team has examined the experiences of working families through analyses of large, nationally representative, closed-ended, publicly available household-level surveys of more than 55,000 households from countries around the world. To date, surveys from Botswana, Brazil, Mexico, Russia, South Africa, the United States, and Vietnam have been analyzed.

The specific analyses conducted for each country varied according to the nature of the information gathered in each survey. Whenever available, the analyses conducted included an assessment of the following variables:

- *caretaking* as indicated by household composition, including the age and number of children; the number of adults older than sixty-five; whether the employed adult was caring for children, children with chronic health conditions, elderly parents, or disabled family members; and the dependency ratio (the ratio of dependents to working-age adults)
- *work status and conditions* as measured by the number of working household members; the average hours per week worked; parental

work conditions, including the availability of paid leave, flexibility, and health insurance; job autonomy; work schedules and shifts; and the household labor force participation rate

■ *social supports* as measured by frequent contact with or support given by family, friends, and coworkers

In addition, we examined the associations among

■ socioeconomic status and work and caregiving conditions
■ gender and work and caregiving conditions
■ family structure and work and caregiving conditions

Botswana

Botswana, located in sub-Saharan Africa, had an estimated population of 1.7 million and an annual population growth rate of 0.6 percent in 2003. Forty-one percent of the Botswanan population was younger than fifteen. Botswana has been rapidly urbanizing. In contrast to 1960, when 93 percent of labor force participants were involved in agriculture, in 2000, only 20 percent worked in agriculture.[1] Of adults between the ages of fifteen and sixty-four, 62.2 percent of men and 42.9 percent of women were economically active in 2001.[2] Botswana has maintained a peaceful multiparty democracy since its independence in 1966.

Yet the Botswanan population presently is plagued by a catastrophic level of HIV infection. Prior to the HIV epidemic, Botswana was one of the most rapidly growing economies in sub-Saharan Africa, fueled primarily by mining and exporting minerals, especially diamonds, and the production and sales of beef.[3] However, despite this macroeconomic performance, 47 percent of the population (38 percent of all households) was still living below the poverty line in 1993 and 1994.[4] Livelihoods and lives were threatened by rapidly rising rates of HIV/AIDS throughout the 1990s. By 1999, Botswana had a staggering adult HIV seroprevalence rate of 36 percent.[5] Infection rates of this magnitude dramatically and tragically added to the caregiving burdens of working adults, making it particularly urgent to understand the conditions they face at work and at home.

DATA SOURCE

The secondary data source used to examine working and caregiving conditions in Botswana was the 2000 round of the Multiple Indicator Survey conducted by the Central Statistics Office, Gaborone.[6] The special focuses of the survey were fertility and the health of mothers and children from birth to age five. It also contained information on household-level demographics, education, school enrollment, employment status, occupation, socioeconomic indicators, and measures of social support. Of the survey's 6,188 households, we analyzed 2,259 households that had a child younger than five and 3,506 households that had a child younger than fourteen.

Households were selected systematically from a list of households that was prepared when the survey fieldwork began. The survey had a high response rate of 92 percent. Because the selection of households was stratified by the fourteen districts in the country, corrective weights were used in all of our analyses.

See table A-1 for a description of the demographic characteristics of the households surveyed.

MEASURES ANALYZED

In addition to the analyses described above, which were conducted in all countries, our analysis of the Botswana data included an examination of enrollment in early childhood education programs, enrollment of children aged six to fourteen in schools, whether or not children were breast-fed, whether or not children were immunized, and how these factors interacted with the working conditions faced by adults in the household. As there were no data on family income in this survey, no analyses by income could be conducted.

Russia

Russia's transition to a market economy in the 1990s was anything but smooth. The consequences of the associated job losses, abrupt increases in income inequality, and loss of social supports were costly to health. Between 1987 and 1994, women's life expectancy dropped from 74.3 to 71.2 and men's life expectancy from 64.9 to 57.7.[7] During the financial crisis, the government ceased to pay social assistance and pension allowances,[8] and social supports such as subsidized childcare programs,[9] subsidized education through the tertiary levels,[10] and subsidized health care[11]—which were once available to all citizens—were reduced. While not yet returning to the precrisis level, life expectancy of men in 1999 was 60 and of women was 72.[12] As a result of a devalued currency, loss of price controls, inflation, and job loss, 26 percent of the Russian population, 36.5 million people, was still living below the poverty line of 1,817 rubles ($57) a month in 2002.[13] As in other former communist countries, capitalism in Russia has brought with it a decline in women's participation in the labor force. From 1980 to 1999, women's labor force participation rate declined from 74.7 percent to 63.9 percent.[14] It is critically important to examine the impact of these major socioeconomic transitions, similar to others in Eastern Europe, on children and working families.

Table A-1. Demographic Characteristics of National Survey Populations

	Botswana Percentage of adults	Russia Percentage of adults
Highest education level achieved		
No schooling	21	0
Primary	31	41
Secondary	46	43
College and above	2	16
Marital status		
Single	55	12
Living with spouse or partner	38	68
Divorced or separated	1	7
Widowed	6	13
Number of children under 18 in household		
0	27	49
1	15	31
2	15	17
3 or more	43	4
Age of children in household		
At least one child between 0 and 5 in household	48	17
At least one child between 6 and 14 in household	59	33
At least one child between 15 and 17 in household	31	14
Per capita household income		
Below $10/day	**	85
At or above $10/day	**	15
Respondent's wage income		
Below $10/day	**	64***
At or above $10/day	**	36***

* For all countries other than the United States, percentages describe all adults in the national household surveys. For the United States, percentages describe respondents in the cohort followed over time.

** The Botswana survey does not provide this information.

*** In Russia, respondent's wage income as reported in the survey is after taxes.

**** In the Vietnam survey, respondent's income is reported. At the household level, expenditure data are reported. In all other surveys, income data were available for both respondents and households.

Notes: Income data reported in each survey have been converted to a common currency using the World Bank's purchasing power parity (PPP) conversion factors. All percentages are rounded to the nearest whole number. As a result of rounding, percentages may not always sum to 100. The table reports the ages of children in the household to provide important information on the frequency of households with preschool, young school-age, and older school-age children. These percentages may sum to over 100 because households with multiple children would fall into multiple categories if their children are in different age groupings.

Vietnam Percentage of adults	United States Percentage of respondents*	Brazil Percentage of adults	Mexico Percentage of adults	South Africa Percentage of adults
11	0	16	14	16
34	3	55	46	28
51	76	20	32	53
5	21	9	9	3
24	20	40	24	30
66	58	49	67	48
2	21	5	5	13
9	1	7	5	10
20	34	31	23	25
24	21	26	20	16
26	28	23	22	19
30	18	21	35	41
37	24	33	44	48
56	50	45	54	59
35	22	25	29	30
96****	9	54	28	71
4****	91	46	72	29
79	5	40	9	14
21	95	60	91	86

We analyzed the 1998–1999 round of the Russian Longitudinal Monitoring Survey conducted by the Institute of Sociology, Russian Academy of Sciences.[15] This survey had a response rate of 84 percent and includes detailed demographic, health, education, employment, and socioeconomic information on household members. Data from the eighth round (November 1998–January 1999) of the survey were examined instead of the most recent 2002 round because the eighth round is the latest round which includes a detailed time-use module. Of the survey's 3,466 households, there were 420 households that had a child younger than five and 1,214 households that had a child younger than fourteen.

See table A-1 for a description of the demographic characteristics of the households surveyed.

MEASURES ANALYZED

In addition to the analyses described that were conducted in all countries, we examined the survey's detailed questions on family illness burden. These included the occurrence and number of household members with health problems in the thirty days immediately preceding the survey, the occurrence and number of household members with health problems for which professional assistance was sought in the thirty days preceding the survey, the number of household members who missed work due to illness in the previous thirty days, the time spent on travel for medical care, and the incidence and duration of hospitalizations of household members in the preceding three months.

We examined social and family supports (as measured by the presence of a grandparent living in the household and hours of care provided to children by both resident and nonresident relatives) and data on the immunization of children and frequency of common illnesses among children under age five. We also analyzed hours spent on childcare and examined children's school and early childhood program enrollment rates, their time spent in school, their time spent studying outside of school, and their relationship to the work status of the household.

One key component of the Russia survey was the inclusion of a time-use module. The time-use section specifies a number of activities and asks whether the person spent any time in the previous seven days on that activity, and if so, how much. We examined time spent on household chores, time spent providing childcare among the household members, childcare provided by non–household members, childcare provided by other children, and time spent providing elderly care.

Vietnam

Vietnam had a population of 81.3 million, 31 percent of whom were children, in 2003.[16] In recent years, women's participation in the labor market has continued to increase from already high levels, rising from 75 percent in 1980 to 79 percent in 1995.[17] While a majority of Vietnam's population remains rural, increasing numbers of rural residents are migrating to cities in search of higher-wage jobs— and the actual numbers are probably higher than official statistics because "unregistered" citizens are overrepresented in urban areas.[18] The United Nations estimates that by 2025 the percentage of Vietnam's population living in cities will be double what it was in 1994.[19] In the late 1980s, the government of Vietnam initiated a series of far-reaching economic reforms. These reforms, involving increased economic freedoms and reduced government spending, are widely credited with having spurred Vietnam's high economic growth rate of 7.8 percent in the 1990s.[20]

At the same time, working families face real dilemmas. In Vietnam in 1994, working hours in many industries ranged from ten to twelve hours per day, six days per week.[21] Another element of Vietnam's economic transition that potentially threatens working families is the reduction in government spending on services such as health care, education, and childcare, leading to the reduction in availability or the imposition of user fees for these services.[22]

DATA SOURCE

We analyzed data on work and family conditions from the Vietnam Household Living Standards Survey 1997–1998.[23] The survey sampled 28,633 individuals in 6,002 households. Of the 6,002 households interviewed, we analyzed 2,105 households that had a child between birth and age five and 4,209 that had at least one child between birth and age fourteen.

Households surveyed were selected from throughout the country, and the sampling frame was nationally representative with the exception of individuals living on the country's islands who, for logistical reasons, were not included.[24] The survey had a 76 percent response rate for the employment module and 70 percent for the health and education modules.

Please see table A-1 for a description of the survey sample we analyzed.

MEASURES ANALYZED

In addition to the analyses described that were conducted in all countries, we examined social and family supports. We also examined the frequency of common childhood illnesses among zero- to four-year-olds and the availability of workplace benefits, specifically, paid medical leave. In addition, our analyses included an examination of children's school and early childhood program enrollment rates, whether children were immunized, whether children were breast-fed and the duration of breast-feeding, and their relationship to the household members' work status.

This survey had detailed questions on family illness burden, which we analyzed. They included the occurrence of health problems in the two weeks preceding the survey, the number of household members who had stopped normal activities due to health problems in the previous thirty days, the number of days of work or school missed due to health problems, and whether any children younger than fourteen had an illness or injury in the previous thirty days.

Lastly, this data source contained questions regarding migration from which we could ascertain whether respondents moved from the province of birth, from rural to urban areas, and vice versa.

United States

Sixty-six percent of adults aged sixteen to sixty-four, including 74 percent of men and 60 percent of women, either worked for pay or were seeking work in 2003. As a result, the majority of American children are raised in families in which all parents work for pay.[25] In addition, most elderly, sick, and disabled Americans must depend on working family members for the routine care and support they need. Our research has explored the prevalence of caregiving burdens for employees and the supports available to them to meet these demands. We have examined differences in these caregiving demands and how workplace supports vary across socioeconomic class and gender. Furthermore, we have analyzed the effects that workplace policies have on employed parents' ability to care for their families' health and educational needs.

DATA SOURCE

The National Longitudinal Survey of Youth (NLSY) is sponsored by the Department of Labor's Bureau of Labor Statistics and is conducted in collaboration with the Center for Human Resource Research at Ohio State University.[26] The NLSY includes detailed measures of children's outcomes and parents' working conditions. The NLSY consists of a nationally representative probability sample of 11,406 civilian young men and women who were aged fourteen to twenty-one at the start of the survey in 1979 and who in 2004 were between thirty-nine and forty-six. Multistage stratified area sampling was used to select the civilian respondents; poor and minority populations were oversampled. Data have been collected annually since 1986, and in addition women and their children are observed biannually. NLSY data from 1994 to 2000 were examined.

See table A-1 for a description of the demographic characteristics of the households surveyed.

MEASURES ANALYZED

Our analyses included an examination of the resources that are available to families in the form of parental work schedules, parental work hours, and the availability of paid leave and job flexibility. Too frequently, surveys examine what benefits companies offer without asking what benefits families actually receive. While these may appear to be the same thing, many companies offer benefits to only some of their employees, for example, to those who have worked for a certain length of time, those who are not temporary or part-time workers, or those who have a minimum job grade. Thus, company managers might say they offer paid leave, but a significant number of their employees might not be receiving that leave.

We examined what resources are available to working Americans across social classes. Many previous studies of working families have interviewed primarily or disproportionately middle-income families. Because of its nationally representative sample and because for many years it contained an oversampling of poor families, the NLSY provides detailed data on the working conditions faced by low-income working families.

We also conducted a detailed examination of the working conditions faced by high-need and resource-poor families. Parents who have a child with a chronic health problem, a learning disability, or a behavioral or emotional problem face greater time demands. The NLSY has conducted detailed developmental and educational examinations of children and has collected information on their health, behavioral, developmental, and educational problems.

Brazil

Brazil has undergone rapid urbanization and labor force transformation. From 1960 to 2003, the percentage of Brazilians living in urban areas increased from 45 percent to 83 percent.[27] As of 1998, services made up the largest sector of the labor force (57 percent of employed persons), far ahead of agriculture (23 percent of employed persons). Women have been rapidly entering the workforce: 57 percent of adult women were in the formal labor market in 1998, compared to only 32 percent in 1980.[28] Still, with its large number of children and youth, Brazil's caregiving demands are high. Brazil had a population of 177 million with 48.5

million children aged fifteen or younger in 2003.[29] Understanding the conditions that working families face under the new economy and current demographics is critical.

DATA SOURCE

We analyzed data on work and family conditions from the Brazilian Living Standards Measurement Survey (Pesquisa Sobre Padroes de Vida) 1996–1997.[30] This survey offers a rich array of work and caregiving measures. Sponsored by the World Bank and the Brazilian Geographical and Statistical Foundation (IBGE), the survey sampled 19,409 individuals in 4,940 households representing the northeastern and southeastern regions of Brazil and reported a response rate of 99 percent.[31] As of 1996, these two regions made up 71 percent of the national population and included both the most- and least-developed areas, as indicated by income, literacy, and infant mortality levels.[32] Of the survey's 4,940 households, we analyzed 1,594 households that had a child younger than five and 2,955 households that had a child younger than fourteen.

See table A-1 for a description of the demographic characteristics of the households surveyed.

MEASURES ANALYZED

In addition to the analyses described that were conducted in all countries, we also analyzed the survey questions regarding family illness burden. This included the occurrence of health problems in the thirty days preceding the survey, the number of household members who had stopped normal activities due to health problems in the previous thirty days, and the number of days of work or school missed due to health problems.

Questions on children's common illnesses and health status were assessed, including whether any children younger than fourteen had missed school for illness or other family reasons, whether the household contained a child from birth to age fourteen with a chronic condition, whether any of the children were not breast-fed, and the average age when children were first fed bottled milk. In addition, we examined social and family supports. For three- to five-year-olds, we examined the proportion attending early education and the number of hours spent in the program. Other survey measures that were analyzed included school enrollment rates of children aged six to fourteen, the number of hours spent in school, the shift attended, commuting time to and from school, indicators of whether homework was completed daily, and the impact these factors had on children's well-being. For each potential outcome, we examined its relationship to parental working conditions.

Mexico

Mexico, with a population of 105 million[33] and a gross domestic product (GDP) of 626 billion (US) dollars in 2003, is one of the largest economies in the developing world. Mexico had 33 million children aged fifteen or younger as of 2003.[34] From 1960 to 2003, the percentage of Mexicans living in urban areas increased from 51 percent to 76 percent, while the percentage of the labor force working in agriculture fell from 24 percent in 1988 to 18 percent in 2001. Services made up the largest sector of the economy—69 percent of GDP and 56 percent of the labor force—with industry occupying the second largest portion of the economy: 27 percent of GDP and 26 percent of employed persons.[35] Women have been entering the workforce rapidly, with 41 percent of adult women in the formal labor market in 1999, compared to 31 percent in 1980. These figures understate the extent to which women work because they do not include informal employment, which in Mexico was estimated to have been 30 percent of total female urban employment in 1999.[36] While most Mexicans consider themselves *mestizo*, or of mixed race, 5.5 million are indigenous minorities and retain their native languages. Indigenous Mexicans are disadvantaged in educational and work opportunities, income, and assets.[37]

DATA SOURCE

We analyzed data on work and family conditions from the 1996 round of the National Survey of Household Income and Expenditure (ENIGH).[38] The survey contains demographic, educational, employment, and socioeconomic data on all household members. Data from the 1996 round was examined instead of the 2000 round because it includes a detailed time-use module, which was administered to 4,985 of the surveyed households. Sponsored by the Instituto Nacionál de Estadística, Geografía y Informática (INEGI), the survey sampled 64,916 individuals in 14,042 households. The survey had a response rate of 83 percent. Of the survey's 14,042 households, there were 5,915 households that had a child younger than five and 9,484 households that had a child younger than fourteen.

See table A-1 for a description of the demographic characteristics of the households surveyed.

MEASURES ANALYZED

In addition to the analyses described that were conducted in all countries, our analyses included the relationship of working conditions to school enrollment rates of children aged five to fourteen. Also, using the time-use module, we examined the number of hours that adult men and women and children aged five to nineteen provided childcare during the last week prior to the survey administration. Finally, we analyzed unpaid work hours, including hours spent on household work.

South Africa

South Africa had a population of 45.3 million with 14.3 million children under the age of fifteen in 2003. By 1980, 45 percent of women were in the labor force; women's labor force participation rose to 62 percent in 1999.[39] Fifty-seven percent of the South African population lived in urban areas in 2003, up from 46.6 percent in 1960. Only 11 percent of the labor force worked in agriculture in 1999. Services made up the largest sector of the labor force (61 percent of employees), with industry occupying the second largest portion of the labor force (25 percent of employees).[40] The rise of the AIDS epidemic is confronting South Africa with particularly difficult work and caregiving challenges: 21.5 percent of South African adults of reproductive age are HIV positive.[41]

DATA SOURCE

We examined data on work and family conditions from the South Africa Integrated Household Survey 1994, which was conducted during the months leading up to the country's first democratic elections.[42] The survey, conducted by the South Africa Labour Development Research Unit (University of Cape Town) in collaboration with the World Bank, sampled 43,687 individuals in 8,809 households. Of these, 2,928 had at least one child between birth and age five, and 4,595 had at least one child between birth and age fourteen. Data from the 1994 survey were examined because at the time of this study, the 1994 survey was the most recent publicly available survey available through the World Bank. The survey had a response rate of 95 percent. The survey offers an extensive coverage of key indicators relating to all spheres of life, including a variety of measures relevant to work and caregiving burdens.

Please see table A-1 for a description of the survey sample we analyzed.

MEASURES ANALYZED

In addition to the analyses described that were conducted in all countries, we examined the survey's detailed questions on family illness burden. Specifically, we analyzed the occurrence of health problems in the two weeks preceding the survey, the number of household members who had stopped normal activities due to health problems in those previous two weeks, the number of days of work missed due to health problems, and whether any children younger than fourteen had an illness or injury during that time period.

In addition, we examined the frequency of common childhood illnesses among zero- to four-year-olds and the available social and family supports. Finally, our analysis included an examination of the average duration of breast-feeding, whether children were immunized, and an assessment of the school enrollment rates of children and their relationship to parental working conditions.

Appendix B
Special Topic Large-Scale Surveys Conducted

Work and Caregiving Crisis: The Case of Botswana

The global AIDS pandemic is presenting one of the greatest threats to human health in centuries. Worldwide, 38 million people are infected. In six countries throughout southern Africa, over 20 percent of reproductive-age adults are infected. Where the infection rates are highest, HIV/AIDS undermines the ability of families to economically survive and dramatically raises caregiving burdens while taking lives. Botswana is one of the countries at the epicenter of the epidemic with 37 percent of adults infected.[43] As part of the Project on Global Working Families, we conducted the Botswana Family and Health Needs Survey to better understand the conditions faced at work, at home, and in the community by people who are themselves HIV infected or by those who are caring for others with HIV/AIDS. The project systematically examined the social and structural ways in which the work and social environments in Botswana affect HIV care as well as other care for adults and children.

In 2002, 1,077 individuals waiting to see a health-care provider at outpatient clinics in government hospitals in Gaborone, the capital city; Lobatse, a large town; and Molepolole, an urban village, were invited to participate. The residency characteristics of the sample interviewed reflected the general population in Botswana in which 40 percent live in cities, 16 percent live in major towns, and 44 percent live in urban villages.[44] In Gaborone, 426 individuals were recruited, and the response rate was 95 percent. In Lobatse, 171 individuals were recruited, and the response rate was 97 percent. In Molepolole, 480 individuals were recruited, and the response rate was 95 percent. The survey consisted of 167 questions, the majority of which were focused on the issues surrounding caregiving and working among families including those with a member who was HIV positive. Twelve questions pertained to the respondent's own experience of HIV infection.

Please see table B-1 for a description of this sample.

Transnational Working Families: The Case of Mexico

While migration and family separation across borders is a global phenomenon,[45] the U.S.-Mexican border is a particularly active border. In no other OECD country does the number of immigrants even approach that of Mexicans entering the United States.[46] The U.S. Immigration and Naturalization Service (INS) states that there were 2.25 million authorized entries of Mexicans into the United States in the 1990s.[47] Undocumented entries number millions more. Migration from Mexico to the United States is transforming the social fabric of both the sending and receiving communities.[48] Yet, far more research has focused on the United States than on Mexico, and that which has examined the impact on Mexico has focused on the monetary remittances that are sent from the American side.[49] The impact of migration on the family members who remain in Mexico has been largely unexamined.[50]

In 2004, we conducted the Transnational Working Families Survey to examine how the families of migrant workers in Mexico cope with the departure of a parent or other adult. We developed and administered a closed-ended survey with 257 questions to investigate the impact on the health and welfare of families of transnational life and the role of labor and social conditions in determining health and well-being in transnational families in Mexico. The overall response rate was 81 percent.

We surveyed a representative sample of families residing in municipalities with high migration rates. The sample frame consisted of the municipalities in Mexico that have a population of at least 50,000 (based on the 2000 census) and where at least 20 percent of the households had a member migrate to the United States in the prior five years.[51] In Mexico, five municipalities of 50,000 or more have this high migration rate: Rio Grande, Zacatecas; La Barca, Jalisco; Comonfort, Guanajuato; Romita, Guanajuato; and Ixmiquilpan, Hidalgo.

In total, 1,509 households with working caregivers were interviewed. A total of 755 had a member of the household who had migrated in the last five years, and 754 did not. Note that in the survey, households with migrants were oversampled to obtain equal numbers of migrant and nonmigrant households; all households with a working primary caregiver in which there was a household member who had migrated to the United States were interviewed, while

Table B-1. Sample of Respondents in Our Family and Health Needs Survey in Botswana

	Percentage of overall sample of respondents	Percentage of parents with a 0–17-year-old in the household	Percentage of respondents affected by HIV (caregiver or infected)
Highest education level achieved			
None	14	14	12
Primary	24	25	25
Secondary	35	34	35
Certificate	13	13	12
Diploma	10	12	13
University degree	3	3	3
Marital status			
Married	23	30	28
Living with partner	12	14	11
Separated	17	11	13
Divorced	2	2	2
Widowed	5	5	4
Single	40	37	42
Number of children under 18 in household			
0	18	0	15
1	18	18	14
2	22	27	21
3 or more	42	55	50
Age of children in household			
At least one child between 0 and 5 in household	50	64	55
At least one child between 6 and 14 in household	65	81	71
At least one child between 15 and 17 in household	33	42	37
Per capita household income			
Below $10/day	82	88	83
At or above $10/day	18	12	17
Respondent's wage income			
Below $10/day	37	37	31
At or above $10/day	63	63	69

one in three of the households in which there was no migrant were asked to participate.

Please see table B-2 for a description of this sample.

The Survey of Midlife in the United States and the National Study of Daily Experiences

With our colleagues at the MacArthur Foundation Network on Successful Midlife Development, we developed survey instruments addressing work and caregiving, including sections in the Survey of Midlife in the United States (MIDUS) and in the National Study of Daily Experiences (NSDE). The members of the MacArthur Foundation Network on Successful Midlife Development, consisting of researchers from across the United States and Europe, conducted the MIDUS survey, which involved a nationally representative sample of more than 3,500 adults aged twenty-five to seventy-four and 1,100 employed adults caring for children, parents, or parents-in-law. The survey included both a telephone interview and a lengthy written questionnaire. The telephone survey had a response rate of 70 percent, and 86.8 percent of those completing the telephone survey completed the self-administered survey as well. The MIDUS survey included information on working conditions, work-family interactions, relationships with coworkers and supervisors, and workplace and outside support.

As part of the NSDE with David Almeida, we conducted the first national daily telephone survey of people regarding how their work was disrupted by family needs. A randomized subsample of 1,242 MIDUS respondents were contacted for the NSDE; 83 percent agreed to participate in the daily telephone diary survey. Of the more than 1,000 national respondents, 870 were working. Study participants were asked whether they had cut back on any of their normal activities during the previous twenty-four hours because a family member needed their help. Follow-up questions were asked to explore what happened and how much it interfered with their usual activities. The respondents to the daily diaries study were telephoned for eight days in a row. When study participants were away from their homes, they were given a toll-free number to call and report their experiences. Eighty-seven percent of the respondents completed six or more days.

See table B-3 for a description of the survey samples we analyzed.

Table B-2. Sample of Households in Our Transnational Working Families Survey in Mexico

	Percentage of overall sample of households	Percentage of households with a U.S. migrant	Percentage of households without a U.S. migrant
Highest education level achieved of respondent			
None	7	6	7
Primary	39	43	35
Junior secondary/middle school	31	32	30
Senior secondary/high school	13	12	14
College	10	6	14
Graduate school	1	0	1
Marital status of respondent			
Married	64	53	74
Living with partner	3	2	3
Separated	18	31	5
Divorced	2	2	1
Widowed	5	5	5
Single	9	8	10
Race/ethnicity of respondent			
Latino or Mestizo	96	95	96
Indigenous	4	5	4
Number of children under 18 in household			
1	23	25	21
2	32	34	31
3 or more	44	41	48
Age of children in household			
At least one child between 0 and 5 in household	56	56	56
At least one child between 6 and 14 in household	78	77	79
At least one child between 15 and 17 in household	26	25	28
Per capita household income			
Below $10/day	97	98	95
At or above $10/day	3	2	5
Respondent's wage income			
Below $10/day	73	76	69
At or above $10/day	27	24	31

Table B-3. Sample of Employed Adults in the National Study of Daily Experiences

	Percentage of employed adults	Percentage of employed caregivers*	Percentage of employed parents
Highest education level achieved			
GED, some high school, or less	8	8	8
High school graduate	28	29	30
Some college	27	28	28
College degree	26	26	25
Some graduate school or graduate degree	12	10	10
Marital status			
Married	64	71	78
Living with partner	4	4	3
Separated	2	3	3
Divorced	15	15	13
Widowed	4	2	1
Single	10	5	2
Race/Ethnicity			
White	90	88	88
Black	6	7	8
Native American	1	1	1
Asian or Pacific Islander	1	1	1
Other	2	2	2
Multiracial	1	1	1
Number of children under 18 in household			
0	56	23	0
1	17	30	42
2	18	32	39
3 or more	9	15	19
Age of children in household			
At least one child between 0 and 5 in household	15	28	36
At least one child between 6 and 14 in household	27	49	64
At least one child between 15 and 17 in household	13	24	31
Per capita household income			
Below $10/day	5	8	7
At or above $10/day	95	92	93
Below $20/day	12	17	15
At or above $20/day	88	83	85
Respondent's wage income			
Below $10/day	14	12	13
At or above $10/day	86	88	87
Below $20/day	20	18	19
At or above $20/day	80	82	81

*Caregivers are those adults who have at least one child younger than 18 in the household or are providing 8 or more hours of unpaid assistance to a parent or parent-in-law.

Notes on Tables

Wherever data allowed, parallel demographic characteristics are provided for all surveys in the tables. Surveys reliably provided data on household members' age, education, marital status, and family structure. Data on race, ethnicity, and job sector varied in availability. In some cases only individual income was available and in others only household income.

Income data reported in each survey have been converted to a common currency using the World Bank's purchasing power parity (PPP) conversion factors, which are estimates of the number of units of a country's currency that would be needed to purchase the same amount of goods and services in the local economy as a U.S. dollar would buy in the United States. This PPP adjustment equalizes the purchasing power of different currencies and eliminates differences in price levels across countries.

All percentages are rounded to the nearest whole number. As a result of rounding, percentages may not always sum to 100. Tables report the ages of children in the households to provide important information on the frequency of households with preschool, young school-age, and older school-age children. These percentages may sum to over 100 because households with multiple children would fall into multiple categories if their children are in different age groupings.

Appendix C
In-Depth Interviews of Families and Caregivers
Worldwide in Five Regions

Overview

Central to the Project on Global Working Families have been the in-depth interviews we have conducted of working families, employers, teachers, childcare providers, and health-care providers in a wide variety of global settings in order to examine the differences and commonalities among the experiences of working adults across national borders, social class, occupation, gender, and ethnicity. Semistructured, open-ended interview instruments were used to examine the impact of societal and working conditions on childhood, on children's health and development, and on the well-being of families.[52]

We have conducted and analyzed more than 1,000 in-depth interviews in

Mexico, Botswana, Vietnam, the United States, Honduras, and Russia. The six country sites were chosen on the basis of two criteria. First, all six country sites have experienced the dramatic demographic changes that are transforming families and work around the world. Second, while the sites have these marked demographic transformations in common, they otherwise represent very different settings geographically, politically, economically, and socially. Specifically, in addition to representing different regions around the world, the six countries represent high-, medium-, and low-income nations; have economies driven variously by natural resource extraction, manufacturing, and services; and include democratic as well as socialist governments.

Botswana

IN-DEPTH INTERVIEWS WITH PARENTS

Parents were recruited at government health clinics in Gaborone, Lobatse, and Molepolole. Between 2000 and 2001, a total of 254 interviews were conducted, 38 of which were pilot interviews; 33 interviews were an oversample focused on HIV. The overall response rate was 96 percent. Nonrespondents were asked a brief series of demographic questions to determine whether there were any significant differences between those who chose to participate and those who did not. There were no significant differences between respondents and nonrespondents in terms of marital status, educational attainment, or whether they have formal or informal work.

Please see table C-1 for a description of the sample of parents interviewed.

IN-DEPTH INTERVIEWS WITH PROFESSIONALS

In addition to speaking at great length with working parents, we conducted forty-eight in-depth, semistructured interviews of health professionals, teachers, and childcare providers who were knowledgeable about the communities in which they worked. Participants were recruited at government health clinics and school settings. Sites were chosen to ensure regional variation.

Mexico

IN-DEPTH INTERVIEWS WITH PARENTS

From 1999 to 2000, study participants were recruited at health clinics in Mexico City and in San Cristóbal de las Casas, Chiapas. Clinics were chosen to ensure variation in occupation, socioeconomic status, family structure, and ethnicity. In-

Table C-1. Sample of Parents in Our Ethnographic Study in Botswana

	Percentage of parents
Highest education level achieved	
Did not complete primary school	5
Completed primary/elementary school	24
Completed junior secondary/middle school	43
Completed senior secondary/high school	17
Completed college	11
Marital status	
Married	26
Living with partner	18
Separated	3
Divorced	1
Widowed	1
Single	52
Race/ethnicity	
Bakwena	36
Bangwaketse	20
Bangwato	11
Bakgatla	9
Bakalanga	7
Balete	6
Other	11
Number of children under 18 in household	
1	42
2	22
3 or more	36
Age of children in household	
At least one child between 0 and 5 in household	54
At least one child between 6 and 14 in household	74
At least one child between 15 and 17 in household	44
Age at birth of first child	
Mean	22
Range	13–44
Per capita household income	
Below $10/day	67
At or above $10/day	33
Respondent's wage income	
Below $10/day	39
At or above $10/day	61
Work sector	
Formal	77
Informal	23
Caring for family member or friend with HIV/AIDS	
Yes	53
No	47

terviews were conducted with 136 parents, including a representative sample of 120 parents and 16 pilot interviews. The response rate for Mexico was 87 percent. Nonrespondents were asked a brief series of demographic questions to determine whether there were any significant differences between those who chose to participate and those who did not. There were no significant differences between respondents and nonrespondents in terms of ethnicity, marital status, number of children, or whether they had formal or informal work.

Please see table C-2 for a description of the sample interviewed.

INTERVIEWS WITH PROFESSIONALS

In addition to speaking at length with working parents, we conducted in-depth, semistructured interviews of twenty-eight health professionals, pediatricians, family medicine physicians, childcare providers, educators, and daycare center directors and teachers who were knowledgeable about the communities in which they worked. Participants were recruited at health clinics, hospitals, and daycare centers in Monterrey, Nuevo Leon, Nuevo Laredo, Tamaulipas, and Oaxaca de Juarez. Sites were chosen to ensure regional, demographic, and ethnic variation.

United States

PARENTS INTERVIEWED IN THE URBAN
WORKING FAMILIES STUDY

In the Urban Working Families Study, we conducted surveys to measure the effects of parental working conditions on children's health and development. In this study, we interviewed a random sample of families who were using a city's services. In addition, the medical records of children were carefully reviewed.

Families were eligible for this study if all parents living in the household had worked at least twenty hours per week for at least six months during the preceding year. The response rate was 82 percent with 95 percent of those who agreed to participate completing both the closed-item survey and the in-depth, semistructured interview. Nonrespondents were asked a brief series of demographic questions to determine whether there were any significant differences between those who chose to participate and those who did not. There were no significant differences between respondents and nonrespondents in terms of race, education, health-care coverage, marital status, number of hours worked per week, employment status, age of respondent, ages of children, or number of children. In addition, we interviewed a supplementary sample of low-income families living in subsidized housing and another sample of unilingual Spanish speakers.

Please see table C-3 for a description of the sample that was analyzed.

Table C-2. Sample of Parents in Our Ethnographic Study in Mexico

	Percentage of parents
Highest education level achieved	
Did not complete primary school	32
Completed primary/elementary school	16
Completed junior secondary/middle school	26
Completed senior secondary/high school	22
Completed college	4
Marital status	
Married	67
Living with partner	8
Separated	10
Divorced	5
Widowed	2
Single	8
Race/ethnicity	
Latino or Mestizo	74
Indigenous	26
Number of children under 18 in household	
1	24
2	33
3 or more	34
Age of children in household	
At least one child between 0 and 5 in household	53
At least one child between 6 and 14 in household	63
At least one child between 15 and 17 in household	27
Age at birth of first child	
Mean	22
Range	14–38
Respondent's wage income	
Below $10/day	57
At or above $10/day	43
Work sector	
Formal	60
Informal	40

Table C-3. Sample of Employed Parents in Our Ethnographic Study in the United States

	Percentage of employed parents
Highest education level achieved	
Did not complete primary school	0
Completed primary/elementary school	4
Completed high school/GED	28
Completed some college	29
College graduate	13
Some graduate school or graduate degree	26
Marital status	
Married	57
Living with partner	4
Separated	8
Divorced	8
Widowed	3
Single	21
Race/ethnicity	
White	54
Black	26
Asian or Pacific Islander	8
Native American	1
Multiracial	5
Other	5
Number of children under 18 in household	
1	42
2	42
3 or more	36
Age of children in household	
At least one child between 0 and 5 in household	65
At least one child between 6 and 14 in household	61
At least one child between 15 and 17 in household	15
Age at birth of first child	
Mean	27
Range	15–45
Per capita household income	
Below $10/day	25
At or above $10/day	75
Below $20/day	42
At or above $20/day	58
Work sector	
Formal	90
Informal	10

In addition to speaking at length with working caregivers, we interviewed a representative sample of thirty-two childcare providers in an urban area. We conducted in-depth, semistructured interviews of childcare providers about the daily care they provided for children and the issues they faced in meeting children's health and developmental needs. Of the thirty-two childcare providers interviewed, 34 percent worked in home-based preschool care, 31 percent in school-age after-school programs, 22 percent in public preschool childcare centers, and 13 percent in private preschool childcare centers. Of the childcare centers where interviews were conducted, 53 percent were publicly funded; 34 percent were private, for-profit; and 13 percent were private, nonprofit.

EMPLOYERS INTERVIEWED IN THE URBAN WORKING FAMILIES STUDY

We also interviewed a random sample of employers, stratified by firm size, selected from a complete list of the city's employers. In-depth face-to-face interviews and closed-item surveys were conducted with each employer. Employers were asked about a range of issues related to employees' successes and difficulties on the job, including how extensively family needs affected the workplace, which family needs most affected the workplace, who was affected and how when family needs arose, and when it was or was not the employer's responsibility to provide assistance. The employer study had a response rate of 74 percent.

Vietnam

INTERVIEWS WITH PARENTS

From 2000 to 2001 in Ho Chi Minh City and surrounding periurban and urban areas, 147 interviews were conducted, including 22 pilot interviews. To obtain a sample of working parents with a wide range of economic and living situations, we conducted interviews at three sites in Ho Chi Minh City, including a large hospital for children that serves both urban and rural residents, a government-owned general hospital serving a population of diverse economic backgrounds, and the largest public obstetrics and gynecology teaching hospital in the city.

The overall response rate was 89 percent for fathers and 77 percent for mothers. Nonrespondents were asked a brief series of demographic questions to determine whether there were any significant differences between those who chose to participate and those who did not. There were no significant differences between respondents and nonrespondents in terms of marital status, educational attainment, or whether they had formal or informal work.

Please see table C-4 for a description of the respondents.

INTERVIEWS WITH PROFESSIONALS

In addition to speaking at great length with working parents, we conducted indepth, semistructured interviews of health professionals. Nine physicians were interviewed at the major children's hospital.

Russia

In 2002, we conducted interviews and focus groups in Moscow to learn how the political, economic, and social transitions of the 1990s had affected adults' ability to get and keep jobs while simultaneously caring for children and adult family members in need. Interviews and focus groups were conducted in the offices of the Russian Center for Public Opinion and Market Research (VCIOM) in Moscow,[53] involving fifty participants. Households in which all adults were working for pay were selected from VCIOM's database of Moscow residents.

Please see table C-5 for a description of the sample interviewed.

Honduras

In Honduras in 2001, we interviewed eighty-five working parents, teachers, doctors, and other caregiving professionals. Participants were interviewed in medical clinics, public daycare centers, shelters, and people's homes in the capital, Tegucigalpa, and in the rural towns of Sabana Grande, Montegrande, Adurasta, San Lorenzo, Laure Abajo, Rosario, and El Chiflon.

In addition to examining work and social conditions and their effect on family health and well-being, the interviews in Honduras explored the long-term impact on working families of a natural disaster, Hurricane Mitch, which had devastated Central America in October 1998. In Honduras, 14,600 people had died as a result of the hurricane, and an additional 2.1 million had been affected in a manner requiring medical attention or immediate assistance with essentials such as food, water, or shelter.[54] Of the 661,760 individuals (82,720 families) whose housing had been affected by the hurricane, 265,760 had been forced to relocate to temporary housing, while 396,000 continued to live in substandard, hazardous conditions.[55]

Table C-4. Sample of Parents in Our Ethnographic Study in Vietnam

	Percentage of parents
Highest education level achieved	
Did not complete primary school	9
Completed primary/elementary school	14
Completed junior secondary/middle school	21
Completed senior secondary/high school	32
Completed college	24
Marital status	
Married	94
Living with partner	0
Separated	2
Divorced	3
Widowed	1
Single	0
Race/ethnicity	
Vietnamese	93
Chinese	5
Cambodian	2
Number of children under 18 in household	
1	50
2	39
3 or more	11
Age of children in household	
At least one child between 0 and 5 in household	63
At least one child between 6 and 14 in household	57
At least one child between 15 and 17 in household	7
Age at birth of first child	
Mean	26
Range	16–41
Respondent's wage income	
Below $10/day	36
At or above $10/day	67
Work sector	
Formal	63
Informal	37

Table C-5. Sample of Parents in Our Ethnographic Study in Russia

	Percentage of parents
Highest education level achieved	
Did not complete primary school	0
Completed primary/elementary school	4
Completed senior secondary/high school	26
Completed technical/vocational training after high school	50
Completed college	20
Marital status	
Married	90
Divorced	4
Widowed	4
Single	2
Number of children under 18 in household	
1	52
2	38
3 or more	10
Age of children in household	
At least one child between 0 and 5 in household	24
At least one child between 6 and 14 in household	66
At least one child between 15 and 17 in household	36
Age at birth of first child	
Mean	25
Range	17–37
Per capita household income	
Below $10/day	51
At or above $10/day	49
Respondent's wage income	
Below $10/day	26
At or above $10/day	74
Work sector	
Formal	98
Informal	2

Notes on Tables

Wherever data allowed, parallel demographic characteristics are provided for all surveys in the tables. Surveys reliably provided data on household members' age, education, marital status, and family structure. Data on race, ethnicity, and job sector varied in availability.

Income data reported in each survey have been converted to a common currency using the World Bank's purchasing power parity (PPP) conversion factors, which are estimates of the number of units of a country's currency that would be needed to purchase the same amount of goods and services in the local economy as a U.S. dollar would buy in the United States. This PPP adjustment equalizes the purchasing power of different currencies and eliminates differences in price levels across countries.

All percentages are rounded to the nearest whole number. As a result of rounding, percentages may not always sum to 100. Tables report the ages of children in the households to provide important information on the frequency of households with preschool, young school-age, and older school-age children. These percentages may sum to over 100 because households with multiple children would fall into multiple categories if their children are in different age groupings.

Appendix D
The Work, Family, and Equity Index:
Examining Policies in 180 Countries

Background

We created the first index to measure how public policies in nations around the globe compare in meeting the needs of working families. We have examined available policies in 180 nations regarding such critical issues as infant and toddler care, early education, care for school-age children, elder care, parental leave, and leave to care for other family needs.

Selecting the Measures for the Index

In order to select evidence-based items for the index, my research team conducted a comprehensive review of the academic literature in a wide range of areas using the following databases: Social Science Citation Index, Science Citation Index, Sociofile, Econlit, Medline, and Education Resources Information Center (ERIC).

Our criteria for including a policy on the weight of the research evidence were that the findings regarding the policy's importance to the health and well-being of working families were strong and statistically significant; had been replicated; and were consistent across time, location, and data source. The review included an examination of published research that documented the conditions faced by and the needs of working families, as well as those that investigated the consequences of existing policies and programs (or lack thereof) for the well-being of working families, their children, and their elderly and disabled members. In addition to this review of the literature, we elicited summary analyses of the evidence base on work and family issues from leaders in a variety of academic fields—ranging from child development to employment research to political science—and from public- and private-sector professionals at a series of conferences.

In order to identify the policies that had achieved global consensus, we conducted a comprehensive review of international agreements, treaties, covenants, and other legal documents that were relevant to work and family issues, including the more than 240 treaties proposed by the United Nations and the ILO. Our analysis included an assessment of the number of countries that had signed or ratified treaties and the number of agreements both signed and proposed pertaining to a given issue. The sources with particular relevance to our index items included the United Nations' Universal Declaration of Human Rights,[56] the Convention on the Elimination of All Forms of Discrimination against Women (CEDAW),[57] the Convention on the Rights of the Child (CRC),[58] and the ILO's Holidays with Pay Convention (Convention 132), Workers with Family Responsibilities Convention (156), and Maternity Protection Convention (183).[59]

This comprehensive research and international agreement review, together with a series of meetings with both national and international experts, led to the construction of an index with twenty items. The resulting items are described below.

The first ten items of the index address the ability of working adults to care for children, including children with special needs. The second ten items of the index address the ability of working adults to care for adult family members who are disabled, elderly, or otherwise in need of care.

Index Measures

ITEM 1: *Paid Leave for Childbearing and Childrearing*

Adequate paid leave for childbirth and childrearing (maternity, paternity, or parental leave) is available to all working adults in a manner that allows them to care for infants and toddlers, to maintain job security, and continue to financially contribute to the support of their family.

ITEM 2: *Infant and Toddler Care*

High-quality care for children during the first three years of life is available, affordable, accessible, and provided by well-trained staff in safe and nurturing settings, and paid parental leave is available.

ITEM 3: *Early Childhood Education and Care*

High-quality early childhood education is widely available, affordable, and accessible to all children between three and five years of age.

ITEM 4: *Working Adults' Availability to Provide Routine Care for Children*

Policies exist that assure that all children have a parent or other adult guardian available to support their educational, emotional, and developmental progress during nonschool hours (including evenings, nights, weekends, and holidays). Policies exist to assure that adults can afford necessities and attain a decent standard of living on a reasonable number of hours of paid work.

ITEM 5: *Educational Opportunities and Supervision for School-Age Children throughout the Day*

High-quality educational and/or enrichment opportunities throughout the full day are available, accessible, and affordable for all school-age children.

ITEM 6: *Educational Opportunities and Supervision for School-Age Children throughout the Year*

High-quality educational and/or enrichment opportunities throughout the full year are available, accessible, and affordable for all school-age children.

ITEM 7: *Paid Leave and Flexibility for Children's Educational Needs*

Adequate paid leave is available to all working adults when they need to attend to a child's educational or developmental needs.

ITEM 8: *Paid Leave and Flexibility for Children's Health Needs*

Adequate paid leave is available to all working adults when they need to meet the preventive or curative health needs of a child on a routine or intermittent basis.

ITEM 9: *Access of Children with Special Needs and Disabilities to Equal Educational Opportunities*

Access of children with special needs to educational and community activities is facilitated by policies and programs that promote full participation in these activities.

ITEM 10: *Health Supports for Children with Special Needs and Disabilities*

Health care and developmental assistance for children with special needs is available, accessible, and affordable on a routine, intermittent, or extended basis, as needed by the child.

ITEM 11: *Access of Adults with Disabilities to Equal Employment Opportunities*

Policies and programs exist to protect adults with disabilities who are able and willing to work from discrimination in employment practices, including hiring, training, and promotion, and to support their participation in the workforce.

ITEM 12: *Access of Adults with Disabilities to Participate Fully in Family and Community Activities*

Access of adults with disabilities to family and community activities is facilitated by policies and programs that decrease barriers and support full participation in these activities.

ITEM 13: *Health Supports for Disabled Adults*

Health supports for disabled adults are available, accessible, and affordable on a routine, intermittent, or extended basis, as needed.

ITEM 14: *Access of Older Adults to Equal Employment Opportunities*

Policies and programs exist to protect older persons who are able and willing to work from age-based discrimination in employment practices, including hiring, training, and promotion, and to support their participation.

ITEM 15: *Access of Older Adults to Participate Fully in Family and Community Activities*

Access of older adults to family and community activities is facilitated by policies and programs that decrease barriers and support full participation.

ITEM 16: *Health Supports for Older Adults*

Health supports for older adults are available, accessible, and affordable on a routine, intermittent, or extended basis, as needed.

ITEM 17: *Policies to Meet Basic Needs of Those Unable to Work*

The basic needs of disabled or older adults who are unable to work are met through policies that guarantee adequate economic support, such as old-age and disability pensions.

ITEM 18: *Working Adults' Availability to Provide Routine Care for Older and Disabled Family Members*

Policies exist that assure that working adults have adequate time to care for older or disabled family members if needed when other care is unavailable, such as during evenings, nights, weekends, and holidays. Policies exist to assure that adults can afford necessities and attain a decent standard of living on a reasonable number of hours of paid work.

ITEM 19: *Paid Leave and Flexibility for Adult Family Members' Health and Other Essential Needs*

Adequate paid leave is available to all working adults when they need to attend to an older or disabled adult's preventive or curative health and basic care needs. Discretionary paid leave and paid leave for family events is available to all working adults to attend to other essential family needs.

ITEM 20: *Paid Leave and Flexibility for Personal Health Needs*

Adequate paid leave is available to all working adults to attend to personal health needs.

Role of Equity

We believe it is critical that countries' performance on this index be measured against criteria of equity. In assessing a country's policies as they relate to working families, it is essential to know whether the policies are equally available and affordable to men and women and across social class, generations, and the diverse demographic groups that comprise a given society. It is equally essential to be certain that making use of these policies does not disadvantage or lead to discrimination against caregivers.

CAREGIVERS FACE INEQUITIES IN THE WORKPLACE IN HIRING, WAGES, PROMOTION, AND JOB STABILITY

While caregivers are often women, men who are caregivers also face penalties. They may lose jobs when they take time off to care for a child or an elderly parent. Even when family-friendly policies are in place, there are frequently unspoken penalties for taking advantage of them. An employee who takes time off for family needs may not advance in a firm as quickly as employees who do not. There may be no or only poor career tracks for part-time workers or workers who temporarily exit the labor force for caregiving. Preventing explicit and implicit discrimination against caregivers is essential to meeting the needs of working families.

THE POOR DISPROPORTIONATELY BEAR THE CARETAKING BURDENS IN MANY SOCIETIES

Moreover, lower-income working caregivers are more likely to lack essential benefits and to have poor working conditions than are middle-income caregivers. As a result, low-income families often find themselves trapped. With higher caregiving burdens and lower hourly wages, they often must chose between working long hours to get their families out of poverty while having no time for caregiving and spending time caring for their families but staying below the poverty line. Poor working conditions place barriers to parental involvement in their children's education and development, often resulting in lower academic achievements, increased behavioral problems, and poorer health outcomes for children being raised in poverty.

MORE EQUITABLE PROVISION OF THESE BASIC SOCIAL SERVICES CAN HELP TO BREAK THE CYCLE OF POVERTY

Low-income families have greater needs for health services than do wealthier families and fewer resources with which to meet these needs. Affordable, high-quality childcare is also difficult for poor families to find. Without access to quality childcare, children are less ready for school and more likely to have poor health and developmental outcomes.

Collecting Global Data

The data sources for the index items fall into two categories: those related to workplace policies and those related to services and programs. For example, in the area of children's care, we examined a set of labor-related measures—the availability of paid leave at an infant's birth or to care for children's health needs, the wage replacement rate, and duration of the leave—as well as a set of measures related to public services: the availability of early education for four- to five-year-olds and out-of-school care for school-age children.

In order to assess how countries around the world perform on each of the index measures, we searched for and reviewed both primary and secondary sources of data. Our primary data sources include actual labor codes and data from national governments on their programs and services. Secondary sources include data, documents, and reports from global intergovernmental organizations, such as UNESCO and the World Bank; national collections of international data; and, where globally comparable data were unavailable, regional sources, such as documents published by the OECD, regional branches of intergovernmental organizations such as UNESCO, and regional academic studies. The data we examined included conducting a detailed review of labor codes from 128 countries and examining information on social security systems in 160 countries.

Notes

Preface

1. S. J. Heymann, *The Widening Gap: Why Working Families Are in Jeopardy and What Can Be Done about It* (New York: Basic, 2000). A. Earle and S. J. Heymann, "What Causes Job Loss among Former Welfare Recipients? The Role of Family Health Problems," *Journal of the American Medical Women's Association* 57 (2002): 5–10. S. J. Heymann and A. Earle, "Low-income Parents: How Do Working Conditions Affect Their Opportunity to Help School-Age Children at Risk?" *American Educational Research Journal* 37, no. 2 (2000): 833–48. S. J. Heymann, "What Happens during and after School: Conditions Faced by Working Parents Living in Poverty and Their School-Age Children," *Journal of Children and Poverty* 6, no. 1 (2000): 5–20. S. J. Heymann and A. Earle, "The Impact of Welfare Reform on Parents' Ability to Care for Their Children's Health," *American Journal of Public Health* 89, no. 4 (1999): 502–5. S. J. Heymann and A. Earle, "The Work Family Balance: What Hurdles Are Parents Leaving Welfare Likely to Confront?" *Journal of Policy Analysis and Management* 17, no. 2 (1998): 312–21.

2. For example the World Bank, *World Development Indicators 2004* (Washington, DC: World Bank, 2004). Full data available online from the World Bank and partner institutions; select indicators available online at http://devdata.world bank.org/data-query.

3. For example the World Health Organization's Statistical Information System

(WHOSIS) and Basic Health Indicators (BHI) database. Available online at http://www3.who.int/whosis/core/core_select.cfm.

4. For example, the ILO's Key Indicators of the Labour Market. Available online at http://www.ilo.org/public/english/employment/strat/kilm/index.htm.

5. For example, UNESCO Institute for Statistics, *Global Education Digest 2003* (Montreal: UNESCO, 2003). Available online at http://www.uis.unesco.org/TEMPLATE/pdf/ged/GED_EN.pdf (accessed June 7, 2005).

6. To estimate this figure, detailed household survey information was used from a sample of widely divergent countries.

7. Everyone who conducts research involving interviews must decide how many people to interview and how deeply to pursue questions. In addition, they must determine something as or more important—namely, how representative of the general population their respondents are, as a group. Both the method of selecting people to participate and the rate at which people accept can profoundly affect whether the findings are representative of the experiences of a broader population. Snowball samples, in which a researcher or a journalist begins with a group of acquaintances and then asks them to suggest other people, may move beyond the bounds of the individual interviewer's personal circle, but the participants still are very unlikely to provide a sense of an entire community. The same glue that binds them together as friends or acquaintances—whether it is that all their children go to the same school, all the fathers play in the same league, or all the parents work at the same institution—is likely to make them different from other groups. Furthermore, those who have wider support networks, have more friends, and know more people are more likely to be named in a snowball sample. People who are more isolated, have less support, or are facing enough problems that they have little time to interact with others are unlikely to be picked up. Similarly, studies that interview respondents all from one workplace or one industry may be able to describe that workplace or industry well but will not be able to give insights into the experience of families working in a range of occupations. Too often, reports of extensive interviews have been based on very self-selective, not representative samples, but this threatens their generalizability. To avoid this pitfall, we have worked hard to interview representative populations, within the bounds of available resources.

8. Equally important as who is invited to participate in a study is how many agree—or the response rate. If only 10 percent of those asked agree to participate, the end result is that those interviewed may differ in significant ways from the general population. They may have agreed to participate for any number of reasons that differentiate them from the 90 percent who declined. While some of these differences may not matter to how valid a study's findings are, others would be significant. If 90 percent of a population worked eighty or more hours a week

but none of them were willing to participate in a lengthy study, it could well be that the 10 percent who agreed were the small number working twenty hours or less a week. Thus, those interviewed would present a biased sample, not a representative one, of the general experience, even if the sample had been drawn from across the nation. Many national and international studies that have gotten a lot of press have, in fact, had very low response rates, and this threatens their reliability. Because of this, we have committed substantial efforts and resources to ensure high response rates.

Chapter 1

1. All names have been changed to protect respondents' confidentiality. While recognizing cultural differences in the practice of referring to individuals by name, for consistency each person is introduced by full name and then the first name only is used in subsequent references to that person.
2. To calculate this figure, detailed household survey information was used from a sample of widely divergent countries.
3. The movement of single women without children into the paid labor force, like the movement of men, precedes much of the available globally comparative data.
4. Regional estimates of the percentage of the total labor force that is made up of women were calculated using data from the World Bank's *World Development Indicators 2002*. The percentage of the labor force that is female in each region was calculated as the weighted average of the female share of the labor force across all countries in that region using the total population of each country as the weighting factor. Only countries with data available in both 1960 and 2000 were used in calculating the regional estimates.
5. These figures are based on our analysis of the Botswana Multiple Indicator Survey; Russia Longitudinal Monitoring Survey; Vietnam Household Living Standards Survey; Brazil Living Standards Survey (Pesquisa Sobre Padroes de Vida); and Mexico Encuesta Nacional de Ingresos y Gastos de los Hogares (ENIGH).
6. M. P. Brockerhoff, "An Urbanizing World," *Population Bulletin* 55, no. 3 (2000): 3–44. J. R. McNeill, *Something New under the Sun: An Environmental History of the Twentieth-Century World* (New York: Norton, 2000).
7. United Nations Population Division (UNPD), *World Urbanization Prospects: The 1999 Revision* (New York: Department of Economic and Social Affairs, UN, 1999).
8. E. Aja, "Urbanization Imperatives in Africa: Nigerian Experience," *Philosophy*

and Social Action 27, no. 1 (2001): 13–22. H. C. Bolak, "Marital Power Dynamics: Women Providers and Working-Class Households in Istanbul," in *Cities in the Developing World: Issues, Theory, and Policy,* ed. J. Gugler, 218–32 (New York: Oxford University Press, 1997). P. Holmes-Eber, "Migration, Urbanization, and Women's Kin Networks in Tunis," *Journal of Comparative Family Studies* 28, no. 2 (1997): 54–72. J. W. Salaff and A. K. Wong, *Women, Work and the Family under Conditions of Rapid Industrialization: Singapore Chinese Women* (Toronto: American Sociological Association, 1981).

Chapter 2

1. The terms *Motswana* (singular) and *Batswana* (plural) are used in Botswana in reference to people from the country of Botswana. The word *Botswana* is only used in reference to the actual country.

2. The analyses in this chapter are based on a sample of households with at least one zero- to five-year-old child unless otherwise noted.

3. A. Elwan, "Poverty and Disability: A Survey of the Literature," *Social Protection Discussion Paper Series,* No. 9932 (Washington, DC: World Bank, 1999).

4. World Bank, *World Development Indicators 2004* (Washington, DC: World Bank, 2004).

5. While little previous research has examined the conditions that working-poor families confront globally, the enormity of the potential impact on children's long-term development of social and physical environments has been extensively documented. See Committee on Integrating the Science of Early Childhood Development, *From Neurons to Neighborhoods: The Science of Early Childhood Development,* ed. Jack P. Shonkoff and Deborah A. Phillips (Washington, DC: National Academy Press, 2000). M. S. Cynader and B. J. Frost, "Mechanisms of Brain Development: Neuronal Sculpting by the Physical and Social Environment," in *Developmental Health and the Wealth of Nations: Social, Biological, and Educational Dynamics,* ed. D. P. Keating and C. Hertzman, 153–84 (New York: Guilford, 1999). C. Bellamy, *The State of the World's Children 2001: Early Childhood* (New York: Oxford University Press for UNICEF, 2000). E. Pollitt, *Early Supplementary Feeding and Cognition: Effects over Two Decades* (Chicago: University of Chicago Press, 1993).

6. The high cost of bringing children to poor work settings was written across the faces of Edith Merino and her daughter. The sequelae of the nature of early childhood care have been documented in research both from industrialized and developing countries. See, for example, R. Myers, *The Twelve Who Survive: Strengthening Programmes of Early Childhood Development in the Third World*

(London and New York: Routledge in cooperation with UNESCO for the Consultative Group on Early Childhood Care and Development, 1992). D. S. Chin-Quee and S. Scarr, "Lack of Early Child Care Effects on School-Age Children's Social Competence and Academic Achievement," *Early Development and Parenting* 3, no. 2 (1994): 103–12.

7. J. Currie and D. Thomas, "Does Head Start Make a Difference?" *American Economic Review* 85, no. 3 (1995): 341–64. A. J. Reynolds et al., "Cognitive and Family-Support Mediators of Preschool Effectiveness: A Confirmatory Analysis," *Child Development* 67, no. 3 (1996): 1119–40. F. Campbell and C. Ramey, "Effects of Early Intervention on Intellectual and Academic Achievement: A Follow-Up Study of Children from Low-Income Families," *Child Development* 65, no. 2 (1994): 684–98. D. Johnson and T. Walker, "A Follow-Up Evaluation of the Houston Parent-Child Development Center: School Performance," *Journal of Early Intervention* 15, no. 3 (1991): 226–36. National Institute of Child Health and Human Development Early Child Care Research Network, "Child Outcomes when Child Care Center Classes Meet Recommended Standards for Quality," *American Journal of Public Health* 89 (1999): 1072–77. W. Barnett, "Long-Term Effects of Early Childhood Programs on Cognitive and School Outcomes," *Future of Children* 5, no. 3 (1995): 25–50. R. McKay, L. Condell, and H. Ganson, *The Impact of Head Start on Children, Families, and Communities: Final Report of the Head Start Evaluation, Synthesis, and Utilization Project* (Washington, DC: CSR, 1985). R. Myers, *The Twelve Who Survive: Strengthening Programmes of Early Childhood Development in the Third World* (London and New York: Routledge in cooperation with UNESCO for the Consultative Group on Early Childhood Care and Development, 1992). E. Chaturvedi et al., "Impact of Six Years Exposure to ICDS Scheme on Psycho-social Development," *Indian Pediatrics* 24 (February 1987): 153–60. W. S. Barnett, *Lives in the Balance: Age 27 Benefit-Cost Analysis of the High/Scope Perry Preschool Program* (Ypsilanti, MI: High/Scope Press, 1996).

Chapter 3

1. Per pupil funding estimates based on data from U.S. Department of Education, "Twenty-First Century Community Learning Centers." Available online at http://www.ed.gov/programs/21stcclc/funding.html (accessed June 10, 2005); U.S. Department of the Census, "Table 1: Annual Estimates of the Population by Sex and Five-Year Age Groups for the United States: April 1, 2000 to July 1, 2004." Available online at http://www.census.gov/popest/national/asrh/NC-EST2004–01.xls (accessed June 10, 2005). In 2005, $991 million was appropri-

ated for after school programs. There were more than 57 million school-age children. The resulting appropriation amounted to less than $18 per child per year.

2. Unless otherwise noted, the analyses in this chapter are based on a sample of households with at least one school-age child between six and fourteen years of age.

3. Countries were selected for analysis when there were at least 100 working families in each household category.

4. B. Iverson, G. Brownlee, and H. Walberg, "Parent-Teacher Contacts and Student Learning," *Journal of Educational Research* 74, no. 6 (1981): 394–96. D. Stevenson and D. Baker, "The Family-School Relation and the Child's School Performance," *Child Development* 58, no. 5 (1987): 1348–57. R. H. Bradley et al., "Home Environment and School Performance among Black Elementary School Children," *Journal of Negro Education* 56, no. 4 (1987): 499–509.

5. T. Z. Keith et al., "Does Parental Involvement Affect Eighth-Grade Student Achievement? Structural Analysis of National Data," *School Psychology Review* 22, no. 3 (1993): 474–96. P. G. Fehrmann, T. Z. Keith, and T. M. Reimers, "Home Influence on School Learning: Direct and Indirect Effects of Parental Involvement on High School Grades," *Journal of Educational Research* 80, no. 6 (1987): 330–37.

6. A. J. Reynolds, "Comparing Measures of Parental Involvement and Their Effects on Academic Achievement," *Early Childhood Research Quarterly* 7, no. 3 (1992): 441–62. J. Griffith, "Relation of Parental Involvement, Empowerment, and School Traits to Student Academic Performance," *Journal of Educational Research* 90, no. 1 (1996): 33–41. S. Christenson, T. Rounds, and D. Gorney, "Family Factors and Student Achievement: An Avenue to Increase Students' Success," *School Psychology Quarterly* 7, no. 3 (1992): 178–206. D. Miller and M. Kelley, "Interventions for Improving Homework Performance: A Critical Review," *School Psychology Quarterly* 6, no. 3 (1991): 174–85. J. Comer, "Home-School Relationships as They Affect the Academic Success of Children," *Education and Urban Society* 16, no. 3 (1984): 323–37. J. Fantuzzo, G. Davis, and M. Ginsburg, "Effects of Parent Involvement in Isolation or in Combination with Peer Tutoring on Student Self-Concept and Mathematics Achievement," *Journal of Educational Psychology* 87, no. 2 (1995): 272–81.

7. D. Leach and S. Siddall, "Parental Involvement in the Teaching of Reading: A Comparison of Hearing Reading, Paired Reading, Pause, Prompt, Praise, and Direct Instruction Methods," *British Journal of Educational Psychology* 60, no. 3 (1990): 349–55. R. Wilkes and V. Clarke, "Training versus Non-Training of Mothers as Home Reading Tutors," *Perceptual and Motor Skills* 67 (1988): 135–42. Eduardo Velez, Ernesto Schiefelbein, and Jorge Valenzuela, "Factors Affecting

Achievement in Primary Education: A Review of the Literature for Latin America and the Caribbean," working paper (Washington, DC: World Bank, 1993). FŸsun Akkšk, "Parental Involvement in the Educational System: To Empower Parents to Become More Knowledgeable and Effective" (paper presented at the Central Asia Regional Literacy Forum, Istanbul, Turkey, June 25, 1999). Available online at http://www.literacyonline.org/products/ili/webdocs/carlf_akk.html (accessed June 24, 2004). UNICEF, *The State of the World's Children 2001* (New York: Oxford University Press, 2001). World Bank, *Guinea beyond Poverty: How Supply Factors Influence Girls' Education in Guinea* (Washington, DC: World Bank, 1996). A. Edwards and J. Warin, "Parental Involvement in Raising the Achievement of Primary School Pupils: Why Bother?" *Oxford Review of Education* 25, no. 3 (1999): 325–41. G. van der Werf, B. Creemers, and H. Guldemond, "Improving Parental Involvement in Primary Education in Indonesia: Implementation, Effects and Costs," *School Effectiveness and School Improvement* 12, no. 4 (2001): 447–66. Lucia Dellagnelo, "Involving Brazilian Parents in Children's School Education: A Cautionary Note to Educators" (qualifying paper, Harvard Graduate School of Education, 1997).

8. J. Posner and D. L. Vandell, "Low-Income Children's After-School Care: Are There Beneficial Effects of After-School Programs?" *Child Development* 65, no. 2 (1994): 440–56. Department of Education, *Safe and Smart: Making After-School Hours Work for Kids* (Washington, DC: Department of Education, June 1998). Available online at http://www.ed.gov/pubs/SafeandSmart (accessed June 24, 2004). A. Carlisi, *The 3:00 Project Program Evaluation* (Decatur: Georgia School Age Care Association, 1996). T. Fleming-McCormick and N. Tushnet, *4-H After-School Activity Program* (Los Angeles, CA: Southwest Regional Education Laboratory and WestEd, 1996). D. Riley, *Preventing Problem Behavior and Raising Academic Performance in the Nation's Youth: The Impacts of 64 School-Age Child Care Programs in 15 States Supported by the Cooperative Extension Service Youth-at-Risk Initiative* (Madison: University of Wisconsin, 1994). P. Gregory, *Youth Opportunities Unlimited: Improving Outcomes for Youth through After-School Care* (Manchester: University of New Hampshire, 1996). National Federation of High School Associations, *The Case for High School Activities* (Kansas City, MO: National Federation of High School Associations, 1998).

9. Catherine Snow, *Preventing Reading Difficulties in Young Children* (Washington, DC: National Research Council and National Academy of Sciences, 1998).

10. D. Morris, B. Shaw, and J. Perney, "Helping Low Readers in Grades 2 and 3: An After-School Volunteer Tutoring Program," *Elementary School Journal* 91, no. 2 (1990): 133–51.

11. Janie Funkhouser, *Extending the Learning Time for Disadvantaged Students* (Washington, DC: U.S. Department of Education, 1995).

Chapter 4

1. UNICEF, *The State of the World's Children 2001* (New York: Oxford University Press, 2001).

2. WHO, "Reducing Mortality from Major Killers of Children," fact sheet no. 178 (Geneva: WHO Division of Child Health and Development, 1998).

3. K. Dewey, M. J. Heinig, and L. Nommsen-Rivers, "Differences in Morbidity between Breast-fed and Formula-fed Infants. Part 1," *Journal of Pediatrics* 126, no. 5 (1995): 696–702. R. G. Feachem and M. A. Koblinsky, "Interventions for the Control of Diarrhoeal Diseases among Young Children: Promotion of Breast-feeding," *Bulletin of the World Health Organization* 62, no. 2 (1984): 271–91. P. Howie et al., "Protective Effect of Breast-feeding against Infection," *British Medical Journal* 300, no. 6716 (1990): 11–16. P. Lepage, C. Munyakazi, and P. Hennart, "Breastfeeding and Hospital Mortality in Children in Rwanda," *Lancet* 1, no. 8268 (1982): 403.

4. M. Cerqueiro et al., "Epidemiologic Risk Factors for Children with Acute Lower Respiratory Tract Infection in Buenos Aires, Argentina: A Matched Case-Control Study," *Reviews of Infectious Diseases*, Suppl. 8, no. 12 (1990): S1021–28. P. Howie et al., "Protective Effect of Breast-feeding against Infection," *British Medical Journal* 300, no. 6716 (1990): 11–16. C. J. Watkins, S. R. Leeder, and R. T. Corkhill, "The Relationship between Breast and Bottle Feeding and Respiratory Illness in the First Year of Life," *Journal of Epidemiology and Community Health* 33, no. 3 (1979): 180–82. A. Wright et al., "Breast Feeding and Lower Respiratory Tract Illness in the First Year of Life," *British Medical Journal* 299, no. 6705 (1989): 946–49.

5. G. Aniansson et al., "A Prospective Cohort Study on Breast-Feeding and Otitis Media in Swedish Infants," *Pediatric Infectious Disease Journal* 13, no. 3 (1994): 183–88. B. Duncan et al., "Exclusive Breast-feeding for at Least 4 Months Protects against Otitis Media," *Pediatrics* 91, no. 5 (1993): 867–72.

6. C. Arnold, S. Makintube, and G. R. Istre, "Day Care Attendance and Other Risk Factors for Invasive *Haemophilus Influenzae* Type B Disease," *American Journal of Epidemiology* 138, no. 5 (1993): 333–40.

7. A. S. Cunningham, D. B. Jelliffe, and E. F. Patrice Jelliffe, "Breast-feeding and Health in the 1980s: A Global Epidemiologic Review," *Journal of Pediatrics* 118, no. 5 (1991): 659–66. R. G. Feachem and M. A. Koblinsky, "Interventions for the Control of Diarrhoeal Diseases among Young Children: Promotion of Breast-feeding," *Bulletin of the World Health Organization* 62, no. 2 (1984): 271–91.

8. R. G. Feachem and M. A. Koblinsky, "Interventions for the Control of Diarrhoeal Diseases among Young Children: Promotion of Breast-feeding," *Bulletin of the World Health Organization* 62, no. 2 (1984): 271–91. J. Habicht, J. Da-

Vanzo, and W. P. Butz, "Does Breastfeeding Really Save Lives, or Are Apparent Benefits Due to Biases?" *American Journal of Epidemiology* 123, no. 2 (1986): 279–90. J. N. Hobcraft, J. McDonald, and S. O. Rutstein, "Demographic Determinants of Infant and Early Child Mortality: A Comparative Analysis," *Population Studies* 39, no. 21 (1985): 363–85. J. Jason, P. Nieburg, and J. S. Marks, "Mortality and Infectious Disease Associated with Infant-feeding Practice in Developing Countries, Part 2," *Pediatrics* 74, no. 4 (1984): 702–27.

9. J. Coreil et al., "Social and Psychological Costs of Preventive Child Health Services in Haiti," *Social Science and Medicine* 38, no. 2 (1994): 231–38. J. E. Fielding, W. G. Cumberland, and L. Pettitt, "Immunization Status of Children of Employees in a Large Corporation," *Journal of the American Medical Association* 271, no. 7 (1994): 525–30. C. Lannon et al., "What Mothers Say about Why Poor Children Fall Behind on Immunizations: A Summary of Focus Groups in North Carolina," *Archives of Pediatrics and Adolescent Medicine* 149, no. 10 (1995): 1070–75. L. K. McCormick et al., "Parental Perceptions of Barriers to Childhood Immunization: Results of Focus Groups Conducted in an Urban Population," *Health Education Research* 12, no. 3 (1997): 355–62.

10. P. R. Mahaffy, "The Effects of Hospitalization on Children Admitted for Tonsillectomy and Adenoidectomy," *Nursing Research* 14, no. 1 (1965): 12–19. S. J. Palmer, "Care of Sick Children by Parents: A Meaningful Role," *Journal of Advanced Nursing* 18, no. 2 (1993): 185–91. G. van der Schyff, "The Role of Parents during Their Child's Hospitalization," *Australian Nurses Journal* 8, no. 11 (1979): 57–61.

11. I. Kristensson-Hallstron, G. Elander, and G. Malmfors, "Increased Parental Participation in a Pediatric Surgical Day-Care Unit," *Journal of Clinical Nursing* 6, no. 4 (1997): 297–302. M. R. Taylor and P. O'Connor, "Resident Parents and Shorter Hospital Stay," *Archives of Disease in Childhood* 64, no. 2 (1989): 274–76.

12. S. Carlton-Ford et al., "Epilepsy and Children's Social and Psychological Adjustment," *Journal of Health and Social Behavior* 36, no. 3 (1995): 285–301.

13. B. J. Anderson et al., "Family Characteristics of Diabetic Adolescents: Relationship to Metabolic Control," *Diabetes Care* 4, no. 6 (1981): 585–94. K. W. Hamlett, D. S. Pellegrini, and K. S. Katz, "Childhood Chronic Illness as a Family Stressor," *Journal of Pediatric Psychology* 17, no. 1 (1992): 33–47. A. LaGreca et al., "I Get By with a Little Help from My Family and Friends: Adolescents' Support for Diabetes Care," *Journal of Pediatric Psychology* 20, no. 4 (1995): 449–76.

14. S. J. Heymann, S. Toomey, and F. Furstenberg, "Working Parents: What Factors Are Involved in Their Ability to Take Time Off from Work when Their Children Are Sick?" *Archives of Pediatrics and Adolescent Medicine* 153, no. 8 (1999): 870–74. S. Jody Heymann, *The Widening Gap: Why America's Working Families Are in Jeopardy and What Can Be Done about It* (New York: Basic, 2000).

S. J. Heymann and A. Earle, "Parental Availability for the Care of Sick Children," *Pediatrics* 98, no. 2 (1996): 226–30.

15. UNICEF, *Education Update: Children with Disabilities*, vol. 2, no. 4 (New York: UNICEF Programme Division, Education Section, October 1999). Available online at http://www.unicef.org/girlseducation/vol2disabileng.pdf (accessed July 30, 2004).

Chapter 5

1. The social class disparities existed whether measured by income or education. Parents who had not completed high school and thus had the fewest job choices consistently paid the highest price for caring for their children and other family members. Those who had not completed high school were more likely to lose pay while caring for a sick child (43 percent versus 34 percent), to lose pay for other caregiving responsibilities (22 percent versus 14 percent), to face difficulty retaining jobs or loss of job promotions because of caring for sick children (13 percent versus 8 percent), and to face difficulty retaining jobs or loss of job promotions because of other caregiving responsibilities (14 percent versus 7 percent). Those who had not completed high school were more likely to face difficulty because of work responsibilities when caring for their sick children (55 percent versus 46 percent). They were also more likely to leave their children home alone sick (24 percent versus 4 percent) and to report negative impacts of their own working conditions on their children's health (34 percent versus 16 percent).

2. J. Melendez and E. Rodriguez-Oreggia, *The Americas Social Security Report 2003: Evaluation of the Reforms* (report presented at a conference entitled "Strengthening Social Security in the Americas," Barbados, November 3, 2003). For further information, see http://natlex.ilo.org, where the full text of the Mexican social security law can be readily accessed.

Chapter 6

1. UNAIDS and WHO, *Global Summary of the HIV/AIDS Epidemic December 2003* (Geneva: UNAIDS and WHO, 2003).

2. UNAIDS and WHO, *AIDS Epidemic Update December 2001* (Geneva: UNAIDS and WHO, 2001).

3. UNAIDS and WHO, *Global Summary of the HIV/AIDS Epidemic December 2003* (Geneva: UNAIDS and WHO, 2003).

4. UNAIDS and WHO, *Global Summary of the HIV/AIDS Epidemic December 2003* (Geneva: UNAIDS and WHO, 2003).

5. UNAIDS and WHO, *AIDS Epidemic Update December 2002* (Geneva: UNAIDS and WHO, 2002).

6. UNAIDS and WHO, *Global Summary of the HIV/AIDS Epidemic December 2003* (Geneva: UNAIDS and WHO, 2003).

7. UN Population Division, "World Population Prospects, the 2002 Revision" (2002). Available online at http://www.un.org/esa/population/publications/wpp2002/wpp2002annextables.pdf (accessed July 2, 2004).

8. UNAIDS/WHO/UNICEF, "Epidemiological Fact Sheets by Country" (2002). Available online at http://www.who.int/emc-hiv/fact_sheets/All_countries.html (accessed July 2, 2004). Specific sites used from this directory were http://www.who.int/emchiv/fact_sheets/pdfs/Southafrica_EN.pdf;http://www.who.int/emc-hiv/fact_sheets/pdfs/Zimbabwe_EN.pdf; http://www.who.int/emc-hiv/fact_sheets/pdfs/Botswana_EN.pdf; http://www.who.int/emc-hiv/fact_sheets/pdfs/Swaziland_EN.pdf; http://www.who.int/emc-hiv/fact_sheets/pdfs/Lesotho_EN.pdf; http://www.who.int/emc-hiv/fact_sheets/pdfs/Namibia_EN.pdf; http://www.who.int/emc-hiv/fact_sheets/pdfs/Zambia_EN.pdf; http://www.who.int/emc-hiv/fact_sheets/pdfs/Malawi_EN.pdf.

9. UNAIDS/UNICEF/USAID, *Children on the Brink 2004: A Joint Report on New Orphan Estimates and a Framework for Action* (Washington, DC: USAID, 2004). Available online at http://www.unaids.org/Unaids/EN/in+focus/topic+areas/children-orphans.asp (accessed July 28, 2004).

10. Commonwealth Secretariat and UNIFEM, *The HIV/AIDS Epidemic: An Inherent Gender Issue* (London: Commonwealth Secretariat, 2001).

11. UNICEF, *Mother-to-Child Transmission of HIV: A UNICEF Fact Sheet* (New York: UNICEF, 2002). Available online at http://www.unicef.org/publications/pub_factsheet_mtct_en.pdf (accessed July 2, 2004).

12. UNICEF, *The Progress of Nations 2000* (New York: UNICEF, 2000). Available online at http://www.unicef.org/pon00/data3.htm (accessed July 2, 2004).

13. UN Office for the Coordination of Humanitarian Affairs, *AFT Africa AIDS Campaign: AFRICA: HIV-Related Deaths among Teachers Alarming* (Washington, DC: Integrated Regional Information Network, May 3, 2003). Available online at http://www.aft.org/partners/africa-aids/articles/un0503.htm (accessed July 2, 2004).

14. UNAIDS/UNICEF/USAID, *Children on the Brink 2004: A Joint Report on New Orphan Estimates and a Framework for Action* (Washington, DC: USAID, 2004). Available online at http://www.unaids.org/Unaids/EN/in+focus/topic+areas/children-orphans.asp (accessed July 28, 2004).

15. Gloria Jacques, "Orphans of the AIDS Pandemic: The Sub-Saharan Africa Expe-

rience," in *AIDS and Development in Africa: A Social Science Perspective*, ed. Ronald Hope Kempe, 93–108 (New York: Haworth, 1999).

16. UNAIDS/UNICEF/USAID, *Children on the Brink 2002: A Joint Report on Orphan Estimates and Program Strategies* (Washington, DC: USAID, 2002). Available online at http://www.unicef.org/publications/files/pub_children_on_the_ brink_en.pdf (accessed July 2, 2004).

17. AIDS/STD Unit, *The Rapid Assessment on the Situation of Orphans in Botswana* (Gaborone: Government of Botswana, 1998). Namposya Nampanya-Serpell, "Children Orphaned by HIV/AIDS in Zambia: Social and Economic Risk Factors of Premature Parental Death" (paper presented at a conference entitled Orphans and Vulnerable Children in Africa: Victims or Vestiges of Hope, Uppsala, Sweden, September 13–16, 2001). E. Procek, *Situational Analysis, Orphans and Vulnerable Children: Institutional and Community Responses to Orphans and Vulnerable Children*, vol. 1 (Francistown, Botswana: Social Welfare and Development Services, 2002). UNAIDS/UNICEF/USAID, *Children on the Brink 2002: A Joint Report on Orphan Estimates and Program Strategies* (Washington, DC: USAID, 2002). Available online at http://www.unicef.org/publications/files/ pub_children_on_the_brink_en.pdf (accessed July 2, 2004). G. Mutangadura, "Women and AIDS in Southern Africa: The Case of Zimbabwe and Its Policy Implications," *Jenda: A Journal of Culture and African Women's Studies* 11, no. 2 (2001): 1–11. J. P. Ntozi and J. Mukiza-Gapere, "Care for AIDS Orphans in Uganda: Findings from Focus Group Discussions," *Health Transition Review* 5, Suppl. (1995): 245–52.

18. G. Foster and J. Williamson, "A Review of Current Literature on the Impact of HIV/AIDS on Children in Sub-Saharan Africa," *Aids* 14, Suppl. 3 (2000): S275–84.

19. Martha Ainsworth and Innocent Semali, "The Impact of Adult Deaths on Children's Health in Northwestern Tanzania" (policy research working paper 2266, Washington, DC: World Bank, 2000). Namposya Nampanya-Serpell, "Children Orphaned by HIV/AIDS in Zambia: Social and Economic Risk Factors of Premature Parental Death" (paper presented at a conference entitled Orphans and Vulnerable Children in Africa: Victims or Vestiges of Hope, Uppsala, Sweden, September 13–16, 2001). K. Lindblade et al., "Health and Nutritional Status of Orphans <6 Years Old Cared for by Relatives in Western Kenya," *Tropical Medicine and International Health* 8, no. 1 (2003): 67–72.

20. G. Bicego, S. Rutstein, and K. Johnson, "Dimensions of the Emerging Orphan Crisis in Sub-Saharan Africa," *Social Science and Medicine* 56, no. 6 (2003): 1235–47. M. Ainsworth and I. Semali, "The Impact of Adult Deaths on Children's Health in Northwestern Tanzania" (policy research working paper 2266, Washington, DC: World Bank, 2000). Namposya Nampanya-Serpell, "Children

Orphaned by HIV/AIDS in Zambia: Social and Economic Risk Factors of Premature Parental Death" (paper presented at a conference entitled Orphans and Vulnerable Children in Africa: Victims or Vestiges of Hope, Uppsala, Sweden, September 13–16, 2001). S. Hunter, "Orphans as a Window on the AIDS Epidemic: Initial Results and Implications of a Study in Uganda," *Social Science and Medicine* 31, no. 6 (1990): 681–90. R. Abrahamsen, "Gender Dimensions of AIDS in Zambia," *Journal of Gender Studies* 6, no. 2 (1997): 177–89. AIDS/STD Unit, *The Rapid Assessment on the Situation of Orphans in Botswana* (Gaborone: Government of Botswana, 1998). H. R. Aspaas, "AIDS and Orphans in Uganda: Geographical and Gender Interpretation of Household Resources," *Social Science Journal* 36, no. 2 (1999): 201–26. G. Mutangadura, "Women and AIDS in Southern Africa: The Case of Zimbabwe and Its Policy Implications," *Jenda: A Journal of Culture and African Women's Studies* 11, no. 2 (2001): 1–11. E. O. Nyambedha, S. Wandibba, and J. Aagaard-Hansen, "Policy Implications of the Inadequate Support Systems for Orphans in Western Kenya," *Health Policy* 58, no. 1 (2001): 83–96. R. Sayson and A. F. Meya, "Strengthening the Roles of Existing Structures by Breaking Down Barriers and Building Up Bridges: Intensifying HIV/AIDS Awareness, Outreach and Intervention in Uganda," *Child Welfare* 53, no. 5 (2001): 541–50. World Bank, *Confronting AIDS: Public Priorities in a Global Epidemic* (Oxford: Oxford University Press, 1997).

21. J. Sengendo and J. Nambi, "The Psychological Effect of Orphanhood: A Study of Orphans in Rakai District," *Health Transition Review* 7, Suppl. (1997): 105–24.

22. V. Makame, C. Ani, and S. Grantham-McGregor, "Psychological Well-Being of Orphans in Dar Es Salaam, Tanzania," *Acta Paediatrica* 91, no. 4 (2002): 459–65.

23. Interviews of 1,033 adults who worked within the past year were conducted. Presented in the following sections are analyses of 913 respondents who reported caregiving responsibility for a zero- to seventeen-year-old (either their own child or an orphaned or ill child) as well as in-depth interviews of more than 250 working families.

24. BIDPA, *Macro-Economic Impacts of the HIV/AIDS Epidemic in Botswana* (Gaborone: UNDP/Government of Botswana, 2000). R. Greener, K. Jefferis, and H. Siphambe, "The Impact of HIV/AIDS on Poverty and Inequality in Botswana," *South African Journal of Economics* 68, no. 5 (2000): 888–915.

25. S. Hunter, "Orphans as a Window on the AIDS Epidemic: Initial Results and Implications of a Study in Uganda," *Social Science and Medicine* 31, no. 6 (1990): 681–90. T. Barnett and P. Blaikie, *AIDS in Africa: Its Present and Future Impact* (London: Belhaven, 1992). M. E. Ankrah, "The Impact of HIV/AIDS on the Family and Other Significant Relationships: The African Clan Revisited," *AIDS Care* 5, no. 1 (1993): 5–22. J. Seeley et al., "The Extended Family and Support for People with AIDS in a Rural Population in Southwest Uganda: A Safety

Net with Holes?" *AIDS Care* 5, no. 1 (1993): 117–22. J. P. Ntozi and J. Mukiza-Gapere, "Care for AIDS Orphans in Uganda: Findings from Focus Group Discussions," *Health Transition Review* 5, Suppl. (1995): 245–52. H. R. Aspaas, "AIDS and Orphans in Uganda: Geographical and Gender Interpretation of Household Resources," *Social Science Journal* 36, no. 2 (1999): 201–26. UNICEF, *Children Orphaned by AIDS: Frontline Response from Eastern and Southern Africa* (New York: UNICEF, 1999). G. Foster, "The Capacity of the Extended Family Safety Net for Orphans in Africa," *Psychology, Health, and Medicine* 5, no. 1 (2000): 55–62. G. Foster and J. Williamson, "A Review of Current Literature on the Impact of HIV/AIDS on Children in Sub-Saharan Africa," *Aids* 14, Suppl. 3 (2000): S275–84. UNAIDS/UNICEF/USAID, *Children on the Brink 2002: A Joint Report on Orphan Estimates and Program Strategies* (Washington, DC: USAID, 2002). Available online at http://www.unicef.org/ publications/files/pub_children_on_the_brink_en.pdf (accessed July 2, 2004). Namposya Nampanya-Serpell, "Children Orphaned by HIV/AIDS in Zambia: Social and Economic Risk Factors of Premature Parental Death" (paper presented at a conference entitled Orphans and Vulnerable Children in Africa: Victims or Vestiges of Hope, Uppsala, Sweden, September 13–16, 2001). G. Rugalema, "Coping or Struggling? A Journey into the Impact of HIV/AIDS in Southern Africa," *Review of African Political Economy* 28, no. 86 (2000): 537–45. Tony Barnett and Alan Whiteside, *AIDS in the Twenty-First Century* (London: Palgrave, 2002). L. Z. Gilborn, "In the Public Eye: Beyond Our Borders: The Effects of HIV Infection and AIDS on Children in Africa," *Western Journal of Medicine* 176, no. 1 (2002): 12–14.

26. Rene Bonnel, *HIV/AIDS: Does It Increase or Decrease Growth in Africa?* (Washington, DC: World Bank, 2000).

27. Steven Forsythe, "How Does HIV/AIDS Affect African Businesses?" in *State of the Art: AIDS and Economics* (prepared by International AIDS Economics Network for IAEN symposium, Barcelona, Spain, June 2002). David Bloom, Ajay Mahal, and River Path Associates, "HIV/AIDS and the Private Sector: A Literature Review" (draft paper presented to the American Foundation for AIDS Research, 2002). P. M. Pronyk, J. C. Kim, and B. Bates, *HIV/AIDS and Businesses in South Africa: Interventions, Opportunities and the Private Sector Response to the Epidemic* (Johannesburg: Canadian Business Alliance of South Africa, 2002). S. Rosen et al., "AIDS Is Your Business," *Harvard Business Review* 81, no. 1 (February 2003): 5–11.

28. BIDPA, *Macro-Economic Impacts of the HIV/AIDS Epidemic in Botswana* (Gaborone: UNDP/Government of Botswana, 2000).

29. United Nations World Food Programme (UNWFP), "WFP Emergency Report,

No. 43," October 30, 1998. Available online at http://www.cidi.org/humanitar ian/wfp/98b/0018.html (accessed July 2, 2004). UNICEF, "United Nations Children's Fund Provides Emergency Support to Victims of Hurricane Mitch," November 3, 1998. Available online at http://www.unicef.org/newline/98pr56 .htm (accessed June 7, 2005).

30. A. Marrison, "Legacy: War, Aftermath and the End of the Nineteenth-Century Liberal Trading Order, 1914–1932," in *The First World War and the International Economy*, ed. Chris Wrigley, 119–64 (Cheltenham, UK: Elgar, 2000).

31. R. Mayne, *Postwar: The Dawn of Today's Europe* (London: Thames and Hudson, 1983).

32. Cyril E. Black, Robert D. English, and A. James McAdams, *Rebirth: A History of Europe since World War II* (Boulder, CO: Westview, 1992).

33. Brian W. Blouet, *Geopolitics and Globalization in the Twentieth Century* (London: Reaktion, 2001).

34. B. O. Daponte, "A Case Study in Estimating Casualties from War and Its Aftermath: The 1991 Persian Gulf War," *PSR Quarterly* 3, no. 2 (1993): 57–66.

35. R. Garfield and C. Leu, "A Multivariate Method for Estimating Mortality Rates among Children under 5 Years from Health and Social Indicators in Iraq," *International Journal of Epidemiology* 29 (2000): 510–15. Richard Garfield, "Morbidity and Mortality among Iraqi Children from 1990 through 1998: Assessing the Impact of Economic Sanctions" (occasional paper commissioned by the Joan B. Kroc Institute for International Peace Studies, University of Notre Dame, and the Fourth Freedom Forum, Goshen, Indiana, March 2000).

36. UNICEF, *Overview of Nutritional Status of Under-fives in South/Centre Iraq* (Baghdad: UNICEF, November 2002). Available online at http://www.casi.org. uk/info/unicef/0211nutrition.pdf (accessed June 7, 2005).

37. UNICEF, *Promotion and Protection of the Rights of Children: Impact of Armed Conflict on Children* (New York: UNICEF, 1996). Available online at http:// www.unicef.org/graca/a51-306_en.pdf (accessed July 2, 2004).

38. UNICEF, *The State of the World's Children 1996* (New York: Oxford University Press, 1996). Available online at http://www.unicef.org/sowc96/ (accessed July 2, 2004).

39. UNICEF, "Facts on Children" (2003). Available online at http://www.unicef .org/media/media_9482.html (accessed July 2, 2004).

40. UNICEF, "Facts on Children" (2003). Available online at http://www.unicef .org/media/media_9482.html (accessed July 2, 2004).

41. UNICEF, *The State of the World's Children 2002* (New York: Oxford University Press, 2002). Available online at http://www.unicef.org/publications/pub_ sowc02_en.pdf (accessed July 2, 2004).

42. UNICEF, "UNICEF Calls on Angola to Lead by Example" (April 21, 2003). Available online at http://www.unicef.org/media/media_7696.html (accessed July 2, 2004).

43. Graça Machel, *Impact of Armed Conflict on Children* (New York: UNICEF, 1996). Available online at http://www.unicef.org/graca/a51–306_en.pdf (accessed July 2, 2004).

44. WHO, *World Report on Violence and Health* (Geneva, WHO, 2002). Available online at http://www.who.int/violence_injury_prevention/en/ (accessed July 2, 2004).

45. Vietnam Courier, *U.S. Chemical Warfare and Its Consequences* (Hanoi: 1980).

46. Melanie Beresford, *Vietnam: Politics, Economics, and Society* (London: Pinter, 1988).

47. Denying employment to those under political suspicion or blacklisting them is not a form of political and economic repression limited to the government that Vietnam had at the time. To cite only one of many possible examples, during the McCarthy era in the United States in the 1950s, a large number of U.S. citizens were blacklisted for their political views. The destruction wrought on individuals and families because their beliefs are taken to be outside of those in power— whether on the Right or the Left, capitalist or communist—has occurred in a wide range of countries.

48. WHO, *World Report on Violence and Health* (Geneva: WHO, 2002). Available online at http://www.who.int/violence_injury_prevention/violence/world_report/en/Front%20and%20intro%20WRVH.pdf (accessed July 2, 2004). A. Ugalde et al., "The Health Costs of War: Can They Be Measured? Lessons from El Salvador," *British Medical Journal* 321 (2000): 169–72. G. Gururaj et al., *Suicide Prevention: Emerging from Darkness* (New Delhi: WHO Regional Office for South-East Asia, 2001). D. Silove, S. Ekblad, and R. Mollica, "The Rights of the Severely Mentally Ill in Post-Conflict Societies," *Lancet* 355 (2000): 1548–49.

49. J. de Jong et al., "The Prevalence of Mental Health Problems in Rwandan and Burundese Refugee Camps," *Acta Psychiatrica Scandinavica* 102 (2000): 171–77.

50. J. de Jong et al., "Lifetime Events and Posttraumatic Stress Disorder in 4 Post-conflict Settings," *Journal of the American Medical Association* 286, no. 5 (2001): 555–62.

51. Joanna Santa Barbara, "The Psychological Effects of War on Children," in *War and Public Health*, ed. Barry S. Levy and Victor W. Sidel, pp. 168–76 (New York: Oxford University Press, 1997).

52. Myron Allukian, Jr., and Paul L. Atwood, "Public Health and the Vietnam War," in *War and Public Health*, ed. Barry S. Levy and Victor W. Sidel, pp. 215–37 (New York: Oxford University Press, 1997).

53. UNAIDS and WHO, *AIDS Epidemic Update December 2002* (Geneva: UNAIDS and WHO, 2002).

54. National Intelligence Council, *The Next Wave of HIV/AIDS: Nigeria, Ethiopia, Russia, India, and China* (Washington, DC: 2002).

Chapter 7

1. World Bank, *World Development Indicators 2004* (Washington, DC: 2004).

2. Exceptions to this generalization include South American countries such as Uruguay and Chile. World Bank, *World Development Report* (New York: World Bank, 2000). See United Nations Development Programme, *Human Development Report 2000* (New York: Oxford University Press, 2000).

3. John McCarthy, "3.3 Million U.S. Services Jobs to Go Offshore," Business View and IT View Brief, *Forrester Research*, November 11, 2002. M. Gongloff, "U.S. Jobs Jumping Ship," *CNNMoney*, May 2, 2003. Available online at http://money.cnn.com/2003/05/01/news/economy/jobless_offshore (accessed June 7, 2005).

4. E. Luce and D. Roberts, "Outsourcing Spreads to Highest-Paid Jobs," *Canadian Business and Current Affairs, Financial Post (National Post)*, September 2, 2003.

5. A. Pollack, "Who's Reading Your X-Ray?" *New York Times*, November 16, 2003.

6. N. Klein, "Miami or Bust," *Guardian*, October 27, 2003.

7. A. Tonelson, *Race to the Bottom* (Boulder, CO: Westview, 2000).

8. K. Bronfenbrenner, "We'll Close! Plant Closings, Plant-Closing Threats, Union Organizing, and NAFTA," *Multinational Monitor* 18, no. 3 (1997): 8–13. K. Bronfenbrenner, "Trade in Traditional Manufacturing" (testimony before the U.S. Trade Deficit Review Commission, October 29, 1999). Available online at http://www.ustdrc.gov/hearings/20Oct99/29Oct99con.html (accessed July 23, 2004).

9. J. Brannen, "Time and the Study of Women's Work-Family Lives: Autonomy or Illusion?" (paper presented at seminar on the relationship between employment and care, Cumberland Lodge, Windsor Great Park, UK, October 27–28, 2003).

10. For a full summary of the evidence base on all twenty items in the Work, Family, and Equity Index, please see S. J. Heymann et al., *The Work, Family, and Equity Index: Where Does the United States Stand Globally?* (Cambridge, MA: Project on Global Working Families, Harvard School of Public Health, June 2004). Available online at http://www.globalworkingfamilies.org (accessed June 7, 2005).

11. C. J. Ruhm, "Parental Leave and Child Health," *Journal of Health Economics* 19, no. 6 (2000): 931–60.

12. R. G. Feachem and M. A. Koblinsky, "Interventions for the Control of Diar-

rhoeal Diseases among Young Children: Promotion of Breast-Feeding," *Bulletin of the World Health Organization* 62, no. 2 (1984): 271–91. J. P. Habicht, J. Da-Vanzo, and W. P. Butz, "Does Breastfeeding Really Save Lives, or Are Apparent Benefits Due to Biases?" *American Journal of Epidemiology* 123, no. 2 (1986): 279–90. J. N. Hobcraft, J. McDonald, and S. Rutstein, "Demographic Determinants of Infant and Early Child Mortality: A Comparative Analysis," *Population Studies* 39, no. 21 (1985): 363–85. J. Jason, P. Nieburg, and J. S. Marks, "Mortality and Infectious Disease Associated with Infant-feeding Practice in Developing Countries. Part 2," *Pediatrics* 74, no. 4 (1984): 702–27.

13. A. S. Cunningham, D. B. Jelliffee, and E. F. Jelliffee, "Breast-feeding and Health in the 1980s: A Global Epidemiologic Review," *Journal of Pediatrics* 118, no. 5 (1991): 659–66. K. Dewey, M. Heinig, and L. Nommsen-Rivers, "Differences in Morbidity between Breast-Fed and Formula-Fed Infants. Part 1," *Journal of Pediatrics* 126, no. 5 (1995): 696–702. R. G. Feachem and M. A. Koblinsky, "Interventions for the Control of Diarrhoeal Diseases among Young Children: Promotion of Breast-Feeding," *Bulletin of the World Health Organization* 62, no. 2 (1984): 271–91. P. Howie et al., "Protective Effect of Breast Feeding against Infection," *British Medical Journal* 300, no. 6716 (1990): 11–16. P. Lepage, C. Munyakazi, and P. Hennart, "Breastfeeding and Hospital Mortality in Children in Rwanda," *Lancet* 1, no. 8268 (1982): 403.

14. M. Cerqueriro et al., "Epidemiologic Risk Factors for Children with Acute Lower Respiratory Tract Infection in Buenos Aires, Argentina: A Matched Case-Control Study," *Reviews of Infectious Diseases* 12, Suppl. 8 (1990): S1021–28. P. Howie et al., "Protective Effect of Breast Feeding against Infection," *British Medical Journal* 300, no. 6716 (1990): 11–16. C. J. Watkins, S. R. Leeder, and R. T. Corkhill, "The Relationship between Breast and Bottle Feeding and Respiratory Illness in the First Year of Life," *Journal of Epidemiology and Community Health* 33, no. 3 (1979): 180–82. A. Wright et al., "Breast Feeding and Lower Respiratory Tract Illness in the First Year of Life," *British Medical Journal* 299, no. 6705 (1989): 946–49.

15. C. Arnold, S. Makintube, and G. Istre, "Daycare Attendance and Other Risk Factors for Invasive *Haemophilus Influenzae* Type B Disease," *American Journal of Epidemiology* 138, no. 5 (1993): 333–40.

16. G. Aniansson et al., "A Prospective Cohort Study on Breast-Feeding and Otitis Media in Swedish Infants," *Pediatric Infectious Disease Journal* 13, no. 3 (1994): 183–88. B. Duncan et al., "Exclusive Breast-Feeding for at Least 4 Months Protects against Otitis Media," *Pediatrics* 91, no. 5 (1993): 867–72. A. S. Cunningham, D. B. Jelliffee, and E. F. Jelliffee, "Breast-Feeding and Health in the 1980s: A Global Epidemiologic Review," *Journal of Pediatrics* 118, no. 5 (1991): 659–66. R. G. Feachem and M. A. Koblinsky, "Interventions for the Control of Diar-

rhoeal Diseases among Young Children: Promotion of Breast-Feeding," *Bulletin of the World Health Organization* 62, no. 2 (1984): 271–91.

17. L. D. Lindberg, "Women's Decisions about Breastfeeding and Maternal Employment," *Journal of Marriage and the Family* 58, no. 1 (1996): 239–51. S. Noble, "Maternal Employment and the Initiation of Breastfeeding," *Acta Paediatrica* 90, no. 4 (2001): 423–28. V. Hight-Laukaran et al., "The Use of Breast Milk Substitutes in Developing Countries: The Impact of Women's Employment," *American Journal of Public Health* 86, no. 9 (1996): 1235–40.

18. A. C. Gielen et al., "Maternal Employment during the Early Postpartum Period: Effects on Initiation and Continuation of Breast-Feeding," *Pediatrics* 87 (1991): 298–305. M. H. Kearney and L. Cronenwett, "Breastfeeding and Employment," *Journal of Obstetric, Gynecologic, and Neonatal Nursing* 20 (1991): 471–80. B. Winikoff and V. Laukaran, "Breast Feeding and Bottle Feeding Controversies in the Developing World: Evidence from a Study in Four Countries," *Social Science and Medicine* 29 (1989): 859–68. C. W. Binns and J. A. Scott, "Factors Associated with the Initiation and Duration of Breastfeeding: A Review of the Literature," *Australian Journal of Nutrition and Dietetics* 55, no. 2 (1998): 51–61. Y. O. Chee and L. Horstmanshof, "A Review of Breastfeeding Practices in Hong Kong, 1994/1995," *Breastfeeding Review* 4, no. 1 (1996): 7–12. A. L. Wright, C. Clark, and M. Bauer, "Maternal Employment and Infant Feeding Practices among the Navajo," *Medical Anthropology Quarterly* 7, no. 3 (1993): 260–80. N. Kurinij et al., "Does Maternal Employment Affect Breast-feeding?" *American Journal of Public Health* 79, no. 9 (1989): 1247–50.

19. V. Escriba et al., "Working Conditions and the Decision to Breast-feed in Spain," *Health Promotion International* 9, no. 4 (1994): 251–58. S. Yimyam and M. Morrow, "Maternal Labor, Breast-Feeding, and Infant Health," in Global Inequalities at Work: Work's Impact on the Health of Individuals, Families, and Societies, ed. S. J. Heymann, pp. 105–35 (New York: Oxford University Press, 2003).

20. A. L. Wright, C. Clark, and M. Bauer, "Maternal Employment and Infant Feeding Practices among the Navajo," *Medical Anthropology Quarterly* 7, no. 3 (1993): 260–80. G. Yilmaz et al., "Factors Influencing Breastfeeding for Working Mothers," *Turkish Journal of Pediatrics* 44, no. 1 (2002): 30–34.

21. M. H. Labbok, "Health Sequelae of Breastfeeding for the Mother," *Clinics in Perinatology* 26, no. 2 (1999): 491–503.

22. M. H. Labbok, "Health Sequelae of Breastfeeding for the Mother," *Clinics in Perinatology* 26, no. 2 (1999): 491–503. Collaborative Group on Hormonal Factors in Breast Cancer, "Breast Cancer and Breastfeeding: Collaborative Reanalysis of Individual Data from 47 Epidemiological Studies in 30 Countries, including 50302 Women with Breast Cancer and 96973 Women without the Disease," *Lancet* 360, no. 9328 (2002): 187–95.

23. M. H. Labbok, "Health Sequelae of Breastfeeding for the Mother," *Clinics in Perinatology* 26, no. 2 (1999): 491–503.

24. M. E. Avery, "A 50-Year Overview of Perinatal Medicine," *Early Human Development* 29, nos. 1–3 (1992): 43–50. M. Crouch and L. Manderson, "The Social Life of Bonding Theory," *Social Science and Medicine* 41, no. 6 (1995): 837–44. C. K. Johnson, M. D. Gilbert, and G. H. Herdt, "Implications for Adult Roles from Differential Styles of Mother-Infant Bonding: An Ethological Study," *Journal of Nervous and Mental Disease* 167, no. 1 (1979): 29–37. E. Anisfeld and E. Lipper, "Early Contact, Social Support, and Mother-Infant Bonding," *Pediatrics* 72, no. 1 (1983): 79–83. M. E. Lamb, "Early Contact and Maternal-Infant Bonding: One Decade Later," *Pediatrics* 70, no. 5 (1982): 763–68. P. G. Mertin, "Maternal-Infant Attachment: A Developmental Perspective," *Australian and New Zealand Journal of Obstetrics and Gynaecology* 26, no. 4 (1986): 280–83. A. M. Taubenheim, "Paternal-Infant Bonding in the First-Time Father," *JOGN Nursing* 10, no. 4 (1981): 261–64. P. Nettelbladt, "Father/Son Relationship during the Preschool Years: An Integrative Review with Special Reference to Recent Swedish Findings," *Acta Psychiatrica Scandinavica* 68, no. 6 (1983): 399–407.

25. G. C. Dalto, "A Structural Approach to Women's Hometime and Experience Earnings Profiles: Maternity Leave and Public Policy," *Population Research and Policy Review* 8 (1989): 247–66. C. J. Ruhm, "The Economic Consequences of Parental Leave Mandates: Lessons from Europe," *Quarterly Journal of Economics* 113, no. 1 (1998): 285–317.

26. J. Waldfogel, "The Family Gap for Young Women in the United States and Britain: Can Maternity Leave Make a Difference?" *Journal of Labor Economics* 16, no. 3 (1998): 505–45.

27. J. Waldfogel, Y. Higuchi, and M. Abe, "Family Leave Policies and Women's Retention after Childbirth: Evidence from the United States, Britain, and Japan," *Journal of Population Economics* 12, no. 4 (1999): 523–45. S. Macran, P. Dex, and H. Joshi, "Employment after Childbearing: A Survival Analysis," *Work, Employment, and Society* 10, no. 2 (1996): 273–96.

28. F. Campbell and C. Ramey, "Effects of Early Intervention on Intellectual and Academic Achievement: A Follow-up Study of Children from Low-Income Families," *Child Development* 65, no. 2 (1994): 684–98. S. Andrews et al., "The Skills of Mothering: A Study of Parent Child Development Centers," *Monographs of the Society for Research in Child Development* 46, no. 6 (1982): 1–83. D. Johnson and T. Walker, "A Follow-up Evaluation of the Houston Parent-Child Development Center: School Performance," *Journal of Early Intervention* 15, no. 3 (1991): 226–36. H. Garber, *The Milwaukee Project: Preventing Mental Retardation in Children at Risk* (Washington, DC: American Association on Mental Retardation, 1988). National Institute of Child Health and Human Develop-

ment Early Child Care Research Network, "Child Outcomes when Child Care Center Classes Meet Recommended Standards for Quality," *American Journal of Public Health* 89 (1999): 1072–77. W. Barnett, "Long-Term Effects of Early Childhood Programs on Cognitive and School Outcomes," *Future of Children* 5, no. 3 (1995): 25–50. R. McKay, L. Condell, and H. Ganson, *The Impact of Head Start on Children, Families, and Communities: Final Report of the Head Start Evaluation, Synthesis, and Utilization Project* (Washington, DC: CSR, 1985). R. Myers, *The Twelve Who Survive: Strengthening Programmes of Early Childhood Development in the Third World* (London: Routledge in cooperation with UNESCO for the Consultative Group on Early Childhood Care and Development, 1992). E. Chaturvedi et al., "Impact of Six Years Exposure to ICDS Scheme on Psycho-social Development," *Indian Pediatrics* 24 (February 1987): 153–60. S. Grantham-McGregor et al., "The Long-Term Follow-up of Severely Malnourished Children Who Participated in an Intervention Program," *Child Development* 65 (1994): 428–39. Q. Xie and M. E. Young, *Integrated Child Development in Rural China* (Washington, DC: World Bank, 1999). S. S. Boocock, "Early Childhood Programs in Other Nations: Goals and Outcomes," *Future of Children* 5, no. 3 (1995): 94–114. C. Kagitcibasi, "Parent Education and Child Development," in *Early Child Development: Investing in Our Children's Future: Proceedings of a World Bank Conference on Early Child Development: Investing in the Future, Atlanta, Georgia, April 8–9, 1996,* ed. M. E. Young, 243–72 (Amsterdam: Elsevier, 1997). D. Wagner and J. Spratt, "Cognitive Consequences of Contrasting Pedagogies: The Effects of Quranic Pre-schooling in Morocco," *Child Development* 58 (1987): 1209–19.

29. S. Kamerman and A. Kahn, *Child Care, Parental Leave, and the Under Threes: Policy Innovation in Europe* (New York: Auburn, 1991). T. E. David, *Researching Early Childhood Education: European Perspectives* (London: Sage, 1998). S. S. Boocock, "Early Childhood Programs in Other Nations: Goals and Outcomes," *Future of Children* 5, no. 3 (1995): 94–114. R. Myers, *The Twelve Who Survive: Strengthening Programmes of Early Childhood Development in the Third World* (London: Routledge in cooperation with UNESCO for the Consultative Group on Early Childhood Care and Development, 1992). M. E. Young, *Early Child Development: Investing in the Future* (Washington, DC: World Bank, 1996). A. Jaramillo and K. Tietjen, *Early Childhood Development in Africa: Can We Do More and Better for Less? A Look at the Impact and Implications of Preschools in Cape Verde and Guinea* (Washington, DC: World Bank, 2001). I. Goduka, "Rethinking the Status of Early Childhood Care and Education (ECCE) in Rural and Urban Areas of South Africa," *Early Education and Development* 8, no. 3 (1997): 307–21. M. S. Khattab, "Early Childhood Education in Eighteen Countries in the Middle East and North Africa," *Child Study Journal* 26, no. 2

(1996): 149–59. World Bank, *Brazil: Early Child Development: A Focus on the Impact of Preschools* (Washington, DC: World Bank, September 2001). M. Herczog, "Assessing Child Welfare Outcomes in Central and Eastern Europe," *Children and Society* 12, no. 3 (1998): 223–27. S. Feeney, *Early Childhood in Asia and the Pacific: A Source Book* (New York: Garland, 1992).

30. F. Campbell and C. Ramey, "Effects of Early Intervention on Intellectual and Academic Achievement: A Follow-up Study of Children from Low-Income Families," *Child Development* 65, no. 2 (1994): 684–98. S. Andrews et al., "The Skills of Mothering: A Study of Parent-Child Development Centers," *Monographs of the Society for Research in Child Development* 46, no. 6 (1982): 1–83. D. Johnson and T. Walker, "A Follow-up Evaluation of the Houston Parent-Child Development Center: School Performance," *Journal of Early Intervention* 15, no. 3 (1991): 226–36. H. Garber, *The Milwaukee Project: Preventing Mental Retardation in Children at Risk* (Washington, DC: American Association on Mental Retardation, 1988). National Institute of Child Health and Human Development Early Child Care Research Network, "Child Outcomes when Child Care Center Classes Meet Recommended Standards for Quality," *American Journal of Public Health* 89 (1999): 1072–77. W. Barnett, "Long-Term Effects of Early Childhood Programs on Cognitive and School Outcomes," *Future of Children* 5, no. 3 (1995): 25–50. R. McKay, L. Condell, and H. Ganson, *The Impact of Head Start on Children, Families, and Communities: Final Report of the Head Start Evaluation, Synthesis, and Utilization Project* (Washington, DC: CSR, 1985). R. Myers, *The Twelve Who Survive: Strengthening Programmes of Early Childhood Development in the Third World* (London and New York: Routledge, in cooperation with UNESCO for the Consultative Group on Early Childhood Care and Development; 1992). E. Chaturvedi et al., "Impact of Six Years Exposure to ICDS Scheme on Psycho-social Development," *Indian Pediatrics* 24 (February 1987): 153–60. S. Grantham-McGregor et al., "The Long-Term Follow-up of Severely Malnourished Children Who Participated in an Intervention Program," *Child Development* 65 (1994): 428–39. Q. Xie and M. E. Young, *Integrated Child Development in Rural China* (Washington, DC: World Bank, 1999). S. S. Boocock, "Early Childhood Programs in Other Nations: Goals and Outcomes," *Future of Children* 5, no. 3 (1995): 94–114. C. Kagitcibasi, "Parent Education and Child Development," in *Early Child Development: Investing in Our Children's Future: Proceedings of a World Bank Conference on Early Child Development: Investing in the Future, Atlanta, Georgia, April 8–9, 1996*, ed. M. E. Young, 243–72 (Amsterdam: Elsevier, 1997). D. Wagner and J. Spratt, "Cognitive Consequences of Contrasting Pedagogies: The Effects of Quranic Pre-schooling in Morocco," *Child Development* 58 (1987): 1209–19.

31. J. Currie and D. Thomas, "Does Head Start Make a Difference?" *American Economic Review* 85, no. 3 (1995): 341–64.

32. R. Myers, *The Twelve Who Survive: Strengthening Programmes of Early Childhood Development in the Third World* (London: Routledge in cooperation with UNESCO for the Consultative Group on Early Childhood Care and Development, 1992). E. Chaturvedi et al., "Impact of Six Years Exposure to ICDS Scheme on Psycho-social Development," *Indian Pediatrics* 24 (February 1987): 153–60.

33. R. Myers, *The Twelve Who Survive: Strengthening Programmes of Early Childhood Development in the Third World* (London: Routledge in cooperation with UNESCO for the Consultative Group on Early Childhood Care and Development, 1992). E. Chaturvedi et al., "Impact of Six Years Exposure to ICDS Scheme on Psycho-social Development," *Indian Pediatrics* 24 (February 1987): 153–60. L. Schweinhart and D. Weikart, *Young Children Grow Up: The Effects of the Perry Preschool Program on Youths through Age 15* (Ypsilanti, MI: High/Scope Press, 1980). F. Campbell and C. Ramey, "Effects of Early Intervention on Intellectual and Academic Achievement: A Follow-up Study of Children from Low-Income Families," *Child Development* 65, no. 2 (1994): 684–98. W. Barnett, "Long-Term Effects of Early Childhood Programs on Cognitive and School Outcomes," *Future of Children* 5, no. 3 (1995): 25–50. A. J. Reynolds et al., "Cognitive and Family-Support Mediators of Preschool Effectiveness: A Confirmatory Analysis," *Child Development* 67, no. 3 (1996): 1119–40.

34. S. Kamerman and A. Kahn, *Child Care, Parental Leave, and the Under Threes: Policy Innovation in Europe* (New York: Auburn, 1991). T. E. Dave, *Researching Early Childhood Education: European Perspectives* (London: Sage, 1998). S. S. Boocock, "Early Childhood Programs in Other Nations: Goals and Outcomes," *Future of Children* 5, no. 3 (1995): 94–114. R. Myers, *The Twelve Who Survive: Strengthening Programmes of Early Childhood Development in the Third World* (London and New York: Routledge, in cooperation with UNESCO for the Consultative Group on Early Childhood Care and Development, 1992). M. E. Young, *Early Child Development: Investing in the Future* (Washington, DC: World Bank, 1996). A. Jaramillo and K. Tietjen, *Early Childhood Development in Africa: Can We Do More and Better for Less? A Look at the Impact and Implications of Preschools in Cape Verde and Guinea* (Washington, DC: World Bank, 2001). I. Goduka, "Rethinking the Status of Early Childhood Care and Education (ECCE) in Rural and Urban Areas of South Africa," *Early Education and Development* 8, no. 3 (1997): 307–21. M. S. Khattab, "Early Childhood Education in Eighteen Countries in the Middle East and North Africa," *Child Study Journal* 26, no. 2 (1996): 149–59. World Bank, *Brazil: Early Child Development: A Focus*

on the Impact of Preschools (Washington, DC: World Bank, 2001). M. Herczog, "Assessing Child Welfare Outcomes in Central and Eastern Europe," *Children and Society* 12, no. 3 (1998): 223–27. S. Feeney, *Early Childhood in Asia and the Pacific: A Source Book* (New York: Garland, 1992).

35. C. Kagitcibasi, "Parent Education and Child Development," in *Early Child Development: Investing in our Children's Future: Proceedings of a World Bank Conference on Early Child Development: Investing in the Future, Atlanta, Georgia, April 8–9, 1996,* ed. M. E. Young, 243–72 (Amsterdam: Elsevier, 1997).

36. E. Chaturvedi et al., "Impact of Six Years Exposure to ICDS Scheme on Psychosocial Development," *Indian Pediatrics* 24 (February 1987): 153–60.

37. R. Myers, *The Twelve Who Survive: Strengthening Programmes of Early Childhood Development in the Third World* (London: Routledge in cooperation with UNESCO for the Consultative Group on Early Childhood Care and Development, 1992).

38. Committee on Integrating the Science of Early Childhood Development, *From Neurons to Neighborhoods: The Science of Early Childhood Development,* ed. J. P. Shonkoff and D. A. Phillips (Washington, DC: National Academy Press, 2000). M. S. Cynader and B. J. Frost, "Mechanisms of Brain Development: Neuronal Sculpting by the Physical and Social Environment," in *Developmental Health and the Wealth of Nations: Social, Biological, and Educational Dynamics,* ed. D. P. Keating and C. Hertzman, 153–84 (New York: Guilford, 1999). C. Bellamy, *The State of the World's Children 2001: Early Childhood* (New York: Oxford University Press for UNICEF, 2000).

39. D. Anderson and P. Levine, "Child Care and Mother's Employment Decisions," in *Finding Jobs: Work and Welfare Reform,* ed. D. Card and R. Blank, 420–62 (New York: Russell Sage Foundation, 2000). R. Wong and R. E. Levine, "The Effect of Household Structure on Women's Economic Activity and Fertility: Evidence from Recent Mothers in Urban Mexico," *Economic Development and Cultural Change* 41, no. 1 (1992): 89–102. E. Bonilla de Ramos, "Working Mothers of Pre-school Children in an Underdeveloped Society," *Women's Studies International Forum* 7, no. 6 (1984): 415–22. R. M. Doan and B. M. Popkin, "Women's Work and Infant Care in the Philippines," *Social Science and Medicine* 36, no. 3 (1993): 297–304. M. Lokshin, *Effects of Child Care Prices on Women's Labor Force Participation in Russia* (Washington, DC: Development Research Group, World Bank, 2000). Available online at http://siteresources.worldbank.org/INTGENDER/Resources/wplo.pdf (accessed June 7, 2005). A. P. Brayfield. "A Bargain at Any Price: Child-Care Costs and Women's Employment," *Social Science Research* 24, no. 2 (1995): 188–214. B. D. Meyer and D. T. Rosenbaum, "Welfare, the Earned Income Tax Credit, and the Labor Supply of Single Mothers," *Quarterly Journal of Economics* 116, no. 3 (2001): 1063–1114.

40. J. L. Glass and S. B. Estes, "Workplace Support, Child Care, and Turnover Intentions among Employed Mothers of Infants," *Journal of Family Issues* 17, no. 3 (1996): 317–35. R. J. Erickson, L. Nichols, and C. Ritter, "Family Influence on Absenteeism: Testing and Expanded Process Model," *Journal of Vocational Behavior* 57, no. 2 (2000): 246–72.

41. S. L. Grover and K. J. Crooker, "Who Appreciates Family-Responsive Human-Resource Policies: The Impact of Family-Friendly Policies on the Organizational Attachment of Parents and Non-Parents," *Personnel Psychology* 48, no. 2 (1995): 271–88.

42. S. J. Heymann, S. Toomey, and F. Furstenberg, "Working Parents: What Factors Are Involved in Their Ability to Take Time Off from Work When Their Children Are Sick?" *Archives of Pediatrics and Adolescent Medicine* 153 (1999): 870–74.

43. J. Coreil et al., "Social and Psychological Costs of Preventive Child Health Services in Haiti," *Social Science and Medicine* 38, no. 2 (1994): 231–38. K. Streatfield and M. Singarimbun, "Social Factors Affecting the Use of Immunization in Indonesia," *Social Science and Medicine* 27, no. 11 (1988): 1237–45. L. K. McCormick et al., "Parental Perceptions of Barriers to Childhood Immunization: Results of Focus Groups Conducted in an Urban Population," *Health Education Research* 12, no. 3 (1997): 355–62. C. Lannon et al., "What Mothers Say about Why Poor Children Fall Behind on Immunizations: A Summary of Focus Groups in North Carolina," *Archives of Pediatrics and Adolescent Medicine* 149, no. 10 (1995): 1070–75.

44. M. B. Woods, "The Unsupervised Child of the Working Mother," *Developmental Psychology* 6 (1972): 4–25. P. A. Nash and J. M. Murphy, "An Approach to Pediatric Perioperative Care: Parent-Present Induction," *Nursing Clinics of North America* 32 (1997): 183–99. A. George and J. Hancock, "Reducing Pediatric Burn Pain with Parent Participation," *Journal of Burn Care and Rehabilitation* 14 (1993): 104–7. G. Van der Schyff, "The Role of Parents during their Child's Hospitalization," *Australian Nurses Journal* 8 (1979): 57–61. J. Bowlby, *Child Care and the Growth of Love* (London: Pelican, 1964). J. Robertson, *Young Children in Hospital* (London: Tavistock, 1970). T. McGraw, "Preparing Children for the Operating Room: Psychological Issues," *Canadian Journal of Anaesthesia* 41 (1994): 1094–103.

45. P. Mahaffy, "The Effects of Hospitalization on Children Admitted for Tonsillectomy and Adenoidectomy," *Nursing Review* 14 (1965): 12–19. G. Van der Schyff, "The Role of Parents during their Child's Hospitalization," *Australian Nurses Journal* 8 (1979): 57–61. S. J. Palmer, "Care of Sick Children by Parents: A Meaningful Role," *Journal of Advanced Nursing* 18 (1993): 185. J. Bowlby, *Child Care and the Growth of Love* (London: Pelican, 1964). J. Robertson, *Young Children in Hospital* (London: Tavistock, 1970).

46. M. R. H. Taylor and P. O'Connor, "Resident Parents and Shorter Hospital Stay," *Archives of Disease in Childhood* 64 (1989): 274–76.

47. I. Kristensson-Hallstron, G. Elander, and G. Malmfors, "Increased Parental Participation on a Pediatric Surgical Daycare Unit," *Journal of Clinical Nursing* 6 (1997): 297–302.

48. T. A. Waugh and D. L. Kjos, "Parental Involvement and the Effectiveness of an Adolescent Day Treatment Program," *Journal of Youth and Adolescence* 21 (1992): 487–97. C. P. Q. Sainsbury et al., "Care by Parents of Their Children in Hospital," *Archives of Disease in Childhood* 61 (1986): 612–15.

49. UNICEF, *Education Update: Children with Disabilities*, vol. 2, no. 4 (New York: UNICEF Programme Division, Education Section, October 1999). Available online at http://www.unicef.org/girlseducation/vol2disabileng.pdf (accessed July 30, 2004).

50. UNICEF, *The State of the World's Children 2000* (New York: Oxford University Press, 2000).

51. L. Montgomery, J. Kiely, and G. Pappas, "The Effects of Poverty, Race, and Family Structure on U.S. Children's Health: Data from NHIS, 1978 through 1980 and 1989 through 1991," *American Journal of Public Health* 86, no. 10 (1996): 1401–5. B. Starfield, "Effects of Poverty on Health Status," *Bulletin of the New York Academy of Medicine* 68, no. 1 (1992): 17–24. R. Bradley et al., "Early Indications of Resilience and Their Relation to Experiences in the Home Environments of Low Birthweight, Premature Children Living in Poverty," *Child Development* 65, no. 2 (1994): 346–60. P. McGauhey et al., "Social Environment and Vulnerability of Low Birth Weight Children: A Social-Epidemiological Perspective," *Pediatrics* 88, no. 5 (1991): 943–53.

52. D. Cantor et al., *Balancing the Needs of Families and Employers: The Family and Medical Leave Surveys 2000 Update* (Rockville, MD: Westat, 2001). Available online at http://www.dol.gov/asp/fmla/main2000.htm (accessed January 31, 2003).

53. C. Wolman et al., "Emotional Well-Being among Adolescents with and without Chronic Conditions," *Adolescent Medicine* 15, no. 3 (1994): 199–204. C. L. Hanson et al., "Comparing Social Learning and Family Systems Correlates of Adaptation in Youths with IDDM," *Journal of Pediatric Psychology* 17, no. 5 (1992): 555–72.

54. S. Carlton-Ford et al., "Epilepsy and Children's Social and Psychological Adjustment," *Journal of Health and Social Behavior* 36, no. 3 (1992): 285–301. K. W. Hamlett, D. S. Pellegrini, and K. S. Katz, "Childhood Chronic Illness as a Family Stressor," *Journal of Pediatric Psychology* 17, no. 1 (1992): 33–47. A. M. LaGreca et al., "I Get By with a Little Help from My Family and Friends: Adolescents' Support for Diabetes Care," *Journal of Pediatric Psychology* 20, no. 4 (1995): 449–76. B. J. Anderson et al., "Family Characteristics of Diabetic

Adolescents: Relationship to Metabolic Control," *Diabetes Care* 4, no. 6 (1981): 586–94.

55. The experiences of Tshegofatso Walone, Ngo Van Cuong, and Kereng Seetasewa are detailed in chapter 4. The experiences of Dipogiso Motlhagomile are detailed in chapter 6.

56. If one-third of the money that the affluent nations spend providing subsidies to farmers in their own nations (often to *not* produce goods) were instead spent supporting the world's children, there would be more than enough funds to ensure that all children would receive early childhood care and education. There are two types of farm subsidies in the North and West that are particularly egregious. The first are subsidies to farmers to not produce—these are the cases where farmers are paid to actually keep their land fallow to artificially raise prices but not to increase the availability of agricultural products. The second are subsidies which artificially lower the cost of farm products from affluent nations and make it far more difficult for developing countries to compete in sales of such produce as cotton. These subsidies help impoverish those developing countries whose most viable exports are agricultural without, in any way, improving the welfare of the majority of citizens in affluent nations. They have been supported primarily by the strong lobbying of agribusiness in industrialized nations. For more information on this topic, see the debate surrounding the World Trade Organization meetings in Cancun, September 2003. For example, see N. Mathiason, "World Trade Crisis: Subsidies Sow Seeds of Ruin," *Observer*, September 7, 2003; E. Becker, "Western Farmers Fear Third-World Challenge to Subsidies," *New York Times*, September 9, 2003; M. Lind, "The Cancun Delusion," *New York Times*, September 12, 2003; R. Kuttner, "Poor Nations Revolt at Rigged Trade Talks," *Boston Globe*, September 17, 2003; J. Garten, "Business: Going Up in Flames," *Newsweek*, September 29, 2003.

57. A. Bessenkool and A. Hegewisch, "Working Time for Working Families: Europe and the United States" (presented at the Conference on Working Time, American University Washington College of Law, Washington, DC, June 7–8, 2004).

58. I. Mamic, "Business and Code of Conduct Implementation: How Firms Use Management Systems for Social Performance" (Geneva: ILO, 2003). Available online at http://www.ilo.org/images/empent/static/mcc/download/supply-chain .pdf (accessed June 8, 2005).

59. Charles Kernaghan and Tom Hayden, "Pennies an Hour and No Way Up," Op-Ed, *New York Times*, sec. A, July 6, 2002.

60. P. Krugman, "In Praise of Cheap Labor: Bad Jobs at Bad Wages Are Better than No Jobs at All," *Slate*, March 20, 1997. Available online at http://slate.msn.com/ id/1918 (accessed June 8, 2005).

61. The experiences of Gabriela Saavedra are detailed in chapter 1.

62. The experiences of Ramon Canez are detailed in chapter 2.

63. The experiences of Vuong My Lan are detailed in chapter 3.

64. Social Security Administration, *Social Security Programs throughout the World: Asia and the Pacific, 2002* (2003). Available online at http://www.ssa.gov/policy/docs/progdesc/ssptw/2002–2003/asia/index.html (accessed November 3, 2004).

65. Social Security Administration, *Social Security Programs throughout the World: The Americas, 2003* (2004). Available online at http://www.ssa.gov/policy/docs/progdesc/ssptw/2002–2003/americas/index.html (accessed November 3, 2004).

66. United Nations, *The World's Women 2000: Trends and Statistics*, 3d ed. (New York: United Nations, Division for the Advancement of Women, 2000), 140–43. Available online at http://unstats.un.org/unsd/Demographic/products/indwm/ww2005/tab5c.htm (accessed September 17, 2003).

67. Labor Code, 1999, section 104.1. Available online at http://www.ilo.org/dyn/natlex/docs/WEBTEXT/57592/65206/E99MNG01.htm (accessed May 27, 2004).

68. Social Security Administration, *Social Security Programs throughout the World: Asia and the Pacific, 2002* (2003). Available online at http://www.ssa.gov/policy/docs/progdesc/ssptw/2002–2003/asia/index.html (accessed November 3, 2004).

69. S. J. Heymann et al., *The Work, Family, and Equity Index: Where Does the United States Stand Globally?* (Cambridge, MA: Project on Global Working Families, Harvard School of Public Health, June 2004). Available online at http://www.globalworkingfamilies.org.

70. International Labor Organization, *Night Work of Women in Industry* (Geneva: International Labor Office, 2001), 53–58, 62–65.

71. The experiences of Gabriela Saavedra are detailed in chapter 1.

72. Loi no 38/PR/96 du 11 décembre 1996 portant Code du Travail, articles 194 and 209. Available online at http://www.ilo.org/dyn/natlex/docs/WEBTEXT/47297/65070/F96TCD01.htm (accessed May 27, 2004).

73. Employment and Labour Relations Act, 2004, article 24, no. 6. Available online at http://www.ilo.org/dyn/natlex/docs/SERIAL/68319/66452/F437907581/tza68319.pdf (accessed March 16, 2005).

74. Codificacion del Codigo del Trabajo, 1997, articles 47 and 50. Available online at http://www.ilo.org/dyn/natlex/docs/WEBTEXT/47812/68395/S97ECU01.htm (accessed May 27, 2004).

75. Labour Standards Law of 1947 [Law No. 49 of April 7, 1947, as amended through Law No. 104 of July 4, 2003], article 35. Available online at http://www.jil.go.jp/english/laborinfo/library/documents/llj_law1-rev.pdf (accessed November 3, 2004).

76. Labour Act, 1992, *Nepal Recorder* 16, no. 19 (1992): 220–53, section 16. Available online at http://www.ilo.org/dyn/natlex/docs/WEBTEXT/30019/64854/E92NPL01.htm (accessed November 3, 2004).

77. Ley núm. 185, Código del Trabajo, *La Gaceta* 205 (October 30, 1996): 6109–90, article 64. Available online at http://www.ilo.org/dyn/natlex/docs/WEBTEXT/45784/65050/S96NICo1.htm (accessed November 3, 2004).

78. Working and Rest Time Act of 24 January 2001 (consolidation), chapter 4, section 21. Amended up to March 2003. Available online at http://www.legaltext.ee/text/en/X40079K4.htm (accessed March 16, 2005).

79. Codificacion del Código del Trabajo, 1997, article 55. Available online at http://www.ilo.org/dyn/natlex/docs/WEBTEXT/47812/68395/S97ECUo1.htm (accessed May 27, 2004).

80. Ley núm. 185, Código del Trabajo, *La Gaceta* 205 (October 30, 1996): 6109–90, article 64. Available online at http://www.ilo.org/dyn/natlex/docs/WEBTEXT/45784/65050/S96NICo1.htm (accessed November 3, 2004).

81. Employment and Labour Relations Act, 2004, article 19, no. 6. Available online at http://www.ilo.org/dyn/natlex/docs/SERIAL/68319/66452/F437907581/tza68319.pdf (accessed March 16, 2005).

82. UNESCO Institute for Statistics, *Global Education Digest 2003* (Montreal: UNESCO, 2003). Available online at http://www.uis.unesco.org/TEMPLATE/pdf/ged/GED_EN.pdf.

83. UNESCO Institute for Statistics Table on Pupil Teacher Ratio. Available online at http://portal.unesco.org/uis/ev.php?URL_ID=5187&URL_DO=DO_TOPIC&URL_SECTION=201 (accessed October 24, 2005).

84. UNESCO Institute for Statistics, *Global Education Digest 2003* (Montreal: UNESCO, 2003). Available online at http://www.uis.unesco.org/TEMPLATE/pdf/ged/GED_EN.pdf.

85. UNESCO Institute for Statistics Table on Pupil Teacher Ratio. Available online at http://portal.unesco.org/uis/ev.php?URL_ID=5187&URL_DO=DO_TOPIC&URL_SECTION=201 (accessed October 24, 2005).

86. United Nations, Convention on the Elimination of All Forms of Discrimination against Women (1979). Available online at http://www.un.org/womenwatch/daw/cedaw/text/econvention.htm (accessed October 24, 2005).

87. United Nations, International Covenant on Economic, Social and Cultural Rights (1976). Available online at http://www.unhchr.ch/html/menu6/2/fs16.htm#3 (accessed October 24, 2005).

88. United Nations, Convention on the Rights of the Child (1989). Available online at http://www.unhchr.ch/html/menu3/b/k2crc.htm (accessed October 24, 2005).

89. United Nations, Convention on the Rights of the Child (1989). Available online at http://www.unhchr.ch/html/menu3/b/k2crc.htm (accessed October 24, 2005).

90. United Nations, Convention on the Elimination of All Forms of Discrimination against Women (1979). Available online at http://www.un.org/womenwatch/daw/cedaw/text/econvention.htm (accessed August 5, 2003).

91. United Nations, Universal Declaration of Human Rights (1948). Available online at www.unhchr.ch/udhr/index.htm (accessed October 24, 2005).

92. P. Varley, ed., "The Multilateral Approach," in *The Sweatshop Quandary: Corporate Responsibility on the Global Frontier*, ed. P. Varley, C. Mathiasen, and M. Voorhees, pp. 33–44 (Washington, DC: Investor Responsibility Research Center, 1998).

93. See http://www.ilo.org for details on the specific conventions.

94. See J. C. Gornick and M. K. Meyers, *Families That Work: Policies for Reconciling Parenthood and Employment* (New York: Russell Sage Foundation, 2003); S. I. Greenspan, *The Four Thirds Solution: Solving the Child-Care Crisis in America Today* (Cambridge, MA: Perseus, 2001).

Appendixes

1. World Bank, *World Development Indicators 2004* (Washington, DC: World Bank, 2004). Full data available online from the World Bank and partner institutions; select indicators available online at http://devdata.worldbank.org/data-query.

2. Central Statistics Office, *2001 Population and Housing Census: National Statistical Tables Report* (Gaborone, Botswana: Central Statistics Office, 2003).

3. United Nations Development Programme, *Human Development Report 2000* (New York: Oxford University Press, 2000).

4. United Nations Development Programme, *UNDP: Country Cooperation Frameworks and Related Matters. First Country Cooperation Framework for Botswana (1997–2002)* (New York: United Nations Population Fund, 1997).

5. Botswana Ministry of Health, AIDS/STD Unit, *Sentinel Surveillance Report 1999* (Gaborone, Botswana: Botswana Ministry of Health, 2000).

6. For more information on the 2000 round of the Multiple Indicator Survey, see http://www.cso.gov.bw/html/household/bmisurvey.html (accessed June 7, 2005), or contact the Botswana Central Statistics Office, Private Bag 0024, Gaborone, Botswana. In 2000, the year of the Multiple Indicator Survey used to conduct our research, the estimated population of Botswana was 1.68 million, with an annual population growth rate of 1.69 percent. Forty-two percent of the Botswanan population was younger than fifteen.

7. V. M. Shkolnikov and F. Meslé, "The Russian Epidemiological Crisis as Mirrored by Mortality Trends," in *Russia's Demographic Crisis*, RAND Conference Report, ed. J. DaVanzo, 113–60 (Santa Monica, CA: RAND Center for Russia and Eurasia, 1996).

8. B. Milanovic, *The Role of Social Assistance in Addressing Poverty* (Washington, DC: World Bank, 1998).

9. M. Lokshin, *Effects of Child Care Prices on Women's Labor Force Participation in Russia* (Washington, DC: World Bank, 2000).

10. O. Bain, "The Cost of Higher Education to Students and Parents in Russia: Tuition Policy Issues," *Peabody Journal of Education* 76, nos. 3–4 (2001): 57–80.

11. B. A. Rozenfeld, "The Crisis of Russian Health Care and Attempts at Reform," in *Russia's Demographic Crisis*, RAND Conference Report, ed. J. DaVanzo, 163–74 (Santa Monica, CA: RAND Center for Russia and Eurasia, 1996).

12. World Bank, *World Development Indicators 2004* (Washington, DC: World Bank, 2004). Full data available online from the World Bank and partner institutions; select indicators available online at http://devdata.worldbank.org/data-query.

13. K. Bush, *The Russian Economy in December 2002* (Washington, DC: Russia and Eurasia Program, Center for Strategic and International Studies, 2002).

14. International Labor Organization, *KILM 2001–2002* (Geneva, Switzerland: International Labor Office, 2002).

15. For more information on the Russian Longitudinal Monitoring Survey, see http://www.cpc.unc.edu/projects/rlms/rlms_home.html (accessed June 7, 2005).

16. World Bank, *World Development Indicators 2004* (Washington, DC: World Bank, 2004). Full data available online from the World Bank and partner institutions; select indicators available online at http://devdata.worldbank.org/data-query.

17. International Labor Organization, *Key Indicators of the Labor Market* (Geneva, Switzerland: International Labor Office, 1999).

18. T. C. Wong, "Urbanisation and Sustainability of Southeast Asian Cities," in *Development and Change: Southeast Asia in the New Millennium*, ed. T. C. Wong and M. Singh (Singapore: Times Academic Press, 1999). Bui Thi Kim Quy, "The Vietnamese Woman in Vietnam's Process of Change," in *Vietnam's Women in Transition*, ed. K. Barry, 159–66 (New York: St. Martin's, 1996).

19. United Nations, *World Urbanization: The 1994 Revision* (New York: United Nations, 1995).

20. World Bank, *World Development Indicators 2000* (Washington, DC: World Bank, 2000).

21. I. Noerlund, "The Labour Market in Vietnam: Between State Incorporation and Autonomy," in *Social Change in Southeast Asia*, ed. J. Schmidt, J. Hersh, and N. Fold, 155–82 (Essex, UK: Addison Wesley Longman, 1998).

22. World Bank, Asian Development Bank, and UNDP, *Vietnam 2010: Entering the Twenty-First Century* (Washington, DC: World Bank, 2001). S. Chandrasiri and

A. de Silva, *Globalization, Employment and Equity: The Vietnam Experience* (Geneva, Switzerland: ILO, 1995).

23. For more information on the Vietnam Household Living Standards Survey, 1997–1998, see http://www.worldbank.org/html/prdph/lsms/country/vn98/mansuper.pdf (accessed June 7, 2005). In 1998, the year of the survey used to conduct our research, Vietnam had a population of 76.5 million, 35 percent of whom were children.

24. N. Phong, *Vietnam Living Standards Survey 1997/98* (Hanoi: General Statistics Office, 1998), 1.

25. U.S. Bureau of Labor Statistics, *Current Population Survey, 2004*. Available online at http://www.bls.gov/cps/home.htm (accessed January 18, 2005).

26. Center for Human Resource Research, *NLS Handbook 2000* (Columbus: Center for Human Resource Research, Ohio State University, 2000).

27. World Bank, *World Development Indicators 2004* (Washington, DC: World Bank, 2004). Full data available online from the World Bank and partner institutions; select indicators available online at http://devdata.worldbank.org/data-query.

28. International Labor Organization, *KILM 2001–2002* (Geneva, Switzerland: International Labor Office, 2002).

29. World Bank, *World Development Indicators 2004* (Washington, DC: World Bank, 2004). Full data available online from the World Bank and partner institutions; select indicators available online at http://devdata.worldbank.org/data-query.

30. For more information on the 1996–1997 Brazilian Living Standards Measurement Survey, see http://www.worldbank.org/lsms/country/brazil/br97home.html (accessed June 7, 2005). In 1997, the year of the survey used to conduct our research, 79.1 percent of the Brazilian population lived in urban areas. Brazil had a population of 166 million, 29.9 percent (50 million) of whom were children.

31. Their reported response rate reflects the employment of a rarely used practice of household substitution (from other households in the sector) to compensate for nonresponse. See P. Silva, "Reporting and Compensating for Non-Sampling Errors for Surveys in Brazil: Current Practice and Future Challenges," in *Household Surveys in Developing and Transition Countries: Design, Implementation and Analysis*, ed. I. Yanseneh, 231–48 (New York: United Nations Department of Economic and Social Affairs, 2003). Available online at http://unstats.un.org/unsd/hhsurveys/pdf/chapter_11.pdf (accessed June 7, 2005). For more information on the survey, see http://www.worldbank.org/lsms/country/brazil/br97home.html (accessed June 7, 2005).

32. World Bank, *The Brazil Health System: Impact Evaluation Report* (Washington, DC: World Bank, 1998), 3.

33. CIA, "Mexico," in *The World Factbook* (Washington, DC: CIA, 2004). Available online at http://www.cia.gov/cia/publications/factbook/index.html (accessed October 5, 2004).

34. World Bank, *World Development Indicators 2004* (Washington, DC: World Bank, 2004). Full data available online from the World Bank and partner institutions; select indicators available online at http://devdata.worldbank.org/data-query.

35. World Bank, *World Development Indicators 2004* (Washington, DC: World Bank, 2004). Full data available online from the World Bank and partner institutions; select indicators available online at http://devdata.worldbank.org/data-query.

36. International Labor Organization, *Key Indicators of the Labor Market* (Geneva, Switzerland: International Labor Office, 1999).

37. Instituto Nacionál de Estadística, Geografía y Informática, *Indicadores Sociodemográficos: 1930–1998* (Aguascalientes, Mexico: Instituto Nacionál de Estadística, Geografía y Informática, 2000).

38. For more information, see Instituto Nacionál de Estadística, Geografía y Informática, online at http://www.inegi.gob.mx (accessed October 24, 2005). In 1996, the year of the National Survey of Household Income and Expenditure used to conduct our research, Mexico had a population of 92.6 million, 35 percent (32.6 million) of whom were children. Mexico had a GDP of $333 billion. The percentage of Mexicans living in urban areas was 74 percent.

39. International Labor Organization, *KILM 2001–2002* (Geneva, Switzerland: International Labor Office, 2002).

40. World Bank, *World Development Indicators 2004* (Washington, DC: World Bank, 2004). Full data available online from the World Bank and partner institutions; select indicators available online at http://devdata.worldbank.org/data-query.

41. UNAIDS, *2004 Report on the Global AIDS Epidemic* (Geneva, Switzerland: UNAIDS, June 2004). Available online at http://www.unaids.org/bangkok2004/report.html (accessed June 7, 2005).

42. For more information on the South Africa Integrated Household Survey, see http://www.worldbank.org/lsms/country/za94/docs/za94ovr.txt (accessed October 24, 2005). In 1994, the year of the survey used to conduct our research, South Africa had a population of 38.2 million, 36 percent (14 million) of whom were children. The female share of the labor force was 37 percent. Fifty-two percent of the South African population lived in urban areas in 1994.

43. UNAIDS, *2004 Report on the Global AIDS Epidemic* (Geneva, Switzerland: UNAIDS, June 2004). Available online at http://www.unaids.org/bangkok2004/GAR2004_pdf/UNAIDSGlobalReport2004_en.pdf (accessed October 24, 2005).

44. Botswana population figures are from the 2001 Botswana Census as published in *2002 Population and Housing Census: Population of Towns, Villages and Associated Localities in August 2001* (Botswana: Central Statistics Office, Botswana Government, 2002).

45. D. F. Bryceson and U. Vuorela, "Transnational Families in the Twenty-first Century," in *The Transnational Family: New European Frontiers and Global Networks*, ed. D. F. Bryceson and U. Vuorela, pp. 7–9 (Oxford: Berg, 2002). S. George, "'Dirty Nurses' and 'Men Who Play': Gender and Class in Transnational Migration," in *Global Ethnography: Forces, Connections, and Imaginations in a Postmodern World*, ed. M. Burawoy, 144–74 (Berkeley: University of California Press, 2000). Nina Glick Schiller and Georges Eugene Fouron, *Georges Woke Up Laughing: Long-Distance Nationalism and the Search for Home* (Durham, NC: Duke University Press, 2001).

46. OECD, *Trends in International Migration 2001* (Paris: OECD, 2003). Available online at http://www1.oecd.org/publications/e-book/8101131E.pdf (accessed February 20, 2003).

47. J. Bustamante et al., "Mexico-to-U.S. Migrant Characteristics from Mexican Data Sources," in *Migration between the United States and Mexico: Binational Study*, ed. Mexican Ministry of Foreign Affairs and U.S. Commission on Immigration Reform, pp. 779–817 (Austin, TX: Morgan Printing, 1998).

48. M. Greenwood and M. Tienda, "U.S. Impacts of Mexican Immigration," in *Migration between the United States and Mexico: Binational Study*, ed. Mexican Ministry of Foreign Affairs and U.S. Commission on Immigration Reform, pp. 251–394 (Austin, TX: Morgan Printing, 1998). G. Verduzco and K. Unger, "Impacts of Migration in Mexico," in *Migration between the United States and Mexico: Binational Study*, ed. Mexican Ministry of Foreign Affairs and U.S. Commission on Immigration Reform, pp. 395–436 (Austin, TX: Morgan Printing, 1998).

49. R. De la Garza and B. Lowell, *Sending Money Home: Hispanic Remittances and Community Development* (Lanham, MD: Rowman and Littlefield, 2002); R. Alarcón et al., *Impacto de la migración y las remesas en el crecimiento económico regional* (Mexico City: Senado de la República, Estados Unidos Mexicanos, 1999).

50. A remarkable exception is a twenty-page brochure published by the University of Guanajuato on the living conditions of women in rural communities with high out-migration: M. Cebada, *Genero, Familia y Migración: La condición de la mujer en comunidades rurales de migrantes hacia Estados Unidos* (Guanajuato, Mexico: Universidad de Guanajuato, 1997).

51. Our source was CONAPO, the National Population Council of Mexico. The migration tables and methodology can be found online in Spanish at http://www.conapo.gob.mx/publicaciones/migra4.htm (accessed June 7, 2005).

52. With this method, a structured interview instrument is used to systematically raise a series of topics. Respondents are encouraged to describe their experiences in detailed narrative fashion, and follow-up questions are asked. Respondents provide open-ended answers on the topic asked and related topics. This book reports results from both qualitative and quantitative analyses of these interviews. When quantitative results are reported from these studies, the percentages reported have as a denominator all interviews addressing the specified topic.

53. The English-language site for the Russian Center for Public Opinion and Market Research is http://www.wciom.ru/?new_lang=2 (accessed October 24, 2005).

54. Centre for Research on the Epidemiology of Disasters, *Natural Disaster Profiles: Honduras* (Brussels, Belgium: Université Catholique de Louvain, 2002).

55. Programa de las Naciones Unidas para el Desarrollo, Informe Sobre Desarrollo Humano Honduras, *El Impacto Humano de un Huracán* (Tegucigalpa: Programa de las Naciones Unidas para el Desarrollo, Informe Sobre Desarrollo Humano Honduras, 1999).

56. The full text of the Universal Declaration of Human Rights is available online at http://www.un.org/Overview/rights.html (accessed June 7, 2005).

57. The full text of the Convention on the Elimination of All Forms of Discrimination against Women can be found at http://www.un.org/womenwatch/daw/cedaw/text/econvention.htm (accessed June 7, 2005).

58. The full text of the Convention on the Rights of the Child is available online at http://www.unicef.org/crc/crc.htm (accessed June 7, 2005).

59. All ILO conventions are available online at http://www.ilo.org/ilolex/english/convdisp1.htm.

Index

accidents and injuries
  to children left alone, 27, 40, 81–87
  HIV/AIDS increasing risk of, 151–52
  parental working conditions and, 81–87
  preschool children, 27, 29–30, 40
  school-age children, 46–48
Africa, HIV/AIDS pandemic in, 84, 144–45
age dependency ratio, 188
AIDS. *See* HIV/AIDS
Angola, repercussions of war in, 170
annual leave, 203
Armenia, paid maternity leave in, 206

Bangladesh, 203, 213
barriers to parental involvement
  in children's education, 57–64, 194, 201–2
  in children's health care, 199
Botswana, 224–25
  affordable solutions to caregiving problems
    in, 201
  child health and parental working condi-
    tions, 78, 83–88, 91–94, 98–99, 102–3,
    109–10, 193
  children caring for other children in, 193

demographic characteristics of population,
  224, 226, 237, 243
Dula Sentle, 66–67
economic and employment conditions for
  working parents, 115, 120, 122, 124
Family and Health Needs Survey, 235–37
HIV/AIDS pandemic in. *See* HIV/AIDS
Keletso counseling center, 181–83
methods for in-depth interviews conducted in, 242, 243
methods for survey of HIV-affected families in, 235–36, 237
Multiple Indicator Survey, 224
national survey data analyzed, 223–25, 226
preschool children, caregiving for, 16–18,
  22–24, 29–31, 36–37, 39–40
school-age children, caregiving for, 46–48,
  52–56, 59, 66–67
shift in location and control of work, 7, 8
unequal distribution of household work
  ("second shift"), 128–29
Brazil, 231–32
  child health and parental working condi-
    tions, 89, 90

Brazil (*continued*)
    demographic characteristics of population,
        227, 231
    Living Standards Measurement Survey, 232
    national survey data analyzed, 223–24, 227,
        231–32
    paid maternity leave, 206
    preschool children, caregiving for, 39–40
    school-age children, caregiving for, 52–55
    shift in location and control of work, 8
breast-feeding, child health, and parental
        working conditions, 77–79, 196–97
business
    affordability of programs and improve-
        ments in working conditions for,
        203
    multinational businesses, rise of, 9–10,
        188–90

Cameroon, HIV/AIDS in, 160
caregiving
    children as caregivers. *See* children as care-
        givers to other children
    during crises. *See* crisis, working families
        in times of
    and discrimination in the workplace,
        25–26, 114–15, 255–56
    extended family, role of, 5, 11, 16–19
    formal day care. *See* childcare centers
    HIV/AIDS and. *See* HIV/AIDS
    international recognition of need to assist
        with, 209–10
    night work regulations for, 207
    preschool children. *See* preschool
        children
    school-age children. *See* school-age
        children
    sick children. *See* sick children, caregiving
        for
    sick family members, childcare conse-
        quences of need to care for, 17–18
    work affected by. *See* employers and em-
        ployment
CEDAW (Convention on the Elimination of
        All Forms of Discrimination against
        Women), 209–10, 252
cerebral palsy, 98, 161

Chad, day of rest provisions in, 207
childcare centers (formal)
    availability of, 26, 117–18, 140, 198
    Bana ba Keletso (Botswana), 181–83
    children with special needs and disabilities,
        100–101
    cost of, 198, 202, 285n56
    developmental and educational benefits of,
        35–37, 42–44
    publicly-supported, 22, 117–18, 140
        San Isidro Center (Honduras), 31–34,
        200
        Seguro Social system (Mexico), 37–39, 44
        in Vietnam, 39
        Red Cross Child Care Center (Honduras),
        183–85
    in the workplace, 44, 196
child development
    early childhood care and education, im-
        portance of, 197–98
    formal child care centers and early child-
        hood care and education programs,
        benefits of, 35–37, 42–44
    HIV/AIDS affecting, 151–53
    Hurricane Mitch (Honduras), continuing
        effects of, 183–84
    leaving children home alone or in substan-
        dard care, effects of, 27, 40, 48–50,
        192–94
    preschool children, 27–29, 43–44
    school-age children, 48–50, 60–64
    social and physical environment's effect
        on, 193–94, 263n5
children
    HIV/AIDS and. *See* HIV/AIDS
    international conventions on needs and
        rights of, 209–10
    left alone. *See* children left alone
    in loco parentis. *See* children as caregivers to
        other children
    orphaned
        HIV/AIDS, 153–56, 157, 158
        by war, 169–70
    preschool. *See* preschool children
    school-age. *See* school-age children
    with special needs and disabilities, 98–101,
        183–84, 195, 199–200

UN Convention on the Rights of the
  Child (CRC), 209–10, 252
violence against, 84, 184
war's effects on, 169–70
work, brought to. *See* work, children
  brought to
in workplace of parent or caregiver, 19–22,
  29
children as caregivers to other children,
  190–92
  educational consequences, 15, 42, 51–57,
    152, 193–94
  HIV/AIDS leading to, 152
  preschoolers affected by, 5, 13–16, 23–24,
    42
  school-age children affected by, 45, 47,
    51–57, 62–63, 65
children left alone, 190–94
  accidents and injuries arising due to, 27,
    40, 81–87
  effects on developmental and educational
    outcomes, 27, 40
  HIV/AIDS and, 151–52
  mental health problems of, 49
  preschoolers, 23–27, 41–42
  school-age children. *See* school-age chil-
    dren, caregiving problems of
  sick children, 90–95
  violence against, 84
children's health issues. *See also* HIV/AIDS
  accidents and injuries. *See* accidents and
    injuries
  caregiving options and, 29–30, 42–43
  cerebral palsy, 98, 161
  chronic conditions, 74–75, 103–4, 199–
    200
  diarrheal disease and oral rehydration
    therapy, 80–81
  epilepsy, 72–74, 100–101
  immunization, 73, 79–80, 201, 205
  infectious diseases, 29, 73–74, 80–81, 96
  insomnia, 49
  malnourishment, 14–15, 29–30, 80, 117, 184
  parental involvement in children's treat-
    ment, 199
  parental working conditions and. *See*
    working conditions

rickets, 14
routine and preventive needs, 76–87
special needs and disabled children,
  98–101, 183–84, 195, 199–200
Chile
  early education programs, value of, 198
  paid maternity leave in, 206
collective action. *See* global action
compensation. *See* income
consumers and paying for change, 203–4
Convention on the Elimination of All Forms
  of Discrimination against Women
  (CEDAW), 209–10, 252
Convention on the Rights of the Child
  (CRC), 209–10, 252
corporations. *See* business
CRC (Convention on the Rights of the
  Child), 209–10, 252
crisis, working families in times of, 143–86
  in the aftermath of war (Vietnam). *See*
    Vietnam War; war
  HIV/AIDS pandemic (Botswana). *See*
    HIV/AIDS
  Hurricane Mitch (Honduras). *See* Hurri-
    cane Mitch
  long-term aftereffects vs. immediate prob-
    lems of, 185–86
  outsider vs. insider views of, 143
  solutions and support for, 178–85
Cuba
  early education program enrollment, 208
  student-staff ratio, 208

day care, formal. *See* child care centers
day of rest provisions, 203, 207
debt burden, foreign, 188
democratization of global government
  structures, 214–15
demographic transitions, 6–11
  economic effects of, 113–14
  female labor force participation, 11, 113,
    261n4
  globalization, 9–10, 188–90
  mapping, viii–ix
  shift in location and control of work, 7–8,
    113, 187–88
  urbanization. *See* urbanization

Denmark, early education program enrollment and student-staff ratio in, 208
development. *See* child development
disability
children with special needs, 98–101, 183–84, 195, 199–200
poverty and, 199–200
discrimination
against caregivers, 25–26, 114–15, 255–56
against women, 114–15, 126–28
drinking water safety, 80–81
dual-earner families
ability to keep children in school, 50–52
demographic shift towards, 11, 113, 261n4
hours worked, 130, 132

early childhood care and education (ECCE)
academic and developmental benefits of, 35–37, 42–44
costs of, 202
efficacy of, 197–98
enrollment in, 207–8
global goals for, 218
student-staff ratios, 208
universal parental preference for, 35–37
economic conditions
benefits for working families and productivity levels, 202
demographic transformation affecting, 113–14
employment and. *See* employers and employment
foreign debt burden, 188
HIV/AIDS, financial problems created by, 146, 148, 153–56, 157, 158, 160–64, 165
poverty. *See* poverty
war and postwar effects, 168–73, 176
Ecuador, day of rest provisions and weekend work wage provision in, 207
education
academic and behavioral problems in school
preschool caregiving and, 27–29
school-age children's care and, 48–50, 60–64
children providing childcare affected as to, 15, 42, 51–57, 152, 193–94

costs as a barrier to, 201–4, 218
global goals for, 218–19
HIV/AIDS, impact of, 151–53, 163
importance of parental involvement in, 57, 67–68
length of school day and year, 218–19
parental involvement in
barriers to, 57–64, 194, 201–2
solutions allowing, 67–68, 201–2
in parenting, 63, 94
parents' education level, effect of, 25, 61, 64, 137, 158, 268n1
preschool programs. *See* early childhood care and education
secondary school, 218
sick children sent to school, 95–97
student-staff ratios, 208
value of, 195
war's effect on, 171, 172, 176
elderly. *See also* extended families
as caregivers, 17–19
need for care, viii–ix, xi, 17–19, 75–78, 140, 144
employers and employment. *See also* labor force; working conditions
bad jobs viewed as preferable to no jobs, myth of, 204–5
child health issues affecting parental jobs, 101–4
docked pay and excessive overtime requirements for absences due to family responsibilities, 101–4, 118–20
"downward spiral" of poor jobs and care burdens, 132–35
finding paid work, 114–15
gender discrimination in, 114–15, 126–28
informal sector. *See* informal sector employment
job loss due to family responsibilities, 101–4, 123–25
poor jobs, having to settle for, 115–18
preschool childcare
children brought to work by parents, 19–22, *22,* 29
problems affecting parental jobs, 30–31
solutions to problems in, 139–41

health care
    access to, 32, 176, 195, 205, 254
    cost of, 161, 201–4
    insurance and, 75, 136, 161, 181, 195, 200,
        224
HIV/AIDS, 144–64
    accident and injury risks related to, 151–52
    affected children, caring for
        infected children, 84, 156–57
        Keletso counseling center (Botswana),
            181–83
        orphans, 153–56, 157, 158
    affordable solutions to caregiving prob-
        lems, 201
    burden of caregiving increased by, 153–60
    caregivers infected with, 157–59
    extended family, unavailability of care-
        giving help from, 159–60
    financial problems created by, 146, 148,
        153–56, 157, 158, 160–64, 165
    impact on education and education sys-
        tems, 151–53, 163
    impact on national economies, 160–64
    infected adults, 84, 157–59
    permeating effects of, 145–53
    prevention vs. treatment, 178–79
    single-parent families, 146–48
    solutions and support for families affected
        by, 178–83, 201
    vertical transmission, 149, 158
    workplace adaptations for, 179–81
Honduras
    child health and parental working condi-
        tions, 77–78, 79, 80, 81–83, 88
    children as caregivers in, 13–16
    demographic transitions in, 3–6, 190
    economic and employment conditions for
        working parents, 124–25
    Hurricane Mitch affecting. See Hurricane
        Mitch
    methods for in-depth interviews con-
        ducted in, 248
    San Isidro Center, 31–34, 200
    school-age children, caregiving for, 49–50
Hungary, early education program enroll-
    ment and student-staff ratio in,
    208

Hurricane Mitch (Honduras)
    continuing effects of, 13–14, 167–68, 205
    initial effects of, 164–67
    preschool children, care of, 13–14, 34
    Red Cross Child Care Center, 183–85

ICC (International Criminal Court), 214
ICESCR (International Covenant on Eco-
    nomic, Social and Cultural Rights),
    209
IGOs (intergovernmental organizations), 214
illness, See entries at sick
ILO. See International Labor Organization
IMF (International Monetary Fund), 214–15
immunization, 73, 79–80, 201, 205
in loco parentis, children acting as. See chil-
    dren as caregivers to other children
income
    living family wage, need for, 219–20
    loss of wages due to family responsibilities,
        101–4, 118–20
    weekend work, wage premiums for, 207
India, 198
inequalities. See also discrimination
    economic. See employers and employment;
        poverty
    gender. See gender issues
    reduction strategies, 139–41
    unequal distribution of household work
        ("second shift"), 127–32
    Work, Family, and Equity Index, 195, 206,
        251–57
informal caregivers. See caregiving
informal sector employment
    benefits of, 117–18
    improving working conditions in, 200
    problems with, 120–23
    San Isidro Center (Honduras) providing
        care for children of parents in, 31–34,
        200
    Seguro Social system (Mexico) not cover-
        ing childcare for those in, 38
    of women, 122–23
intergovernmental organizations (IGOs), 214
International Covenant on Economic, Social
    and Cultural Rights (ICESCR), 209
International Criminal Court (ICC), 214

international issues. *See* entries at global

International Labor Organization (ILO), 210–11

  Conventions, 210, 252

  demographic data provided by, ix

  enforcement mechanisms, 214–15

  Work, Family, and Equity Index, 252

International Monetary Fund (IMF), 214–15

interview methods, 241–51

  in Botswana, 242, 243

  in Honduras, 248

  in Mexico, 242–44, 245

  open-ended vs. closed-ended questions, x–xi, 241, 293n52

  representativeness of respondents, 260n7

  response rate, 260–61n8, 290n31

  in Russia, 249, 250

  in United States, 244–47

  in Vietnam, 247–48, 249

Japan

  day of rest provisions, 207

  early education program enrollment, 208

  night work regulations for caregivers, 207

jobs. *See* employers and employment

Kenya, HIV/AIDS in, 154, 160

Krugman, Paul, 204

labor force

  demographic shift in location and control of work, 7–8, 113, 187–88

  women's participation in, 11, 113, 261n4

labor standards, 210–11, 219–20

land mines, 169

leave. *See also* working conditions

  annual leave, 203

  for children's health needs

    caring for children with acute and chronic illnesses, 74–75

    immunization, 73, 79–80, 201, 205

    paid leave, 106–9, 199–200

  globalization, effects of, 189

  ILO Conventions regarding, 210, 252

  maternity, 195, 196–97, 203, 206–7, 209

  paid parental leave, 60, 67–68, 106–9, 136, 195–97, 199–200

paternity, 195, 196–97, 206–7, 209

sick leave, 203

unpaid, 68, 94, 96, 164, 197

legislation and labor laws, 126, 203, 205–7

Lesotho, HIV/AIDS pandemic in, 145

living family wage, 219–20

Malawi, HIV/AIDS pandemic in, 145

maternity leave, 195, 196–97, 203, 206–7, 209

mental health

  of children left alone, 49

  Hurricane Mitch (Honduras), continuing effects of, 184

  parents affected by children's illnesses, 104–6

  war's effect on, 173, 177

Mexico, 233–34

  child health and parental working conditions, 83, 88, 91, 103, 105, 110, 193

  childcare policy in, 138, 141

  children caring for other children in, 193

  demographic characteristics of population, 227, 233, 239, 245

  early education program enrollment, 208

  economic and employment conditions for working parents, 114, 119, 125, 138, 141

  methods for in-depth interviews conducted in, 242, 244–45

  methods for survey of transnational families in, 236, 238, 239

  migration to the U.S., 236

  NAFTA's effect on, 189

  national survey data analyzed, 223–24, 227, 233–34

  National Survey of Household Income and Expenditure (ENIGH), 233

  poverty and children left home alone in, 191

  preschool children, 20–21, 24, 27–29, 37–39, 44

  school-age children, 48–49, 52–55, 57–59, 67–68

  Seguro Social system, 37–39, 44

  shift in location and control of work, 7, 8

equity and, 255–56

and health care costs, 161, 201–4

inability to meet basic family needs due to, 137

intergenerational cycle, means of breaking, 68–69

"race to the bottom" or "downward spiral" of, vii, 132–35, 203

reduction strategies, 139–41

single-parent households more likely to be, 191

pregnancy

employment and, 115, 123, 126

maternity leave, 195, 196–97, 203, 206–7, 209

preschool children, 13–44

accidents and injuries, 27, 29–30, 40

children as caregivers of preschoolers, 5, 13–16, 23–24, 42

developmental issues, 27–29, 43–44

extended family as caregivers, 16–19

health issues, 29–30, 42–43

informal arrangements, 22–25

leaving preschoolers home alone, 23–27, 41–42

parental employment impacted by care needs of, 30–31

paucity of quality care, consequences of, 26–31

solutions to caregiving problems of, 31–44, 195, *See also* early childhood care and education

local vs. universal contexts, 35–37

San Isidro Center (Honduras), 31–34, 200

Seguro Social system (Mexico), 37–39

setting goals, 40–44

work, taking children to, 19–22, 29

Project on Global Working Families, viii–xi

demographic characteristics of populations, 226–27

Family and Health Needs Survey (Botswana), 235–37

in-depth ethnographic studies, viii–xi, 151, 241–51, *See also* interviews

national and regional household surveys, ix–x, 223–41

National Study of Daily Experiences (NSDE), 238

public policy analysis, xi

Survey of Midlife in the United States (MIDUS), 238, 240

Transnational Working Families Survey (Mexico), 236–48, 239

Work, Family, and Equity Index, 195, 206, 251–57

public policy

coordination of workplace and childcare policies within countries, 110–11

myths leading to inaction in

affordability issues, 201–4

bad jobs viewed as preferable to no jobs, 204–5

global action viewed as difficult or impossible, 208–12

inability to help informal sector workers, 200

individual countries' inability to act alone, 206–8

lack of understanding as to what works, 195–200

parental ability to solve problems alone, 205–6

"race to the bottom," vii, 132–35, 203

Russia, 225–28

changes after perestroika, 225

child health and parental working conditions, 88

demographic characteristics of population, 225, 226, 250

economic and employment conditions for working parents, 114–17, 132–33

extended families, preschool-age childcare provided by, 16

Longitudinal Monitoring Survey, 228

methods for in-depth interviews conducted in, 248, 250

national survey data analyzed, 223–24, 225, 226, 228

shift in location and control of work, 8

unequal distribution of household work ("second shift"), 127–28, 130

Rwanda, repercussions of war in, 170

working conditions (*continued*)

    coordination of public workplace and childcare policies, 110–11

    diarrheal and other infectious diseases, 80–81

    immunization, 73, 79–80, 201, 205

    parental involvement in children's treatment, 199

    parents affected by, 101–6

    sick children. *See* sick children, caregiving for

    solutions to, 106–11, 199–200

    special needs and disabled children, 98–101, 183–84, 195, 199–200

    violence against children left home alone, 84

    day of rest provisions, 203, 207

    flexibility of work schedule, 60, 67–68, 87, 106–10, 136, 151

    global goals regarding, 219–20

    globalization, effects of, 189–90

    HIV/AIDS, workplace adaptations for, 179–81

    ILO on. *See* International Labor Organization

    informal sector conditions, improvement of, 200

    international recognition of basic rights in, 209–12

    leave. *See* leave

    long hours, 3–6, 57–59

    multiple jeopardy, 137, 139

    night work regulations for caregivers, 126, 207

working families

    collective action in favor of, 208–12

    during crises. *See* crisis, working families in times of

    dual-earner. *See* dual-earner families

    extended families in which all adults work, 7–8, 131

    productivity levels and benefits for, 202

    research on, vii, 220–22

    single-parent. *See* single-parent households

World Bank, ix, 214, 241, 251, 257

World Health Organization (WHO), ix, 214–15

World Trade Organization (WTO), 214–15, 221

Zambia, HIV/AIDS pandemic in, 145, 154, 160

Zimbabwe, HIV/AIDS pandemic in, 145, 154